California's Best Fly Fishing

California's Best Fly Fishing

PREMIER STREAMS
AND RIVERS
**FROM NORTHERN CALIFORNIA
TO THE EASTERN SIERRA**

Chip O'Brien

HEADWATER
BOOKS

STACKPOLE
BOOKS

Published by
HEADWATER BOOKS
531 Harding Street
New Cumberland, PA 17070
www.headwaterbooks.com

STACKPOLE BOOKS
5067 Ritter Road
Mechanicsburg, PA 17055
www.stackpolebooks.com

Printed in China

First edition

10 9 8 7 6 5 4 3 2 1

Photos by the author unless otherwise noted
Cover design by Wendy Reynolds

ISBN: 978-1-934753-03-3

Library of Congress Control Number: 2009932463

CONTENTS

To my wife, Marlee LeDai,
for missing me so much when I traipse off
on yet another outdoor adventure.

A book of this scope would be impossible without the help of a network of generous friends, many of whom happen to be among California's best fly-fishing guides.

I would like to thank Dick Galland, former owner of Clearwater House on Hat Creek; Bill Lowe and his wife, Michelle; Tom Peppas; Dax Messet; Andrew Harris; Mark Buljan; Brannon Santos; Jay Cockrum; Billy and Vanessa Downs; Brooke Matteson; Mike Peters; Ed Volpe; Mike Mercer and Tim Fox of The Fly Shop; Ken Morrish; Dave Sloan; Brad McFall; Clearwater Lodge on the Pit River; Chris Conaty at Idylwilde Flies; Mark Thau Photography; Jim Reid, owner of Ken's Sporting Goods in Bridgeport, and his brother Bill; Bob Quigley; Pat Jaeger; Zach O'Brien; The Big Fisherman; Confluence Guide Service; Tim Haddon; Perry Sims; Gary Eblen at American Flyfishing; John Sherman; Glenn Yoshioka; California Trout; Richard May; Richard Anderson of *California Fly Fisher*; Steve Probasco and John Shewey of *Northwest Flyfishing*; Dave Hughes; Rick Hafele; and Jay Nichols.

All played a part in bringing this project into reality.

Guide Brad McFall makes one last cast on the Upper Owens. JOHN SHERMAN PHOTO

Who would attempt to write another guidebook on California fly fishing, and why now? That someone might consider such a task is perhaps a bit revealing in itself, perhaps a fool's errand. But as the old saying points out, the more things stay the same, the more they don't.

There are already excellent references available on the fisheries explored in this text. But most of these do not tap into what I consider the primary source of up-to-date essential information, the critical facts and foibles of each destination. In my opinion no one knows these better than the cadre of fly-fishing guides who ply their living from these waters, and I am fortunate beyond words to call many of them my friends. As a group, they are generous to a fault, optimistic, and highly skilled. The other common trait is that they are an absolute blast to spend time with, catching fish or not, on or off the water. It is their voices, hard-earned knowledge, wit, and wisdom that you are reading in these chapters.

Fisheries change at an astonishing pace. The Upper Sacramento River, for example, is a completely different river than the one anglers fished with their fathers and grandfathers for generations. Most of the same rocks are in all the same places, but natural and human-induced changes have taken their toll over time. It's still a wondrous river, but different in significant ways. In some waters the fish themselves have changed. Manzanita Lake, for example, was for many years primarily a wild rainbow fishery. Ten years ago you might catch a brown trout here and there, but you could also go for days without doing so. Now they seem to outnumber rainbows and catching them is not nearly as easy. Steelhead runs in the Trinity River continue to ebb and flow, but years of habitat restoration are constantly improving the ratio of wild to hatchery steelhead there. And, changes in fisheries management have enhanced numerous fisheries. One fairly recent phenomenon involves the trend toward year-round angling. Learning how to catch fish in some of these rivers in January is a completely new challenge.

I've long been drawn to and fascinated with the aquatic insects that are so important for trout to prosper, and many hatches on California trout streams have come and gone over time. For instance, when I first began fishing Hat Creek in the 1980s, it was half as wide and three times as deep as it is today. In those days trying to stand in Powerhouse 2 Riffle, you were never

Guide Bill Lowe launches a cast on the American River, which provides excellent fly fishing for trout, stripers, and shad.

quite sure if the buzzing noise in the background was coming from the high-voltage wires overhead or the ungainly flight of giant Salmonflies buzzing past your ear. At that time, the river was renowned for its giant Salmonflies, but the last true Salmonfly I saw on Hat was in the early 1990s. Happily, Golden Stones can still be abundant in the early spring and are often mistaken for their even-larger cousins.

One might deduce that the disappearance of Hat Creek Salmonflies had something to do with the plug of sediment working its way through that system, but Salmonflies had also vanished from the Pit, McCloud, and Upper Sacramento rivers over the same period of time. Only a year ago, I noticed the first Salmonfly I had seen in a decade on the McCloud, and I was jubilant. Chances are excellent that this amazing hatch could be coming back. Understanding why it faded in the first place is another thing.

A quick note about the hatch charts and fly patterns included in this book. Because each year is different and the hatches can change from year to year, the hatch charts in this book are intended as general guides only. For up-to-date information on hatches, as well as conditions, you should consult the fly shops listed in the Fly Shops and Guides section of each region. Fly pat-

While this book attempts to provide the most current information on where to go, hatches, and best fly patterns, there is no substitute for the knowledge provided by local fly shops or spending the day on the water with an expert guide.

tern choice is subjective, and many different patterns, as long as they are presented well, will work. However, many of the patterns in this book were designed to catch trout in the fisheries covered in this book. Fly boxes stocked with the patterns appearing throughout the book will stand you in good stead on all California waters. Of course, it is always a good idea to stop by a local shop for up-to-date local knowledge.

Choosing a dozen or so fisheries to include in a guide book is a subjective undertaking, like trying to choose the best grains of sand on a beach. California is simply loaded with great fly-fishing opportunities. New books could easily be written on California's stillwaters, bass-fishing opportunities, salt water, and extensive backcountry. And while I dabble in all of these from time to time, I am a wild-trout guy at heart with a preference for moving water.

When selecting fisheries for this volume I opted toward waters that were already famous, an admitted ploy to avoid death threats and barroom brawls over "spilling the beans" on someone's favorite secret fishing spot. Fortunately, we can all learn to fish the places we already know better. I also avoided focusing on places that could be potentially "loved to death" by increased fishing pressure and stampeding hoards of anglers. Some say the more places there are to fish, the chances of any one place being overrun diminish. I agree with that. But the fact is there is so much good water in California that anglers willing to hike a bit farther than the next guy can often

You can find solitude and unpressured fish simply by walking far from the access parking lots and fishing off the beaten path.

Bill Reid hoists an East Walker brown with obvious enthusiasm. The fact that fish like this are a possibility throughout much of the year adds to the river's legend and popularity. KEN REID PHOTO

find blissful solitude almost anywhere. Access to good fishing in California is fairly simple. If the river is appropriate for boat traffic like the Lower Sacramento, American, Yuba, and Trinity, you are not trespassing as long as you are below the high-water mark. Properties owned by government agencies like the USDA Forest Service are considered to be public property. All other waterways are private property.

By continuing to publicize the places selected in this book, I intentionally offer them up for protection in perpetuity. Few do a better job of fiercely guarding fisheries than fly anglers.

Pit River rainbows very often have small heads and deep bodies, an indicator of rapid growth. The fact that the river is a food factory probably helps.

FLY FISHING
NORTHERN CALIFORNIA

O nce one of the most fertile areas in the world for anadromous fish like salmon and steelhead, most Northern California rivers were shackled between dams and powerhouses in man's lust for cheap energy. What manifested was bad for the ocean-run fish, but a bonanza for wild trout. Streams were no longer as vulnerable to extreme seasonal flooding and the water flowing from beneath dams stayed cold year-round. The tailwater fisheries created protected trout from the harshness of the hot summers and stabilized these streams as great trout habitat. This area of California has more world-class wild-trout streams in a dense concentration than anywhere else I know of, without the bitterly cold winters of Montana, Idaho, and Wyoming.

The successes of California Trout and the fisheries management practices they pioneered in this part of the state also contribute to the area's richness. It started with Hat Creek, but they have been intimately involved in the management of every major California wild-trout stream. The beloved wild-trout section of Hat Creek was created, almost from the ground up, by a few dedicated individuals chasing a dream. The story of how Hat Creek was created is classic in California angling lore with tentacles reaching into the origins of the California Wild Trout Program and California Trout, Inc.

It all started with a group of fishing buddies who loved Hat Creek in the 1960s. The part that would

Northern California Fly Shops and Guides

Hat Creek

Art Teter Guide Service
41075 McArthur Road
Fall River Mills, CA 96028
(530) 336-6110
artteter.com

Clearwater Lodge
P.O. Box 920
Fall River Mills, CA 96028
(888) 600-5451
clearwaterlodge.com

Confluence Outfitters
20735 Manter Court
Red Bluff, CA 96080
(888) 481-1650
confluenceoutfitters.com

Vaughn's Sporting Goods
37307 Main Street
Burney, CA 96013
(530) 335-2381
citlink.net/~vaughnfly/

Fall River

Art Teter Guide Service
41075 McArthur Road
Fall River Mills, CA 96028
(530) 336-6110
artteter.com

Bob Norman
Riverbend Adventures
P.O. Box 281
Douglas City, CA 96024
(530) 778-3540
riverbendadventures.com

(continued)

1

Fall River (continued)

Clearwater Lodge
P.O. Box 920
Fall River Mills, CA 96028
(888) 600-5451
clearwaterlodge.com

Confluence Outfitters
20735 Manter Court
Red Bluff, CA 96080
(888) 481-1650
confluenceoutfitters.com

George Durand
(530) 474-4316

The Fly Shop
Churn Creek Road
Redding, CA 96002
(800) 669-3474
theflyshop.com

McCloud River

Alan Blankenship
Three Rivers Guide Service
Mt. Shasta, CA 96067
(530) 925-7990
threeriversguideservice.com

Art Teter Guide Service
41075 McArthur Road
Fall River Mills, CA 96028
(530) 336-6110
artteter.com

Clearwater Lodge
P.O. Box 920
Fall River Mills, CA 96028
(888) 600-5451
clearwaterlodge.com

Confluence Outfitters
20735 Manter Court
Red Bluff, CA 96080
(888) 481-1650
confluenceoutfitters.com

(continued)

become the wild-trout section looked much different in those days. The stream was narrower and deeper in those days, and there were at least two more islands in Powerhouse 2 Riffle. Hatchery trout were dumped in with abandon, and most of the wild fish were suckers, pikeminnows, and hardheads, not trout. A few visionary anglers decided to do something about it.

I tracked down Richard May, one of the original group of stalwart anglers who conceived and were able to convince others to sign off on a grand experiment to turn a section of Hat into a wild-trout haven. This concept had never been attempted before. According to May, others directly involved were Andre Puyans, Joe Paul, Bob Carroll, and Dr. Herb Joseph.

"Prior to the Hat Creek Project we decided on some broader issues. We wanted to do something about trout management in California. The state was inclined to answer every trout-management problem with the hatchery truck. We thought that bore no resemblance to the kind of trout fishing we knew and wanted to have in the future," said May.

"We searched around and decided that our best deal was to affiliate with Trout Unlimited, which was kind of a fledgling trout conservation organization in Michigan, and use them as a template for going forward with our ideas. After we'd done that, we wanted a demonstration project to show what we meant about wild-trout management.

"Jim Adams, who was the chief fisheries biologist for Pacific Gas and Electric and a friend of many of us, had this idea that had been proposed by one of his biologists years previous to put up a rough-fish barrier on the North Fork of the Feather River. That project never got wheels. But Jim thought the idea would work in lower Hat Creek, which was infested with rough fish. If we could purify that stretch of water, it would be a great place to demonstrate what wild-trout management was all about.

"It was a hard sell, especially locally in Burney and Fall River Mills. Joe used to say it was a project that survived a thousand deaths before it went forward." Finally a rough-fish barrier was constructed just above where Hat flows into Lake Britton.

"After cleansing the stream with rotenone, we restocked it with wild browns and a few hundred Hat

The breathtaking scenery of Northern California's rivers is a bonus to the fantastic trout fishing. There is good fishing up- and downstream of upper Mossbrae Falls, just north of Dunsmuir, accessed by hiking the railroad tracks.

Guide Dax Messet plays a feisty McCloud River rainbow he caught on a nymph. The breathtaking scenery of many of California's rivers is a bonus to the terrific fishing.

McCloud River (continued)

Craig Nielson
Shasta Trout
512 Sarah Bell
Mt. Shasta, CA 96067
(530) 926-5763
shastatrout.com

Hart's Guide Service
(530) 926-2431
snowcrest.net/ronhart/

(continued)

Creek rainbows that we were able to recover during the electroshocking process. After we had done that we set the harvest regulations at a two-fish limit, no restrictions on method. This was a politically feasible approach for the first step in establishing a wild-trout management program where the habitat was managed. The fish were cropped only to the extent they could sustain their numbers in terms of sizes and numbers.

"After those regulations had been in place for a number of years, we could see that the cropping was being excessive. Not the numbers of fish, but the sizes of fish were beginning to descend. We were able to convince the California Fish and Game Commission to put in some restrictions on method of fishing, and a size restriction of 18 inches minimum. That's what really started the momentum for the California Wild Trout Project, which put a dozen streams under similar management with individual regulations depending on habitat and fish population dynamics."

Almost 40 years after this wild experiment, the effects are still being felt. Every fishery in this book is currently protected and managed through the California Wild Trout Program. The best wild-trout fishing in California would not exist without dreams and dreamers. The success at Hat Creek changed the face of wild-trout management forever.

Although more and more streams are staying open to angling year-round, not all have made the change. The traditional angling season runs from the last Saturday in April through November 15. Lakes have always been open all year long. This part of California has somewhat regular weather patterns: cool (not cold) winters; wet, rainy springs; and sweltering summers. The best fishing occurs in spring and fall; July, August, and September are the most challenging months to find consistently good fishing. Surprisingly, even though this is the northernmost part of the state, it is also the hottest during summer, which impacts the quality of the fishing. During summer when other streams in California are fishing well, northern California is subject to doldrums related to the intense heat. You can still have great fishing in the summer, but you have to pick your places wisely—some fisheries are cooler than others. You also have to make allowances for the blast-furnace conditions, choosing to fish early and late and taking a midday siesta.

It's always astounding to me how, in our nation's most populous state, there can be mile after mile of untrammeled blue-ribbon wild-trout water. Between the Upper Sac and the Pit River alone, there is over 50 miles of water to explore. Anglers love to stack up in the easily accessed spots, while there is so much virgin unfished water close by. All it takes is a willingness to hike a little farther. Holiday weekends are the worst and

McCloud River (continued)

McCloud Fly Fishing Adventures
(530) 964-2533
mccloudflyfishing.com

Ted Fay Fly Shop
5732 Dunsmuir Avenue
Dunsmuir, CA 96025
(530) 235-2969
tedfay.com

Pit River

Alan Blankenship
Three Rivers Guide Service
Mt. Shasta, CA 96067
(530) 925-7990
threeriversguideservice.com

Art Teter Guide Service
41075 McArthur Road
Fall River Mills, CA 96028
(530) 336-6110
artteter.com

Clearwater Lodge
P.O. Box 920
Fall River Mills, CA 96028
(888) 600-5451
clearwaterlodge.com

Confluence Outfitters
20735 Manter Court
Red Bluff, CA 96080
(888) 481-1650
confluenceoutfitters.com

Craig Nielson
Shasta Trout
512 Sarah Bell
Mt. Shasta, CA 96067
(530) 926-5763
shastatrout.com

Hart's Guide Service
(530) 926-2431
snowcrest.net/ronhart/

(continued)

Pit River (continued)

Vaughn's Sporting Goods
37307 Main Street
Burney, CA 96013
(530) 335-2381
citlink.net/~vaughnfly/

Upper Sacramento River

Alan Blankenship
Three Rivers Guide Service
Mt. Shasta, CA 96067
(530) 925-7990
threeriversguideservice.com

Art Teter Guide Service
41075 McArthur Road
Fall River Mills, CA 96028
(530) 336-6110
artteter.com

Confluence Outfitters
20735 Manter Court
Red Bluff, CA 96080
(888) 481-1650
confluenceoutfitters.com

Craig Nielson
Shasta Trout
512 Sarah Bell
Mt. Shasta, CA 96067
(530) 926-5763
shastatrout.com

Hart's Guide Service
(530) 926-2431
snowcrest.net/ronhart/

McCloud Fly Fishing Adventures
(530) 964-2533
mccloudflyfishing.com

Ted Fay Fly Shop
5732 Dunsmuir Avenue
Dunsmuir, CA 96025
(530) 235-2969
tedfay.com

The Fly Shop
Churn Creek Road
Redding, CA 96002
(800) 669-3474
theflyshop.com

Lower Sacramento River

Art Teter Guide Service
41075 McArthur Road
Fall River Mills, CA 96028
(530) 336-6110
artteter.com

Bob Norman
Riverbend Adventures
P.O. Box 281
Douglas City, CA 96024
(530) 778-3540
riverbendadventures.com

Confluence Outfitters
20735 Manter Court
Red Bluff, CA 96080
(888) 481-1650
confluenceoutfitters.com

George Durand
(530) 474-4316

Sac River Outfitters
10622 Petunia Lane
Palo Cedro, CA 96073
(888) 722-7483
sacriveroutfitters.com

The Fly Shop
Churn Creek Road
Redding, CA 96002
(800) 669-3474
theflyshop.com

Trinity River

Bob Norman
Riverbend Adventures
P.O. Box 281
Douglas City, CA 96024
(530) 778-3540
riverbendadventures.com

Brad McFall
P.O. Box 2515
Mammoth Lakes, CA 93546
(209) 484-1114
mammothflyfishing.com

Confluence Outfitters
20735 Manter Court
Red Bluff, CA 96080
(888) 481-1650
confluenceoutfitters.com

Ed Duggan
P.O. Box 867
Willow Creek, CA 95573
(530) 629-3554

George Durand
(530) 474-4316

Mike Hibbard
Shasta Outfitters
(530) 247-3970
shastaoutfitters.com

Sac River Outfitters
10622 Petunia Lane
Palo Cedro, CA 96073
(888) 722-7483
sacriveroutfitters.com

The Fly Shop
Churn Creek Road
Redding, CA 96002
(800) 669-3474
theflyshop.com

Trinity Fly Shop
P.O. Box 176
Lewiston, CA 96052
(530) 623-6757
trinityflyshop.com

Trinity River Adventures
361 Ponderosa Pines Road
Lewiston, CA 96052
(530) 623-4179
trinityriveradventures.com

Manzanita Lake

Guiding is not allowed on Manzanita Lake because it is within the national park. The Fly Shop in Redding is the best source of flies and information.

Northern California's challenging trout water provides anglers with the opportunity to hone their skills.

are good times to avoid Hat Creek's Powerhouse 2 Riffle, for instance, but the more remote sections of larger rivers are often blissfully vacant. Sections of Pit 4 see only a few anglers in an entire year, and I live for these remote places. Seek them out and you will agree.

While you can separate yourself from the maddening hordes and find good fishing almost any day of the year in Northern California, this part of the state hoards one more provocative gift for the ardent angler. It is the opportunity to develop skill—an occupation scores of anglers have devoted themselves to. No other part of California offers a better opportunity to learn the nuances of fly fishing. Not only is there a lot of quality water but also an abundance of highly skilled guides, casting instructors, and fly-fishing schools. I know of no better place to become an expert angler.

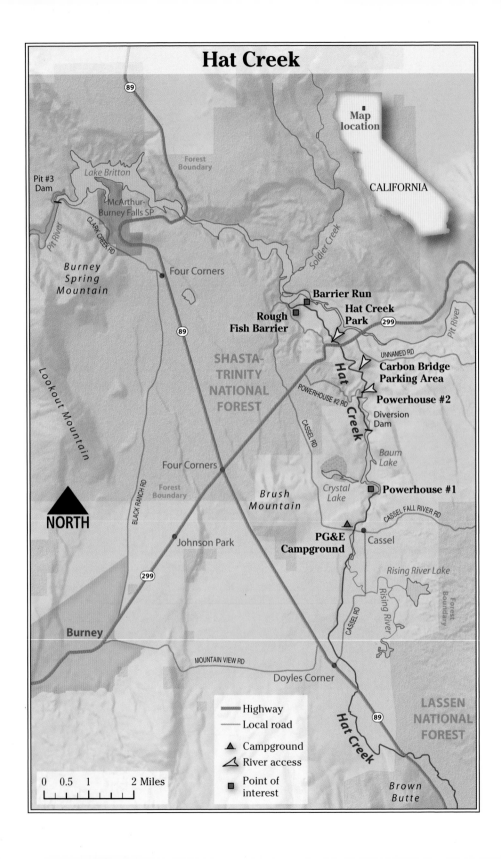

Hat Creek

Map location

CALIFORNIA

89

Forest
Boundary

Lake Britton

Pit #3
Dam

McArthur-
Burney Falls SP

CLARK CREEK RD

Pit River

Burney
Spring
Mountain

Four Corners

Barrier Run

Hat Creek
Park

299

Soldier Creek

Pit River

Rough
Fish Barrier

SHASTA-
TRINITY
NATIONAL
FOREST

89

UNNAMED RD

Carbon Bridge
Parking Area

Hat Creek

POWERHOUSE #2 RD

Powerhouse #2

Diversion
Dam

CASSEL RD

Baum
Lake

Lookout Mountain

Four Corners

Forest
Boundary

Brush
Mountain

Crystal
Lake

Powerhouse #1

CASSEL FALL RIVER RD

BLACK RANCH RD

NORTH

Johnson Park

PG&E
Campground

Cassel

Rising River Lake

299

Rising River

CASSEL RD

Forest
Boundary

Burney

MOUNTAIN VIEW RD

Doyles Corner

LASSEN
NATIONAL
FOREST

Hat Creek

89

Highway

Local road

▲ Campground

◁ River access

■ Point of
interest

0   0.5   1   2 Miles

Brown
Butte

CHAPTER 1

Hat Creek

More words per mile have been written about Hat Creek than there are wild trout per mile beneath its surface. Yet it remains the Mt. Everest of all California spring creeks. While never easy, it certainly is possible to catch fish here, even on the flat water. To succeed against these fish, reputed to be the wariest wild trout in California, is the ultimate validation of your skill as an angler.

Countless articles, reports, studies, surveys, and chapters have been produced, meetings held, and dollars spent on creating and preserving this dream. How could three little miles of spring creek water be worth all that? The perfect idea that became Hat Creek, sometimes as fragile and uncertain as a whiff of smoke in the air, hangs on in this tiny northern California hamlet with the tenacity of a pit bull. To many, Hat Creek is something like a shrine. Anglers come here with and without guides eager to test or improve their spring-creek skills. Many crash and burn, yet failure here isn't the same as in other places. The difficulty of this flat-water fishing is understood and respected by those who fish here often and wouldn't have it any other way.

When fly anglers talk about Hat Creek, they are likely talking about lower Hat, the wild-trout section. From Powerhouse 2 downstream to Lake Britton, it crosses under CA 299 in the shadow of a diatomaceous earth cliff just east of Burney. It's a tranquil setting, but upstream is some of the most intriguing, low-gradient, meandering wild-trout water imaginable. All the fish have PhDs, and to them we are knuckle-dragging Neanderthals. Well, some more than others.

The Wild-Trout Section

From Powerhouse 2 down to Lake Britton, Hat is as picturesque and beautiful a meadow trout stream as you could find anywhere. The stream bubbles out of a powerhouse instead of the ground, but here's where obvious human intervention ends.

Powerhouse 2 Riffle immediately below the powerhouse is the most popular place to fish on Hat Creek if not, as the old joke goes, in all of California. Most Hat regulars know it as "the riffle," simply because it is the only one. I have personally seen 45 anglers stacked up in this section at one time and, as you might imagine, it can get a little crazy. I heard one fellow address another, "If you cast to my trout one more time I'm going to come over there and

Hat has a small population of fussy wild browns. If you can fool these fish, you are well on your way to becoming an expert angler. ANDREW HARRIS PHOTO

Before trying to wade across Hat Creek, watch others doing it first, especially the guides who work here often. It is easy to get in over your waders, and the current is stronger than it appears.

thump your head!" Fortunately Hat is hardly ever this crowded, but you will hardly ever have the place to yourself either.

The riffle is a bug factory and the only place on Hat Creek where an angler of average skill might consistently catch fish. The surface of the water is broken, disguising a slightly deeper trough that holds many fish. This is also the only productive nymphing water above CA 299.

Nymphing the riffle is pretty straightforward. You can get away with fishing a 9-foot leader tapered to 6X. Tie on one or two #16-18 nymphs and one medium-size split-shot about 10 inches above them. Use a small strike indicator about 5 feet above the split-shot. Larger indicators tend to spook these fish. Work out 6 to 8 feet of fly line and flip it in the water quartering upstream. Hold your rod high, and as your indicator passes in front of you,

Anglers line up on both sides of the "slot" in Powerhouse 2 Riffle. Though nymphing is the primary tactic, evenings can bring fantastic dry-fly fishing.

mend upstream so your fly line stays above the indicator. Then lower your rod at the same speed as the current until your rod touches the surface and your flies swing up to the surface.

At times, especially evenings, the riffle can provide outstanding dry-fly fishing for fish less selective than those in the flat water. During daylight hours it isn't common to catch fish over 12 or 13 inches in Powerhouse 2 Riffle. But as a few Hat Creek regulars have discovered, the big boys come out at dark.

It's legal to fish until one hour after sunset in this part of the state. Plan on heading out when you see others wading back to the parking lot for lack of light. I like to use a Type III full-sinking line, a short 1X leader, and a #10 black Woolly Bugger. Cast across the stream, throw a big upstream mend, and just hold on. There is no fly or strike indicator to watch as you swing the fly under the surface, but you will feel the grabs. As in all fishing, some nights you win, sometimes you don't. But I've witnessed some truly impressive Hat Creek rainbows and browns taken this way and never failed to get a murderous grab or two.

Flat-Water Fishing

Once you're below Powerhouse 2 Riffle, the water stays flat all the way down to the CA 299 bridge. The long straightaway immediately below the riffle can provide good fishing depending on the year and the time of year. Sometimes it has lush vegetation; other times all you see is silt. When the vegetation is there, so are the fish. When it's not, move downstream. In the 20-plus years I've been fishing and snorkeling Hat Creek, I've seen two fish approaching 30 inches. One was on this first bend below the riffle.

Downstream of this straightaway, Hat jogs to the left and flows through an area of swampy cattails, muskrat holes, and eroding stream bank. But the vegetation is less seasonal here and the fish seem to like it. Like most of the flat water downstream, there is limited wading in this section and better casters definitely have a leg up. There's no question where the fish are; you can see them rising, but it is difficult to deliver a fly to the feeding lane and get a long enough drag-free drift and not snag a cattail on your backcast. To add to the challenge, the deep water makes it tough to wade into casting range.

Downstream the stream takes a slight right-hand turn against a high bank on the western side. The deeper hole in front of the high bank, which is

Fooling trout from the bank often requires keeping your backcast high enough to prevent snagging surrounding vegetation.

best accessed from the eastern side, is an ideal place to throw leech or Woolly Bugger patterns on a sinking line at dark. Until the stream takes another left-hand turn just above Carbon Bridge, the stream on both sides is almost too marshy for good access.

The Carbon Bridge area takes its name from a historic toll bridge that was here until its removal in 1969. This is one of the most popular sections for dry-fly addicts, and it has its own parking section. The water here could not be more inviting. The clear, glassy flows caress rich, undulating vegetation, providing ideal habitat for trout, and the tawny fields rising from the water into rolling hills give the place a pastoral, peaceful look. If trout are going to be rising on Hat Creek, Carbon is the place to find them.

Unless you are an accomplished caster, the best way to approach the risers in this section is by wading. Be careful though and bring a wading staff. Sediments shift frequently here, and a place you could barely wade to last week may be a no-go this week. In the water you will most likely be concentrating on downstream presentations. Casting isn't a concern here as much as being able to manage slack line as you feed each drift gradually downstream.

The downstream routine goes something like this: Make a short cast with 10 or 15 feet of fly line, and skate your fly until it lines up with your target fish's feeding lane. If you shake line downstream too slowly, you will skate the fly and put the fish down. If you shake line out too fast and the fish grabs your fly, you won't be able to set the hook. The trick is in finding that happy medium and then reacting fast enough when the trout takes your fly. When everything comes together, you feel like Lee Wulff and Ernest Schwiebert rolled into one. When you fail, you feel like the rest of us.

Below Carbon, Hat takes a right-hand swing, and the western side of the river is forested from here on down. There is still good access on the eastern side, and going below the Carbon Bridge straightaway will likely get you away from most other anglers. At this point you will see the upper end of Teal Island (called Wood Duck Island on some maps), another strikingly scenic and popular area. But like Carbon, it can be tough. Both sides of the island offer great fishing and the seam where currents come together below is a natural feeding lane the trout take advantage of.

The far forested section of Hat is special in that it holds some large brown trout. There are a few browns left from the original stocking in 1969–1970, and they can attain substantial size. If you're a good distance caster and don't mind wading to the top of your waders, try throwing Woolly Buggers into the downed sweepers at or near dark.

The last cherished section of great dry-fly water is the long straightaway above the CA 299 bridge known as the 299 Flats. Here there are sporadic areas of vegetation, and the rest of the bottom is more sand-colored silt. Looking into the water might lead you to believe there aren't many fish here, but if you look upstream from the bridge in the evening, you will see rising fish.

You can park at Hat Creek Park immediately downstream from the bridge and hike upstream. Above, the bridge access is better on the western

Simple patterns often work the best for sophisticated fish. This one took a Birds Nest presented on a dead-drift.

side, although a little swampy. The path on the eastern side will take you up a hill and provide better access to water farther upstream.

Downstream of 299

Most of the water downstream of the CA 299 Bridge becomes fairly shallow and fast, providing habitat for small fish at best. Only the areas above and below the rough-fish barrier downstream provide enough deeper water to provide big-fish habitat. You can access this lower section by driving east from the CA 299 bridge and turning right at the first dirt road you come to. There are no signs, but there is an open gate. Take a right turn after the sand quarry and you will soon be driving parallel to lower Hat. Park your car and look for a shallow place to cross the river. The stream is not so deep, but the water moves fairly quickly. Access to Barrier Run, Barrier Pool, and the riffle immediately below are all from the far side.

Barrier Run is a good option if the water above the CA 299 bridge is crowded. You can find good nymphing and dry-fly fishing here (especially in the evenings) without the need for the spring-creek skills so important upstream. Access to the pool leaves room for one angler at best, and he needs to be an accomplished roll-caster. The riffle immediately below the rough-fish barrier, technically Lake Britton, has a few deeper spots and can hold some surprisingly big trout. It also holds Sacramento suckers, pikeminnows, and hardheads—the very fish the barrier was constructed to exclude.

Wading is not always necessary on Hat Creek's flat water, as fish often rise within casting range. Still, merely getting the fly to the fish is not good enough to fool these fussy fish. Anglers must have good line-handling skills and be able to present the fly with a dead-drift.

Upper Hat

Hat first bubbles out of the volcanic landscape within Lassen Volcanic National Park some 40 miles to the south. While not much of a fishery here, there are a few small brookies and rainbows to dally with if you feel the urge. From the park, Hat Creek sets a course almost due north, where it flows through numerous farmers' fields, campgrounds, and day-use areas. Several more springs contribute their flows along the way, broadening the stream and transforming it into a better fishery. The campgrounds along CA 89 and CA 44 are generously planted with hatchery trout and are wildly popular with the catch-and-keep set.

By the time Hat almost reaches the tiny town of Cassel, roughly paralleling CA 44, most of the magic water is lost to irrigation, and much of the rest seeps back down into the volcanic landscape from whence it came. Just when Hat is about to become an afterthought, the broad icy flows of Rising River enter the stream, giving it new life. Like Hat, Rising River also bubbles out of the ground, on Rising River Ranch, and is currently owned by Clint Eastwood and formerly by Bing Crosby.

Upstream of Hat Creek Bridge in Cassel, anglers fish for a combination of wild and hatchery trout in a picturesque setting of cattails, ospreys, red-winged blackbirds, and a backdrop of extinct volcanoes. The evening hatch is reliable in this section, and while most of the trout aren't wild, they do provide some challenging fishing.

Across the road and downstream from the bridge, Hat flows through what is affectionately called "The Ditch," a concrete canal next to a PG&E (Pacific Gas and Electric) campground. This water is also liberally stocked with hatchery fish. Eventually Hat again almost reaches its terminus in a place called Cassel Forebay, a big pool with a grass-catching machine at the bottom where all the water is shunted into a pipe and dropped into Hat 1 Powerhouse at the head of Baum Lake. Another concrete ditch carries water from Baum Lake along the top of a ridge before it is confined in another pipe and dropped into Hat 2 Powerhouse. These are the less-than-glamorous origins of Hat's wild-trout fishery. But what happens to the setting and the stream for the next three miles is truly remarkable.

Early-Season Hatches

Understanding Hat's entomology will certainly help you select the right pattern, but if you haven't mastered spring-creek presentation skills, having the perfect fly is of little consequence. Catching fish on Hat is about presentation, pure and simple. Hat Creek trout will fall for the wrong fly on occasion if it's drifted properly, but they won't abide a dragging fly, period. Slow, flat water gives these trout an opportunity to consider your fly for an exasperatingly long time. Having plenty of food also means the fish aren't motivated by gnawing hunger.

Opening Day (the last Saturday in April) often finds the Powerhouse 2 Riffle alive with activity. Giant Golden Stoneflies are usually clinging on the streamside grasses and hopelessly failing at streamlined flight later in the day. The colony of Lewis woodpeckers, first named on the Lewis and Clark expedition, living in the trees adjacent to the riffle take notice of this and are well-known for preferring to catch their meals in midair. Just at dark, the fish begin looking up for the big mouthful they've learned to expect, and a well-placed Stimulator or Madame X (#8-10) can often induce a murderous strike.

As happens all too frequently at Hat, anglers see the big stoneflies and immediately think that is the fly pattern to fish. Remember the majority of these insects are in the air, and not yet available to the trout. If you see rising fish, try putting your face down closer to the water and perhaps you will notice something smaller that might be stealing the show. Early and again

HAT CREEK HATCHES

	JAN	FEB	MAR	APR	MAY	JUN	JUL	AUG	SEP	OCT	NOV	DEC
Blue-Winged Olive (*Baetis* spp.)					●						●	
Golden Stonefly (*Calineuria* spp.)					●							
Pale Morning Dun (*Ephemerella* spp.)						●						
Trico (*Tricorythodes* spp.)							●					
Caddis (*Brachycentrus/Hydropsyche* spp.)					●	●						
Little Sister Sedge (*Cheumatopsyche* spp.)					●	●						
Little Yellow Stone (*Isoperla* spp.)						●						
Mahogany Dun (*Paraleptophlebia* spp.)									●	●		
October Caddis (*Dicosmoecus* spp.)										●		

Blue-Winged Olive (*Baetis* spp.)
#18-20 olive Mercer's Micro Mayfly, Mercer's Poxyback Baetis, Morrish's Anato-May, Morrish's Hotwire May, Beadhead Pheasant Tail, WD-40, Quigley's Hat Creek Spider, Quigley Cripple, Paradun

Golden Stonefly (*Calineuria* spp.)
#6-8 Morrish's Cone Stone, Mercer's Biot Epoxy Golden Stone, Superfloss Rubberlegs, Idyl-Wired Stone, Mercer's Flush Floater Foam Stone, Stimulator, Madame X

Pale Morning Dun (*Ephemerella* spp.)
#16-18 yellow Morrish's Anato-May, rust Morrish's Hotwire May, Mercer's GB Poxyback PMD, Mercer's Poxyback Emerger, brown or ruby Mercer's Micro Mayfly, Burk's HBI Nymph, P.M.D. Challenger, Sparkle Dun, Paradun, Quigley's Hat Creek Spider, Mercer's PMD Profile Spinner

Trico (*Tricorythodes* spp.)
#20 black Mercer's Micro Mayfly, CDC Biot Spinner, Etha Wing Trico, Quigley's Hat Creek Spider

Caddis (*Brachycentrus/Hydropsyche* spp.)
#12-16 olive or brown Birds Nest, Copper John, Mercer's Z-Wing Caddis, Mercer's Glo-Bubble Caddis, Fox's Poopah, Morrish's Hotwire Caddis, Morrish's Super Pupa, Gordon's Prince Nymph, Mercer's Missing Link, Hot Creek Caddis

Little Sister Sedge (*Cheumatopsyche* spp.)
#18 brown Fox's Micro Poopah, Mercer's Glo-Bubble Caddis, Morrish's Super Pupa, Elk Hair Caddis, Cutter's E/C Caddis, Mercer's Missing Link, Hot Creek Caddis

Little Yellow Stone (*Isoperla* spp.)
#14 Morrish's Iron Sally, Quigley's Stacker Sally

Mahogany Dun (*Paraleptophlebia* spp.)
#12-14 rust Sparkle Dun, Mercer's Foam Parachute, Paradun, Tilt Wing Dun

October Caddis (*Dicosmoecus* spp.)
#8 Mercer's Tungsten October Pupa, orange Mercer's Psycho Prince, Morrish's October Pupa, Morrish's WMD, Puterbaugh's Foam Caddis, Stimulator, Madame X

late in the season tiny Blue-Winged Olive mayflies may actually provide enough strength in numbers to become more important to the fish than their larger brethren. An olive Paradun (#18-20) on a 6X or 7X tippet might be the better choice.

By June, there are so many different bugs—Blue-Winged Olive mayflies, Golden Stoneflies, several different caddisflies, Little Yellow Stones, Pale Morning Duns (PMDs), and Tricos—coming off that matching the hatch becomes a shell game. The good news is that even selective trout will sometimes try something a little different, perhaps just for variety. Also, certain fly patterns will effectively match several different hatches, and this really ups your odds. An Elk Hair Caddis (#12-20), for example, can easily be taken for several different caddisflies, as well as a Little Yellow Stone. Of course, spring-creek trout do not always focus on the most abundant insect. On a typical spring morning on Hat's flat water, the fish rise to Trico or PMD spinners early in the day. If you see rising fish, but no insects on the water, a Trico Spinner (#18-22) or Rusty Spinner (#16-20) are good choices.

By July 4, the air temperatures can soar into triple digits, and the fish hunker down under the weeds until the sun is off the water. Early and late can be wonderful, but midday is a bust unless a rare rainstorm arrives to break the monotony. Other local streams fish better during the high sun and heat, so heading over to the Pit or McCloud until the sun is off the water is a good strategy.

Pale Morning Duns may come off sporadically during the day, but it's rare to find the hatch localized enough to get the fish interested. Better off to wait until evening when all the females flush with ripe egg sacs return to the stream to oviposit. The fish definitely notice this and seem less reticent to rise when the sun is off the water. There are a number of good PMD imitations, and everything from an emerger to a dun or a cripple might prove useful. Good choices include Mercer's Poxyback Emergers, Quigley's Hat Creek Spiders, and P.M.D. Challengers (#16-18).

Like other spring creeks, on Hat the fish show a preference for mayflies. This is important to know when there are mayflies, several different sizes of caddisflies, and Little Yellow Stones all on the water at the same time. More

Keeping Hat a great place to fish requires regular maintenance. Between the muskrat problem and siltation issues, Hat keeps conservation groups busy. Of course, the fishing makes it all worthwhile.

often than not, imitating the small mayfly proves the best way to go. But every day is different, so be ready for anything.

Just when they've got you lulled into a false sense of security, Hat Creek trout will become selective to caddisflies. Hat abounds in Little Western Weedy-Water Sedge (*Amiocentrus* spp.), American Grannom (*Brachycentrus* spp.), and Spotted Sedge (*Hydropsyche* spp.). These are perhaps the most common caddisflies on the West Coast, and they're found in nearly every Pacific trout stream. If you should luck into a major emergence, you're better off fishing nymphs just beneath the surface or emergers. Patterns like Cutter's E/C Caddis, Hot Creek Caddis, or Pettis' Glass Caddis Emerger (#16-18) will be needed to persuade these fish. Of course, there are times when a plain old Elk Hair Caddis will do the trick.

Beginning in September, which can still offer triple-digit weather, things begin to change on Hat. Mahogany Duns, one of my favorite hatches, begin

In order to keep muskrats from burrowing into and eroding the streambanks, volunteers have placed rocks and logs in sections of the river.

emerging, signaling the doldrums of summer are coming to an end. During cloudy or rainy weather, the Mahogany Duns may hatch in the middle of the day and provoke the fish to rise. The long straightaway known as the 299 Flats can provide some fast fishing to this hatch, and fishing a #14-16 Tilt Wing Dun or Haystack is a refreshing change of pace from the small-fly fishing of summer.

The fall October Caddis hatch (*Dicosmoecus* spp.) is interesting in that it comes off best in Powerhouse 2 Riffle and below CA 299. That's not to say you won't see the huge mothlike creatures bobbing up and down in the air like crazed yo-yos on the flat water. They drift both downstream from the riffle and up from below CA 299 to the flat water. But to take a fish on an October Caddis dry fly on the flat water would be a fluke. It might happen, but someday pigs might fly. The best water to fish this hatch is Barrier Run down closer to Lake Britton. Adult October Caddis patterns like a Puterbaugh's Foam Caddis or a Stimulator (#8-10) will usually get the desired response.

Keeping the Dream Alive

The only trouble with creating a virtual paradise is keeping it that way. Truth is, nothing stays the same for very long, and natural and man-made challenges conspire to undermine one of the most famous trout fisheries in the West.

Scientists hesitate to say for sure, but most agree the most likely source of the volcanic sediment that began choking Hat in the early 1990s is a ruptured underground lava tube. Because Hat is essentially a closed system due to the rough-fish barrier just above Lake Britton, sediments do not move through Hat the way they do in a normal stream. Because most dams are built on such a grand scale, no one notices that every dammed piece of water eventually fills in. Hat's dam is small, so changes are more noticeable, and Hat is becoming shallower with every passing year.

Hat has a considerable muskrat population. While these critters don't directly hurt the fish, they burrow into the soft banks to build their dens, and when hapless anglers casting from the bank step on them, they cave, and over time this has caused Hat to become a little wider and a little shallower. Muskrats also munch stream vegetation with a vengeance (at certain times of the year, an adult muskrat can uproot 14 pounds of vegetation in a single day), which also hastens erosion. A 750-foot section of streambank just downstream from the Carbon Bridge parking lot was rebuilt several years ago with provisions to make it "muskrat proof." The fact that it is almost impossible to recognize stands as a testament to its success.

Hat began as a vision, and has rightly taken its place as the most daunting fly-fishing destination in California. As long as there are people willing to dream big, Hat Creek will remain a very special place to fish that will easily get under your skin and keep you coming back.

Bob Quigley's Sparkle Stacker (BWO)

Hook:	#20 Tiemco 100
Thread:	Olive 8/0 Uni-Thread
Tail:	Rusty brown Z-lon
Abdomen:	Olive 8/0 Uni-Thread
Thorax:	BWO Super Fine
Hackle:	Dun hackle, tied Sparkle Stacker style
Wing:	White poly yarn

Mercer's Micro Mayfly (Black)

Hook:	#14-20 Tiemco 3769
Bead:	Copper
Thread:	Black 8/0 Uni-Thread
Tail:	Natural ring-necked pheasant-tail fibers
Rib:	Silver Ultra Wire (small)
Abdomen:	Black Flashabou
Wing Case:	Golden brown mottled turkey tail and pearl Flashabou coated with 5-minute epoxy
Thorax:	Lava brown Buggy Nymph Dubbing
Legs:	Same as tail

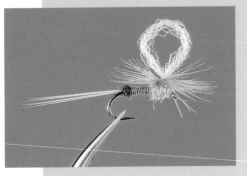

Bob Quigley's Upright Loop Wing Female Spinner (Baetis)

Hook:	#14-22 Tiemco 100
Thread:	Light dun 8/0 Uni-Thread
Tail:	Dun Microfibetts
Egg Sac:	Black Super Fine
Body:	Dark olive stripped saddle
Wing:	Gray dun poly
Thorax:	Medium olive dubbing
Hackle:	Dun

Bob Quigley's Spider Midge

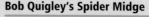

Hook:	#20-22 Tiemco 2488
Thread:	Gray 12/0 Benecchi
Tail:	Z-lon
Underbody:	Green to olive dubbing
Overbody:	Deer hair butts from front wing folded over and tied in behind the front tips tied forward
Overwings:	Two grizzly hackle tips, and two strands of Micro Pearl Krystal Flash
Hackle:	Grizzly

Bob Quigley's Female Baetis Hackle Stacker

Hook:	#16-20 Tiemco 100
Thread:	Olive dun 8/0 Uni-Thread
Tail:	Dun Microfibetts
Body:	Olive saddle hackle quill stripped and wrapped
Thorax:	BWO Super Fine
Hackle:	Grizzly tied Hackle Stacker style

Bob Quigley's Loopy Cripple (PMD)

Hook:	#14-20 Tiemco 2487 or Daiichi 1130
Thread:	Light olive 8/0 Uni-Thread
Tail:	Brown Z-lon spotted with a black Sharpie
Body:	Pheasant tail
Rib:	Copper or red wire (fine)
Hackle:	Light ginger or cream
Thorax:	PMD Super Fine
Wing:	Medium gray poly yarn

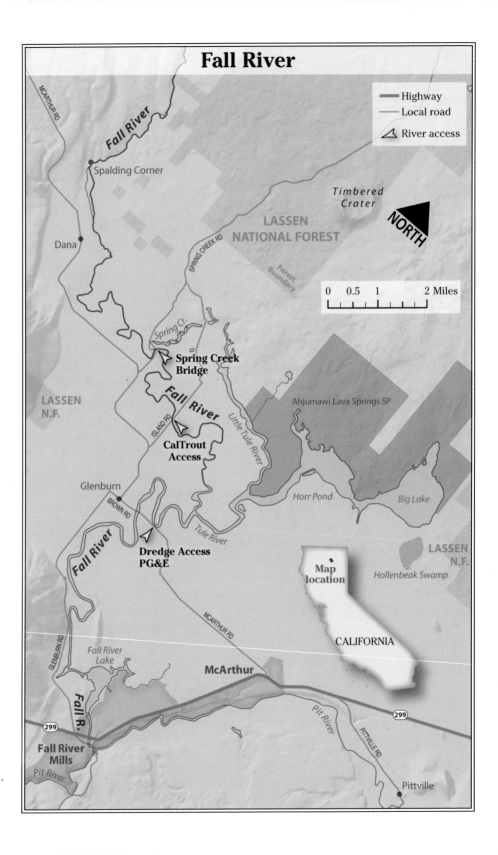

Fall River

Highway
Local road
⊿ River access

Fall River

MCARTHUR RD

Spalding Corner

LASSEN
NATIONAL FOREST

Timbered
Crater

NORTH

Dana

SPRING CREEK RD

Forest
Boundary

0   0.5   1   2 Miles

Spring Cr.

Spring Creek
Bridge

LASSEN
N.F.

Fall River

Ahjumawi Lava Springs SP

ISLAND RD

Little Tule River

CalTrout
Access

Glenburn

BROWN RD

Horr Pond

Big Lake

Fall River

Tule River

Dredge Access
PG&E

LASSEN
N.F.

Map
location

Hollenbeak Swamp

MCARTHUR RD

GLENBURN RD

Fall River
Lake

McArthur

CALIFORNIA

Pit River

PITTVILLE RD

299

Fall R.

299

Fall River
Mills

Pit River

Pittville

CHAPTER 2

Fall River

While floating on Fall River, you find yourself straddling the apex of two worlds. Reflected up are scenes from the bucolic Fall River valley—swaying cattails and ramshackle barns beneath a seemingly endless blue sky. Below is a glistening silent world, the one seen through polarized lenses that is even more verdant, picturesque, and teeming with life than the landscape above. Here is where Fall River holds her secrets, and the sound of what she won't tell you can be deafening.

With 26 miles of flat water; Shasta County's Fall River is the longest spring creek in North America. It literally bubbles out of the earth on private property. There is not a single riffle, run, or pool anywhere along its length, only miles of slow-moving water loaded with trout. Virtually anywhere you consider stepping out of the boat on dry land is private property. Most of the fish are wild, native rainbow trout, thousands of them per mile, with just a sprinkling of browns to keep things interesting. The browns are a vestige of times gone by when fisheries management protocol assumed that dumping nonnative fish into almost any puddle was a good thing.

Fall is a fairly deep river meandering through a scenic valley framed by mountains, hardly any shade except under bridges, and lots of sky. The water looks much different than, say, a freestone stream. This is flat, deep water; every inch of it. Some areas are sandy with little vegetation or places for fish to hide. Generally these are not the best areas to fish, although fish will some-times move into these areas to intercept bugs hatching from up above. Other areas of the stream have lush vegetation, which provides lots of food and cover for fish.

Fishing Fall River is largely an act of working "the line," that skinny playing field where air and water converge. Eyeballs both above and below are fixed upon it. Frequent visitors to that shimmering plane include abundant hatches of mayflies, caddisflies, stoneflies, and damselflies, water snakes, muskrats, birds of every description, anglers dizzy with anticipation, and hungry rainbows and browns.

Fall River provides nothing but lots of glassy spring-creek water and a big sky overhead. As stunning as the scenery is, most anglers direct their attention down toward the water and the great schools of trout scattering as the boats plow through.

Public access is limited to two launch spots, the CalTrout access and the Dredge Site. Low bridges over the river intentionally limit the size of boats anglers may use, and pram-style crafts with small gasoline motors and electric motors are favored. These are best for stability while standing up casting and fishing, which is how most anglers do it. One anchor is a must, but two are much better for positioning your boat perpendicular to the banks and making downstream drifts.

It pays to be fairly well organized before pulling away from the dock, since anything you forget in the car will probably not be accessible for the rest of the day. Fall gets regular attention from area game wardens, so forgetting your fishing license in your car or failing to pinch your barbs in the appropriate areas will cost you big-time; plus they are authorized to confiscate your rod and reel as well. You can leave your waders at home, but water, tackle, boat gear, a brimmed hat, and sunscreen are essential. During summer, Fall River anglers often refer to themselves as "pram potatoes," an apt description of how it feels to bake under the relentless sun.

Guide Andrew Harris shows off a fat rainbow with Soldier Mountain in the background. Large-brimmed hats are a good idea on Fall for protection from the relentless sun. ANDREW HARRIS PHOTO

From Top to Bottom

Unless you have private access, the middle portions of Fall are the most practical to fish, and the most productive. Fortunately the areas up- and downstream from the two public boat-launch ramps give you access to plenty of great water.

The CalTrout access (short for California Trout) just above Island Road Bridge is free, open to the public, and the closest to the upper regions of the river. From here most anglers find more than enough water to fish without venturing too far above Zug Bug Alley, the section of stream immediately downstream of Spring Creek, one of Fall's main tributaries.

While there is a lot of water above Spring Creek, this section doesn't usually get the pressure the middle portions of the river do. Frankly, most anglers feel you don't need to take such a long boat ride to find really good fishing. The upper river is generally used by residents with riverfront property or anglers staying at the one fishing lodge in this section, Spinner Fall Lodge. The busiest section, except during the Hex hatch, is usually the section from Spring Creek downstream several river miles from the CalTrout boat-launch ramp. Despite the likelihood of seeing other anglers, the fishing in this middle section continues to hold up, chiefly because the water is loaded with hungry trout.

Continuing downstream, the river gets wider and cloudier in sections, particularly below the confluence with Tule River, and you tend to see less

Island Road Bridge over Fall River is kept low to the water, intentionally limiting the size of boats that can drift up and down the river. Flat-bottomed prams are typically the best due to their low profile and stability.

Almost the only disturbance to the placid flows on Fall River are made by fish, either rising or battling against someone's bent rod.

vegetation and rising fish. The general impression is that the lower river holds fewer trout than the upper, although there are also some truly huge fish in this lower section.

Tactics and Strategies

Unlike freestone streams where trout can be found in predictable places, the trout in Fall River move around a great deal, similar to the way fish move around in lakes. The good news is there are areas that always seem to hold fish. The downside is there are often other boats stacked every 30 or 40 feet in such places. On the other hand, Fall is so full of healthy trout that finding a good spot is fairly easy.

If fish are taking bugs on the surface, it's fairly obvious where they are. Because the water is so flat, it's easy to spot rising fish from a distance. Resist the urge to chase those intermittent rises, because the river is generally full of intermittently rising fish. Your best chance of success lies in locating a group of fish that are consistently rising.

Motor slowly up- or downstream keeping a sharp eye on the surface of the water. Take care not to spook fish by motoring over them or banging hard objects against the side of the boat. When you think you've spied a bunch of risers, slow down. These fish require a downstream dead-drift presentation. If you're coming from downstream, give them a wide berth as you motor above them. If the risers are downstream from you, cut your gas motor and quietly drift down to within casting distance before you drop anchor. Do not stand in the boat while you are adjusting your position, since as soon as you stand the fish are likely to move 15 more feet downstream.

Finding fish that are not rising is a little more challenging, but with a good pair of polarized sunglasses you can easily see into the clear water, scanning for fish as you motor upstream. Chances are, you will spook them, but mark the spot, anchor above them as quietly as possible, and wait a few minutes for things to settle down. In ten or fewer minutes, they will generally resume rising.

Fall River Twitch

Whether the technique was actually developed on Fall River is speculative, but anyone who learns to catch fish consistently here must first master the "Twitch." The twitch refers to the flipping or twitching motion of the rod tip used in presenting a fly downstream dead-drift, making it one of the best techniques for flat water and fussy fish. The benefit is the fish see the dead-drifting fly first, before they get a look at the tippet, leader, and fly line trailing behind it.

Make a short, downstream cast, stopping the rod high so the leader and tippet fall in lazy curves on the water. As soon as it lands, throw an upstream mend so that the fly goes downstream first and you create some slack between the fly and rod tip. After mending, point the rod tip down at the water and begin shaking loose coils of fly line downstream. It helps to gather up loose fly line in your left hand before shaking the rod with your right (or the reverse for left-handers).

Handling the slack line takes some practice. If too much slack develops between your fly and rod tip, you will likely miss a fish that grabs your fly. If you don't have enough slack going for you, your fly will jerk on the water with each twitch of the rod tip, and your likelihood of success plummets to zero.

Skilled anglers often fish up to three dry flies, each connects to the bend of the preceding fly with clinch knots. Use 6X tippet to all flies, and attach them a foot or less apart. Apply powdered desiccant frequently to keep your flies floating as high as possible on the water. The advantages of mastering the twitch go far beyond just fishing spring creeks. It will allow you to fish any moving water better.

Hatches

Fall River's angling season runs from the last Saturday in April to November 15, and if it's been a relatively normal rain year, the river is likely to be in prime shape. Every so often there is an unusually wet spring season and Fall essentially floods. Intrepid anglers willing to fish in these conditions may encounter the rather odd sensation of catching trout in what is normally some

Brannon Santos searching for rising fish and a target for his dry fly. Regular Fall River anglers have mastered the downstream presentation to rising fish, known as the Fall River Twitch.

*When **Hexagenias** are heavy, birds, fish, and anglers work the hatch simultaneously. The best times are from mid-June through mid-July.*

farmer's field. Otherwise the swollen river restricts up- and downstream traffic by making it impossible to fit under the various bridges. Nevertheless, you can fish Fall successfully when the water is up, though you may not be able to get to all the places you want to fish.

The first major hatch of the season is also the last. While the weather is still cool and the days still cloudy, *Baetis* (#18-22) are in their prime, and the trout know it. Depending on weather and other factors, the next major hatch to expect is the Pale Morning Duns (PMDs), which is Fall's longest-lasting and reliable hatch of the season. PMDs often start in May and slow down some time in October. This is generally a midday hatch, and anglers can take advantage of fishing PMD nymphs, emergers, duns, and spinners through the course of a day's fishing. Compared with the incomprehensible mayfly density on this river, caddisflies are only secondary in importance, except when the fish key on them, which could happen any time May through September.

Fall has a fairly abundant population of Tricos, and their spinner fall is a popular morning to midday event in late summer. Trying to see an all-but-invisible Trico spinner pattern drifting downstream 40 or more feet and knowing when to set the hook can be tricky, however. The only logical alternative is to make your best guess as to where the fly is, and if anything within a 10-foot radius disturbs the water, set the hook. Thank goodness PMDs are still hatching at this time of year as well and, though pretty small themselves, most anglers stand a better chance of seeing these flies.

Fall has a great leech population, and open areas of water are prime targets for swinging or stripping small, sparse leech patterns like a #12 olive or rust Monroe Leech on a clear intermediate sinking line any day of the season. For anglers unable to master the "Fall River Twitch" technique so essential in presenting mayfly and caddis imitations throughout the season, this approach offers hope. Cast as far as you can to the side of your boat, throw a small upstream mend, and then track your line with the rod tip as it swings downstream, pointing your rod at the water. Unusual for this type of fishing, most grabs are fairly soft, so set the hook on the slightest tug.

The Hex Hatch

The Hex hatch from mid-June through mid-July is arguably Fall River's premier hatch. While fishing big Hex nymphs suspended under indicators accounts for many fish, most anglers are here to fish the big, impossibly clumsy Hex dry flies, though some nights the hatch is intense and other nights the bugs don't come off at all. Strangely, large expanses of river can seem all but vacant during daylight hours, with the most popular areas the many miles of the lower river. Fall really sputters to life just before dark to the sound of gas motors cranking and revving in unabashed anticipation of the big event.

This fishing is a matter of finding a good spot, anchoring, and then waiting for the bugs to start. The lower river is considered better than the upper for this hatch, largely due to the muddier bottom below, which these mayflies favor. Surface-feeding fish are easy to see and often work one general area of the stream like a circuit. The game is anticipating which way the fish will go after each rise, and dead-drifting the fly right in the fish's path. This is high-anxiety, fever-pitch fishing, and you will either thrive on it or hate it. One thing is certain: Once you've experienced it, you aren't likely to forget it. You may not see the first few Hexes of an evening. Since the fish are actively watching and waiting for the big meal, you are more likely to *hear* the big grab and merely see the disturbance in the water where the bug used to be.

The annual Hex hatch, for a time, will deposit a carnival atmosphere in the valley. Day in and day out anglers are normally very considerate on Fall River,

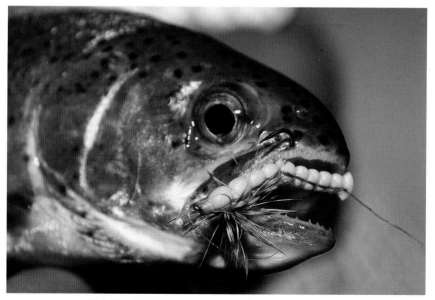

Big buoyant dry flies like this Loco Hex are good choices for this hatch. On some nights a Hex cripple or emerger works better.

Though changes to Fall River might be difficult to notice, it is a much different river than it was before the first pioneers upset the native peoples' way of life. The river above Spring Creek was heavily timbered and typically steeped in shadow. Downstream from Spring Creek the timber diminished, giving way to a ribbon of river bleeding into endless stands of tules and miles of primordial swamp.

The native Achomawi fashioned canoes out of tight bundles of tules and used these for transport up and down the river. The river brought food in the form of trout, pikeminnows, Sacramento suckers, and, in wet years, salmon and steelhead. Local game included deer, elk, antelope, and black and grizzly bears. The Achomawi also ate crayfish, freshwater mussels, grasshoppers, and Salmonflies.

The winter of 1856–1857 brought blood to the alley. One of the first wayfarers to visit the settlement of Lockhart's Ferry (now Fall River Mills) discovered a ghastly scene. The few squat buildings had been plundered and torched while the white residents had been slaughtered, obviously by Indians. Later, it came to light that what came to be called Lockhart's Ferry Massacre was retaliation by the Indians for "depredations" against Indian women by local white men.

In May 1857, U.S. Army Company D under the command of Lieutenant George Crook was ordered to Fall River valley to subdue the hostile natives. The campaign took only four bloody months. A significant number of natives fell before the greater firepower of the U.S. Army, and many more died at the hands of white man's diseases for which the natives had little immunity.

Lieutenant Crook observed Fall River's source while stationed nearby. "The water was so clear in those springs," he wrote "that it was difficult to tell where the atmosphere left off and the water commenced. There was notably one spring that was forty-five feet deep, and so clear that the smallest trout could be seen at its bottom with ease. This water was ice cold and full of magnificent trout." Today these breathtaking springs bubble out of the ground on Thousand Springs Ranch, which is private and available for viewing only from the air.

The early 1900s saw more changes as the burgeoning influx of white settlers removed much of the timber and built lava-rock levees to transform swamp into productive farmland. Today these century-old levees just seem like part of the natural landscape. Natural surroundings, however, are rarely drawn with nice, straight lines, so those stream banks along the lower river didn't happen by accident.

Though not so obvious today, the town of Fall River Mills was built on the fertile delta formed by the junction of the Fall and Pit rivers. Just upstream from Lockhart's Ferry was Manning's Falls (one of three waterfalls for which the river is named). Fall River spilled over these falls and into a series of shallow riffles and runs that extended through the little town.

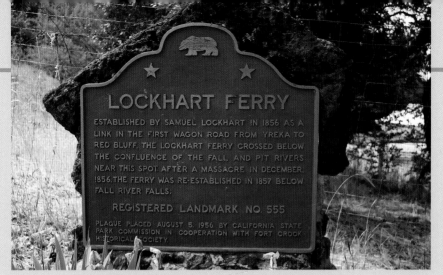

The bloody Lockhart's Ferry Massacre in 1857 is part of Fall River's colorful history. Later it was determined the Native Americans attacked the white settlers because of liberties the white men were taking with Indian women.

An April 1888 edition of the *Shasta Courier* describes the phenomenon of the spring Salmonfly hatch in the colorful prose of the era: "Salmonflies are now ripe and are to be had for the picking. Consequently the small boy is in his glory and may be seen in pairs and gangs hieing their way to Manning's Falls to cast their line with the certainty at each cast of drawing forth the speckled trout that anxiously awaits their coming."

The river provided more than fish; it also provided a unique environment for at least one home. An impressive wood-framed home was built on the island that once existed in Fall River, just upstream from its confluence with the Pit. This 1887 description from the *Shasta Courier* romanticizes the popular landmark:

"On this green spot surrounded by the raging waters, I. H. Winter has erected his residence and can probably claim that nowhere else its equal exists. Owing to the fact that Fall River is fed by springs, its waters are warm in winter and cold in summer, and the temperature of the island is the same. In the spring when the trout bite the family can stand at the kitchen door, and with rod and flies in a few minutes land a sufficient number of the finny tribe for a meal."

Island House and Manning's Falls are now long gone, literally drowned by hydroelectric projects that have turned this stretch of Fall River into the frog water you drive over on your way into town from the west. Also gone is Fall River Falls where the river cascaded 30 feet into the Pit River. It was de-watered when the river was diverted into a two-mile tunnel through Haney Mountain that dumps Fall River water into the Pit 1 Powerhouse.

While lovers of Fall River might ruefully wonder how a river so miraculously born has to end in such pedestrian fashion, perhaps such thoughts are hopelessly out of date. Apparently the world has a shortage of electric lightbulbs, and an overabundance of waterfalls. ▪

FALL RIVER HATCHES

	JAN	FEB	MAR	APR	MAY	JUN	JUL	AUG	SEP	OCT	NOV	DEC

Blue-Winged Olive
(*Baetis* spp.)

#18-20 Mercer's Poxyback Baetis, olive Mercer's Micro Mayfly, Morrish's Anato-May, Morrish's Biotic Nymph, WD-40, Quigley's Hat Creek Spider, Quigley Cripple, Quigley's Loopy Cripple

Pale Morning Dun
(*Ephemerella* spp.)

#16-18 yellow Morrish's Anato-May, rust Morrish's Hotwire May, Mercer's GB Poxyback PMD, brown or ruby Mercer's Micro Mayfly, Burk's HBI Nymph, Sparkle Dun, Paradun, Mercer's PMD Profile Spinner

Trico (*Tricorythodes* spp.)

#20 black Mercer's Micro Mayfly, CDC Biot Spinner, Etha Wing Trico, Quigley's Hat Creek Spider

Caddis
(*Brachycentrus/Hydropsyche* spp.)

#12-16 olive or brown Birds Nest, Copper John, Mercer's Z-Wing Caddis, Mercer's Glo-Bubble Caddis, Fox's Poopah, Morrish's Hotwire Caddis, Morrish's Super Pupa, Gordon's Prince Nymph, Mercer's Missing Link

Little Sister Sedge
(*Cheumatopsyche* spp.)

#18 brown Fox's Micro Poopah, Mercer's Glo-Bubble Caddis, Morrish's Super Pupa, Elk Hair Caddis, Cutter's E/C Caddis, Mercer's Missing Link

Hex (*Hexagenia* spp.)

#6 Mercer's Rag Hex, Mercer's Poxyback Emerger, Loco Hex, Mercer's Foam Dun Profile, Paradrake

Damselflies (Zygoptera)

#12 olive Burk's Sierra Damsel, Foam Swimming Damsel, Living Damsel; blue Deer Hair Adult Damsel

Leeches

#10-12 Monroe Leech, Beadhead Micro Bugger, Fox's Sleech

Reviving each fish properly is important to the future of the fishery. Too many anglers keep fish out of the water much longer than they should.

Mark Buljan kicks back on a guide's night off, chasing the Hex on Fall River. The fish feed on the large bugs until well after dark.

even routinely asking parked anglers on which side they prefer to be passed as they motor upstream. When the Hex is popping, however, it seems as though all bets are off, and tensions can become strained as boats jockey for prime positions. The posted 10-mile-per-hour speed limit goes out the window as boats fly past one another to get their spot and drop anchor. Better areas host virtual flotillas of watercraft, and once everyone is in position, the air can become fairly still as all wait for the first telltale set of huge yellow wings.

Hexagenia limbata is the largest species of the mayfly family, and anglers aren't the only ones who love them. Big fish that normally remain elusive toss caution to the wind and hammer these massive flies. Birds also get into the act creating a real challenge for anglers to cast to the fish while avoiding hooking grebes, mallards, and swallows. Last of all are the ubiquitous bats that skim the surface, picking up struggling Hexes by radar as the last of the bits of light dissolve into darkness.

Eventually it will be too dark to see, and many anglers have to fight the "just one more cast" obsession hoping to hear the take rather than see it. But the feeding often goes on well after dark when the fish have the advantage of seeing a dark silhouette against a lighter background. Hex-addicted fishermen don't share that advantage, and perhaps it's best left that way.

Mercer's Profile Spinner (Hex)

Hook: #6 Tiemco 2499SP
Thread: Yellow 8/0 Uni-Thread
Tail: Yellow dyed grizzly neck hackle,
           stripped
Abdomen: Yellow Larva Lace Dry Fly Foam,
           folded over a needle and colored
           with waterproof marking pens,
           golden on top, yellow on bottom
Rib: Tying thread
Post: Orange and yellow macramé yarn
Wings: Dun Z-lon (straight)
Thorax: Yellow Mercer's Buggy Nymph
           Dubbing
Hackle: Ginger saddle hackle

Mercer's Rag Hex

Hook: #8 Tiemco 2457
Thread: Tan 8/0 Uni-Thread
Eyes: Bead chain painted black
Tail: Natural gray ostrich herl tips
Gills: Natural gray marabou clumps
Abdomen: Golden Stone EZE-Bug yarn,
            colored on top with light tan
            Prismacolor waterproof
            marking pen
Thorax: Golden Stone Mercer's Buggy
            Nymph Dubbing
Wing Case: Dark mottled turkey tail slip,
            coated with 5-minute epoxy
Legs: Pumpkin/black flake Sili Legs

Hex Emerger

Hook: #8-10 Tiemco 200R
Thread: Yellow 8/0 Uni-Thread
Tail: Gray ostrich and pearl Krystal
           Flash
Body: Olive brown Ice Dub
Rib: Yellow Larva Lace
Thorax: Thin strip of yellow foam
Wing: Natural elk hair
Hackle: Yellow dyed grizzly

Hex Cripple

Hook:	#8-10 Tiemco 200R
Thread:	Yellow 8/0 Uni-Thread
Tail:	Light gray dyed marabou
Body:	Light gray dyed marabou
Thorax:	UV light yellow Ice Dub
Wing:	Yellow dyed elk hair

Loco Hex

Hook:	#8-10 Tiemco 100
Thread:	Yellow 8/0 Uni-Thread
Tail:	Moose hair
Body:	Yellow Rainy's Round Float Foam
Wing:	Yellow dyed elk hair
Hackle:	Yellow dyed grizzly

Burk's HBI Nymph

Hook:	#12-22 Tiemco 2487
Thread:	Orange 6/0 Danville
Weight:	.015 lead-free wire (Optional)
Body:	70% rusty brown, 15% hot orange, and 15% light olive brown rabbit dubbing
Rib:	Orange 6/0 Danville
Tail:	Wood-duck fibers
Wing Case:	Dark mottled turkey tail fibers
Thorax:	Same as body
Legs:	Wood-duck fibers

Monroe Leech

Hook:	#8-10 Tiemco 200R
Thread:	Olive 8/0 Uni-Thread
Tail:	Pale olive marabou
Body:	Pale olive marabou

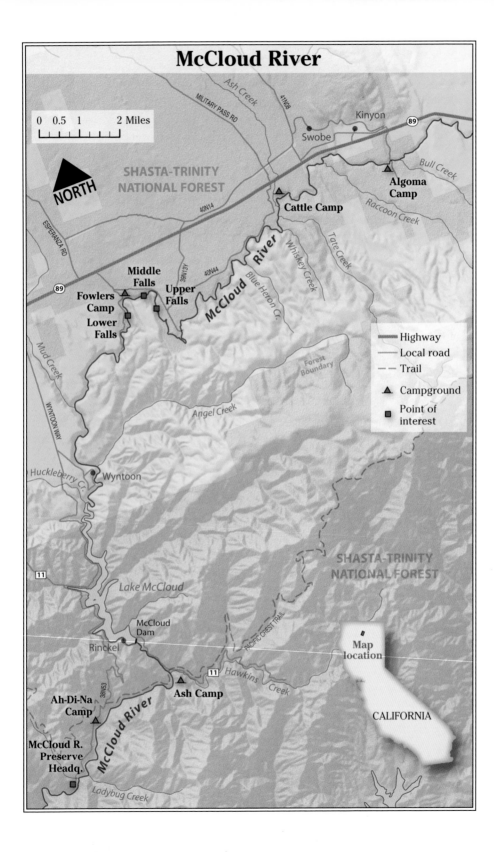

McCloud River

CHAPTER 3

McCloud River

The journey to the lower McCloud is not always easy, but it is an invest-ment to be savored while building anticipation with each dusty turn down a seemingly endless dirt road. The surroundings turn from primi-tive to borderline prehistoric, and when you get there you have truly entered a parallel universe where DEET is the fragrance of choice and GORE-TEX is commonly accepted as dinner attire.

Born in the shadow of northern California's Mount Shasta, the McCloud straddles Siskiyou and Shasta Counties with a reservoir dropped right in the middle. The upper and lower sections are two very different rivers offering a wide variety of angling experiences. Perhaps more than any other California trout stream, the McCloud River is spoken of with the reverence reserved for a small handful of rivers considered to be "holy water."

Hardly any California running water escapes being halted temporarily by dams, and the McCloud is no exception. The upper McCloud, the water above McCloud Reservoir, is a small stream with some wild fish, especially above Upper Falls, and also liberal doses of hatchery trout around the several public campgrounds. The lower McCloud, the water below the reservoir, is a monument to wild trout, and most people here practice catch-and-release.

The Lower McCloud

Although the public section below the dam is only about six miles long, this water is frequently spoken of in terms that would aptly describe a Florentine cathedral. The bluish-green water tinged by glaciers on Mount Shasta flows through a pristine old-growth forest with lots of big wild rainbows and browns. Even around the two campgrounds in this section, Ash Camp and Ah-Di-Nah Campground, you can often find privacy and perhaps as grand a fishing adventure as you are likely to have any place in the world.

Like most of the rivers in California, the McCloud is primarily a nymph-fishing venue. On the other hand, the McCloud is not nearly as exclusively

Anglers tend to ignore the edges on the McCloud, but fish often hold in the deep water in the shade of the overhanging elephant ears, which provide the added bonus of also attracting terrestrial insects.

Beloved by anglers for more than 100 years, the blue-green water of the McCloud is diverse and loaded with trout.

so as other rivers. Perhaps this has to do with the river's unique chemistry or with the fact that the McCloud is the coolest, narrowest canyon in the area. In any case, while nymphing is the most productive method to connect with McCloud River trout most of the time, keep an eye peeled for fish noses at almost any time of the day. Even if there are none, it isn't totally crazy to just start lobbing dry flies to see what happens, especially in the spring and fall when the fish are used to looking up for Golden Stones or October Caddis.

Nymphing the McCloud successfully means using enough weight to suspend your nymphs just off the bottom. The river is deeper than most anglers realize, and most aren't fishing on the bottom. If you are never snagging the bottom, you aren't fishing deep enough. Losing an occasional nymph is the cost of doing business here. There is no lack of hungry fish, but they want to take nymphs that hit them on the nose.

The lower McCloud has an abundance of tiny bugs. It's not that fish won't eat nymphs size 12 and larger, especially during certain times of the year, but they usually eat a lot more bugs in the #16-20 range. If you want to increase your chances of hooking trout, don't be afraid to fish these smaller flies, usually with several split-shot suspended under a floating strike indicator. There are days on the river, however, in the face of either extreme heat or heightened fishing pressure when anglers skilled at nymphing without the

Nymphing the McCloud successfully means using enough weight to suspend your nymphs just off the bottom. The river is deeper than most anglers realize, and most aren't fishing on the bottom.

indicator have an advantage. During these fortunately rare occasions, even a small indicator seems to put the fish down.

Angling regulations from McCloud Dam downstream to Ladybug Creek, which flows into the Nature Conservancy property, are barbless artificial lures or flies only and up to two trout may be harvested. Downstream from Ladybug Creek is the same, only no trout may be harvested.

Ash Camp

Allegedly built on top of an ancient Indian burial ground, Ash Camp sits at the confluence of the McCloud and Hawkins Creek, about a mile below the dam. To get to Ash Camp, take Squaw Valley Road from the town of McCloud, past the reservoir, and drive over the top of McCloud Dam. Take a right on the T at the end of it. In about a mile, keep a sharp eye for the gravel road sloping down to the campground and stream below. It can be easy to miss.

Resist the urge to touch the plants on the driver's side of your rig on the way down to the campground. They are largely poison oak, whose leaves look like average oak leaves, but they are chubby and in groups of three. It is one of the most common plants on the McCloud. The good news is you have to touch it with either your skin or clothing to get it. On one of my first trips to the McCloud in the 1980s I met a young couple on their honeymoon wearing shorts and wading straight through the poison-oak jungle. When I asked if they knew what poison oak looked like they said "no," but were pretty sure they were both really allergic to it. I tried to break the bad news gently, and I sometimes wonder whatever happened to them.

There is great water both up- and downstream, and the charming foot-bridge over the McCloud at Ash Camp is part of the Pacific Crest Trail (PCT). The banks under that bridge also have the dubious distinction of being where I have personally seen more rattlesnakes than anywhere else around. Be careful, but don't let the snakes keep you from going. They really want less to do with you than you do with them. They do not want to bite you.

Fishing above Ash Camp means hugging the rough shoreline on your way up- and downstream. There are no other paths. If you are in good shape, an aggressive wader, and have a staff with you, you can cross in a few places and fish the other side. But these places are few and far between. River right gets fairly steep as it angles up toward the road you drove in on. River right is rough, but it's the better of the two routes upstream. Of course, river right gets less fishing pressure, which will make it more attractive to the hardier types.

Even during those times when you may not be catching a lot of fish, don't give in to the illusion the fish aren't there. The place is absolutely lousy with trout. Rest assured there are trout eyeballs scrutinizing your flies on every single cast. The problem isn't with the fish.

Fishing downstream from Ash Camp offers a few options. You can either wade across Hawkins Creek and jump on the rough trail leading downstream

The numerous well-worn paths along the McCloud offer great access, but always be on the lookout for poison oak, which is one of the most common plants on the river.

*The Salmonfly (**Pteronarcys californica**) gives anglers tired of trying to tie on tiny flies an opportunity to really see something. Trout go crazy for the nymphs and dry flies, a truly huge chunk of protein.*

from here, or cross over the bridge and hike down the PCT. In both cases you will notice trails down to the water, and these are not accidents. If there should happen to be other anglers in sight, consider going somewhere else or watch the direction in which they are fishing and jump in behind them. When in doubt and it is reasonable to do so, just ask if they mind you fishing a certain spot. The answer is usually "no," but in the rare case they have not yet fished that spot and would like to, be considerate. A little etiquette goes a long way.

Ah-Di-Nah Campground

Once part of the Hearst family holdings on the river, Ah-Di-Nah Campground is fairly large and is best for tent camping. To get to Ah-Di-Nah, take Squaw Valley Road from the town of McCloud. Before the dam, the road takes a tight left-hand turn, and a sign marks a gravel road on the right that leads to Ah-Di-Nah and the Nature Conservancy water. It's a good 30-minute drive on a heavily potholed washboard road from Squaw Valley Road to the campground. Make sure you have a spare tire and plenty of gas as there is no cell phone reception.

At Ah-Di-Nah you can pay the fee and park in one of the campsites, or continue to one of the turnouts just past the campground and save the parking fee. Like Ash Camp, there is great water both up- and downstream, even adjacent to the campground. Don't be discouraged if the campground is full either. There are some great "unofficial" campsites between the campground and the Nature Conservancy where you don't have to pay, but there are no toilets either. I've had the unusual experience (more than once) of arriving with Ah-Di-Nah Campground completely full, but no anglers at all on the water. The only time it may be difficult to find privacy is just before dark when many anglers try to avail themselves of the regular evening rise. A lot of anglers seem more intent upon relaxation than fishing and may only fish for an hour or two each day.

In this section there is only a trail on the campground side of the stream. Some anglers make the mistake of bypassing this Ah-Di-Nah section in hopes of finding fewer anglers downstream in the Nature Conservancy, where angling pressure is controlled. Many days, maybe even most days, there are fewer anglers fishing Ah-Di-Nah than the Conservancy. The water is equally good.

About a mile past Ah-Di-Nah the road comes to an abrupt end. Here you will see a sign and trailhead for the McCloud Conservancy, and the Conser-

Like wild trout everywhere, McCloud fish do not take well to flies that drag in the water. Successful anglers learn to mend their drifts as often as necessary to maintain a drag-free drift.

vancy cabin is about a third of a mile hike down the well-maintained trail. If you can handle it, be a good guest and pick up one or two logs from the woodpile and carry them in when you go. The Nature Conservancy owns about six miles of the McCloud in this section but allows nonmembers free access to fishing providing you follow their rules (barbless lures or flies, catch and release). Fishing this water is fairly easy to arrange, and many anglers prize the experience. Up to ten anglers are allowed at a time, five by reservation and five on a walk-in basis. Call (415) 777-0487 for reservations.

The McCloud fishing season is from the last Saturday in April through November 15. Early season can be cold and rainy or warm and sunny. Some years the river is unfishable for a while until large volumes of water move through the system, but once things settle down the river seldom varies.

Insect life in the McCloud is abundant. Though the ecosystem seems to favor mayflies over other species, there are huge hatches of caddisflies and stoneflies, and multiple insects often hatch at the same time. In the spring and fall the fish aren't as picky, but by midsummer they can get focused on one particular bug and challenge anglers to figure out what it is.

Even during big-water springtimes, McCloud trout like little bugs. The early season *Baetis* hatch is often best on drizzly days. Sizes 16-18 match the hatch well. If you encounter rising fish lengthen your leader and drop down to 6X. Great *Baetis* adult imitations include Quigley's Hat Creek Spider, Quigley Cripple, or even an old reliable Adams. When the *Baetis* return on the cold days of fall, they will be one size smaller.

General nymph patterns like the Gold-Ribbed Hare's Ear work well on the McCloud because they resemble so many different kinds of bugs.

Rattlesnakes like this are not uncommon on the McCloud. Despite media hype to the contrary, these reptiles are for the most part shy and passive. Just be aware that they might be around, and watch where you place your hands and feet.

As soon as you get a couple of warmer spring days, rain or shine, McCloud hatches go berserk. Not only do Golden Stones hatch, but also Salmonflies, at least three species of caddis, and assorted species of mayflies. But rather than get overwhelmed by the notion of which hatch to match, take a deep breath and relax. Early season the trout aren't as selective to specific insects. What they will not abide, however, is a bad drift.

If no fish are rising, try a couple of vastly different nymphs under an indicator. A good McCloud River nymphing rig is a 12-foot leader tapered to 6X. If the water is off-color you can get away with 5X. For the top fly I like something larger, like a #12-14 Copper John or Prince Nymph. For the bottom nymph go smaller and dark, such as a #16-18 Micro May or Anato-May. Sink these with three or four medium split-shot around eight feet under a strike indicator buoyant enough to hold it all up. If the water is deep enough that you can't see the bottom, fish it. McCloud River fish could be anywhere that's deep enough.

Spring also can provide hours of dry-fly fishing on some days. Rainy days are usually better. Here is an opportunity to use your powers of observation. Fortunately you needn't know the scientific names for what's on the water. Match size, profile, and then color—in that order. Again, the right drift is more important than the fly you choose. A good leader for this fishing is

MCCLOUD RIVER HATCHES

	JAN	FEB	MAR	APR	MAY	JUN	JUL	AUG	SEP	OCT	NOV	DEC
Blue-Winged Olive (*Baetis* spp.)					▬						▬	
Golden Stonefly (*Calineuria* spp.)					▬							
Salmonfly (*Pteronarcys californica*)					▬							
Caddis (*Brachycentrus/Hydropsyche* spp.)					▬	▬	▬					
Pale Morning Dun (*Ephemerella* spp.)						▬						
Little Sister Sedge (*Cheumatopsyche* spp.)					▬							
Little Yellow Stone (*Alloperla pacifica*)							▬					
Mahogany Dun (*Paraleptophlebia* spp.)										▬		
Isonychia (*Isonychia* spp.)									▬			
October Caddis (*Dicosmoecus* spp.)										▬		

Blue-Winged Olive (*Baetis* spp.)
#18-20 Mercer's Poxyback Baetis, olive Mercer's Micro Mayfly, Morrish's Anato-May, Morrish's Hotwire May, Beadhead Pheasant Tail, WD-40, Quigley's Hat Creek Spider, Quigley Cripple

Golden Stonefly (*Calineuria* spp.)
#6-8 golden Morrish's Cone Stone, Mercer's Biot Epoxy Golden Stone, Superfloss Rubberlegs, Mercer's Poxyback Golden Stone, Idyl-Wired Stone, Stimulator, Madame X, Sloan's Persuader, Mercer's Flush Floater Foam Stone

Salmonfly (*Pteronarcys californica*)
#4-6 Superfloss Rubberlegs, Foam Stone Adult, Rogue Foam Stone

Caddis (*Brachycentrus/Hydropsyche* spp.)
#12-16 olive or brown Birds Nest, Copper John, Mercer's Z-Wing Caddis, Mercer's Glo-Bubble Caddis, Fox's Poopah, Mercer's Missing Link, Morrish's Hotwire Caddis, Morrish's Super Pupa, Gordon's Prince Nymph

Pale Morning Dun (*Ephemerella* spp.)
#16-18 yellow Morrish's Anato-May, rust Morrish's Hotwire May, Mercer's GB Poxyback PMD, brown or ruby Mercer's Micro Mayfly, Burk's HBI Nymph, Sparkle Dun, Paradun, Mercer's PMD Profile Spinner

Little Sister Sedge (*Cheumatopsyche* spp.)
#18 brown Fox's Micro Poopah, Mercer's Glo-Bubble Caddis, Morrish's Super Pupa, Elk Hair Caddis, Cutter's E/C Caddis, Mercer's Missing Link

Little Yellow Stone (*Alloperla pacifica*)
#12-14 yellow Elk Hair Caddis, Morrish's Iron Sally, Quigley's Stacker Sally

Mahogany Dun (*Paraleptophlebia* spp.)
#12-14 rust Sparkle Dun, Mercer's Foam Parachute, Tilt Wing Dun, Paradun

Isonychia (*Isonychia* spp.)
#10-12 Mercer's Poxyback Isonychia, black A.P. Nymph, Birds Nest

October Caddis (*Dicosmoecus* spp.)
#8 Mercer's Tungsten October Pupa, orange Mercer's Psycho Prince, Morrish's October Pupa, Morrish's WMD, Stimulator, Madame X

about 12 feet long, tapered to 6X. Use a powdered desiccant fairly often to keep your fly riding high.

On spring evenings you can go big. Golden Stones and the occasional Salmonfly bob up and down until *splat*, they either lay their eggs or become a bedtime snack for a trout. If the water is flat there is reason for a longer and more delicate presentation. In smaller places like pocketwater you can get away with short, rather abrupt presentations. Try to make your big Mercer's Flush Floater, Stimulator, Madame X, or Sloan's Persuader hit the water like the naturals. Most of us don't need any help making indelicate presentations.

Salmonflies seem to be making a comeback on the McCloud after their disappearance for a few years. No one really knows all the factors that cause insects to cycle in and out of some fisheries. But we know they do cycle. Nothing ever stays completely the same for very long. It's good to see the huge bugs of spring coming back.

Perhaps because the McCloud is cooler than other streams in the area, the big-bug dry-fly fishing may last a good month longer than on other area streams. In some years the Golden Stones are active into mid-July. Typically they go well into June. The good news is you can continue lobbing the big boys at greedy trout well after most other places have moved on.

By summer, caddis hatches take over. Though the fish will take caddis dry flies, they take mayfly patterns better, and at this time I always fish a small mayfly nymph as a dropper. If I see rising fish, I've had far greater success fishing dry flies that imitate mayflies, rather than caddisflies. A good PMD dry fly is hard to beat on summer evenings. It also pays to have a few Little Yellow Stone imitations in your box such as a #12-14 Elk Hair Caddis or Quigley's Stacker Sally. I have seen times when they will be on the water when almost nothing else is, and the trout respond.

Although the McCloud is the coolest river canyon in the area, it can still cook on a summer afternoon July through September. Other places may hit 115 degrees, but I have seen the McCloud at 102 degrees, and that's hot enough for most people. Fishing can be good early and late in the day, but you might as well take a nap in the middle of the afternoon. That's what the trout seem to do.

The fall fishing actually starts in August when the prespawn browns start to get aggressive. There seem to be two distinct groups of brown trout in the McCloud. Some stay in the river year-round, as evidenced by the fact that it isn't unusual to catch one any time in the season. But some McCloud River browns are known to be adfluvial, meaning they migrate in and out of the stream. Biologists are aware of a population of these McCloud fish that tend to migrate down to Shasta Lake after spawning to feed on the lake's threadfin shad. These fish bulk up far faster than those who limit their intake to bugs and may tip the scales at more than ten pounds. After chowing down, they re-enter the McCloud and usually summer in the deepest water they can find. No doubt they also feed on sculpin and immature trout.

While I've never been a fan of casting sinking-tip lines, sometimes they can't be beat. A good rig for this fall streamer fishing is a 9-foot, 7-weight rod and a line with a fairly quick-sinking tip. Zonkers, big leeches, or Woolly Buggers are all good choices, since all you are trying to do is irritate a big brown into striking. When these browns get territorial, they are not trying to *eat* your fly, they are trying to *kill* it.

Quarter your cast well above where you think the deepest water is. Let the fly sink as long as you can, throw an upstream mend, point the rod at the water, and start stripping. You are more likely to get strikes giving the fly some action rather than just letting it swing. Experiment with short strips,

The McCloud was a popular fishing venue long before dams, and even before paved roads for that matter. Considered sacred by the Wintu Indians who made their homes here, the river used to sustain incredible numbers of native rainbows, redband trout, steelhead, Chinook salmon, and bull trout. The McCloud was the southernmost limit of the bull trout's native range, and it was declared officially extinct here in 1975. By the mid-1800s the river had already become a trendy fishing destination for wealthy San Franciscans and U.S. presidents.

Rainbow trout, probably the most ubiquitous trout in the world today, were not all that common. Rainbows are only native to the Pacific West Coast and streams adjacent to these watersheds. A McCloud River rancher named Jeremiah Blizzard Campbell was the first recorded person to send some of his colorful trout to the eastern United States. As early as the 1870s, the East Coast was recognizing that pollution from manufacturing was eliminating native brook trout from their waters and finding that rainbows were a hardier breed. Within ten years rainbows got a foothold on the eastern seaboard and were naturally reproducing in the fisheries vacated by brookies. Perhaps his rainbow trout exporting venture was too successful, but eventually his East Coast market dried up. Taking a more global view, Campbell exported his rainbows to more exotic locales like New Zealand, Argentina, and Peru. McCloud River rainbows are one of the most popular adversaries in some of the most highly touted fly-fishing destinations in the world.

Brown trout were first introduced into the McCloud in the 1920s, where they caught on well. It turns out the hardy browns were more adaptable than the native bull trout, and their introduction combined with the building of the McCloud Dam are considered the most likely causes of the natives' demise. But anglers have taken to these McCloud River browns, especially in late summer and fall when they become more aggressing in preparation for spawning. Some huge browns are taken on streamers and October Caddis patterns almost every fall. Double-digit fish are not out of the question. ■

long strips, fast and slow. Be anticipating a strike up until the last moment as browns will often hit a streamer just as you're about to take it out of the water to recast. You will occasionally also catch huge rainbows this way. Don't worry about fine tippets for this fishing. A 4-foot section of plain 1X mono will do the trick. Dawn, dusk, and other low-light conditions are the best times for this fishing.

In addition to fall mayfly hatches, the McCloud, along with the Upper Sacramento River above Dunsmuir, has the densest October Caddis hatches I have ever seen. This is a major food event for the trout that brings even the big boys who usually sulk on the bottom to the surface. You may only get an hour of dry-fly fishing in right before dark, but it tends to be memorable. Cut back to 4X or 5X tippet and fish these flies in the same way as you would the stonefly patterns of spring.

Be mindful of the substantial black bear population on the McCloud. Like the brown trout, the bruins get more active in the fall trying to build up fat for the long, cold winter. Before they eventually tuck themselves in for a long winter's nap, they become ravenous and very active at nighttime. I once hiked alone deep into the Nature Conservancy to fish the October Caddis hatch. The fishing's done when you can no longer see your hand in front of your face, and there are absolutely no lights out here save the night sky. Wearing a good headlamp, I encountered a bear on the trail back, who quickly ran away. But the rest of the hike was less than enjoyable, since I started seeing imaginary bears everywhere. If confronted by a bear, loud noises will usually scare it off. Bring a friend to chat with and don't be shy about making lots of noise. If given sufficient warning, most wild creatures will do everything they can to avoid human contact. Mountain lions are also a possibility almost anywhere in California. If confronted by a cat, never run or turn your back on it. Avoid eye contact and slowly back away from it.

Guide Dax Messet with a chunky McCloud rainbow. The river provides something for anglers of all levels, and beginners and experts alike are captivated with the river. The McCloud's famous rainbow trout were among the first to ever be exported to other countries, like New Zealand.

Almost every inch of the McCloud holds trout. Pocketwater like this is perfect for high-stick nymphing.

Upper McCloud

The upper McCloud is very different from the lower. Give it another name and you might not suspect they share the same water. The upper McCloud is much smaller with more campgrounds and impressive waterfalls. It has some hatchery fish, and some wild ones as well, which are related to but not quite the same as the ones below McCloud Reservoir.

All of the upper McCloud is accessed off of CA 89 east of the town of McCloud. The most popular section surrounds Upper, Middle, and Lower Falls and the campgrounds close by. These are located off the McCloud River Loop, approximately six miles east of McCloud, well marked on CA 89.

Below Lower Falls, signs indicate the end of public land and the start of the Hearst property just upstream from McCloud Reservoir. This is a pristine area closed to the public where Big Springs contribute their chilly flows to the McCloud. Lower Falls drop about one foot, small enough to be a popular swimming venue despite the chilly water, but tall enough to be worth avoiding if a tumble isn't part of your plan. The fishing generally begins above this waterfall, and every spot at least two or three feet deep in this watershed holds trout.

The most popular fishing area is between Middle and Lower Falls. The wading is fairly easy and the landscape beautiful with lush green trees and bushes adorning the canyon walls and that oh-so-blue California sky. There are special angling regulations in the upper water as there is down below. Any method of take is acceptable, and anglers may harvest up to five trout.

For several days after the hatchery truck has been by, the stream may be crowded. After that there are usually plenty of trout left and many fewer people. The stream is stocked every few weeks during the summer, and always before Fourth of July and Labor Day weekends.

McCloud River Loop Road runs along a high ridge above Middle Falls, so to fish it you have to hike the trail down. The excellent trail is gradual, but the required output of physical energy to get down there and back does a wonderful job of keeping Middle Falls the least crowded part of the upper river. Evening dry-fly fishing below this 46-foot falling monument can be exciting, and a good angler can reasonably expect to hook ten or more fish in an evening.

A narrow 25-foot drop, Upper Falls is the barrier above which the California Department of Fish and Game considers all the fish to be wild native redband trout. Robert J. Behnke in *Trout and Salmon of North America* lists these fish above Upper Falls as McCloud River redband trout (*Oncorhynchus mykiss stonei*), a more primitive form of rainbow trout. Primitive or not, they are as colorful as the most garish tropical fish and will slam a fly as readily as any other trout.

Mercer's Poxyback Hare's Ear

Hook:	#10-16 Tiemco 2302
Bead:	Gold
Thread:	Camel 8/0 Uni-Thread
Tail:	Gray turkey biot
Rib:	Pearl Flashabou
Abdomen:	Dark hare's ear Hareline Dubbing
Thorax:	Same as abdomen
Wing Case:	Dark mottled turkey-tail slip and a strip of pearl Flashabou coated with 5-minute epoxy
Head:	Same as thorax

Fred Gordon's Prince Nymph

Hook:	#10-16 Tiemco 3761
Bead:	Copper
Thread:	Dark brown 8/0 Uni-Thread
Tail:	Dark brown turkey or goose biots
Rib:	Gold tinsel (fine) and copper wire (fine)
Body:	Peacock herl
Wings:	Gold turkey or goose biots
Legs:	Dark brown webby hackle

Mercer's Biot Epoxy Golden Stone

Hook:	#6-18 Tiemco 2302
Bead:	Gold
Thread:	Tan 8/0 Uni-Thread
Tail/	Sulphur-orange turkey biots,
Antennae:	mottled with brown water-proof pen
Underbody:	Round lead-substitute wire strips
Abdomen:	Sulphur-orange turkey biots, mottled with brown water-proof pen
Wing Case:	Golden brown mottled turkey tail coated with 5-minute epoxy
Thorax:	Golden Stone Mercer's Buggy Nymph Dubbing
Legs:	Golden brown mottled hen-back feather
Head:	Same as thorax, colored with brown waterproof pen on top

Mercer's Flush Floater Foam Stone (Salmonfly)

Hook:	#4-6 Tiemco 2302
Thread:	Camel 8/0 Uni-Thread
Tail:	Black round rubber
Abdomen:	Orange Larva Lace Dry Fly Foam (color last segment with dark gray Prismacolor pen)
Thorax:	Dark Stone Mercer's Buggy Nymph Dubbing
Collar:	Orange dubbing and Dark Stone Mercer's Buggy Nymph Dubbing
Underwing:	Elk body hair over black moose mane over pearl Krystal Flash
Overwing:	Yellow over orange macramé yarn
Legs:	Black round rubber
Head:	Same foam as abdomen, marked on top with dark gray Prisma-color pen
Antennae:	Black round rubber

Mercer's Flush Floater Foam Stone (Golden Stone)

Hook:	#8-10 Tiemco 2302
Thread:	Camel 8/0 Uni-Thread
Tail:	Pumpkin/black flake Sili Legs
Abdomen:	Yellow Larva Lace Dry Fly Foam colored with light tan Prisma-color pen
Thorax:	Golden Stone Mercer's Buggy Nymph Dubbing
Collar:	Same as thorax
Underwing:	Elk body hair over black moose mane over pearl Krystal Flash
Overwing:	Yellow over orange macramé yarn
Legs:	Pumpkin/black flake Sili Legs
Head:	Same foam as abdomen, marked on top with light tan Prismacolor pen
Antennae:	Pumpkin/black flake Sili Legs

Gold Ribbed Hare's Ear

Hook:	#8-18 Tiemco 3761
Thread:	Black 8/0 Uni-Thread
Tail:	Hare's mask guard hairs
Rib:	Gold mylar tinsel
Abdomen:	Blended hare's ear; sparse
Wing Case:	Turkey tail coated with Flexament
Thorax:	Same as abdomen, only thicker, with hairs picked out

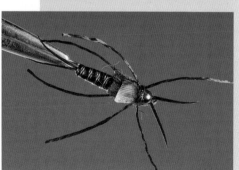

Morrish's WMD (Dark Stone)

Hook:	#6-8 Tiemco 5263
Bead:	Black nickel
Weight:	.025-.035 lead or lead-free wire
Thread:	Black 6/0 Danville
Tail:	Black goose biots
Antennae:	Black goose biots
Abdomen:	Copper brown and black Ultra Wire (large)
Back:	Black 1/8" Scud Back
Thorax:	Equal parts of chocolate brown and UV black Ice Dub
Wing Case:	Dark turkey shorts, coated and folded
Legs:	Black Super Floss
Head:	Same as thorax

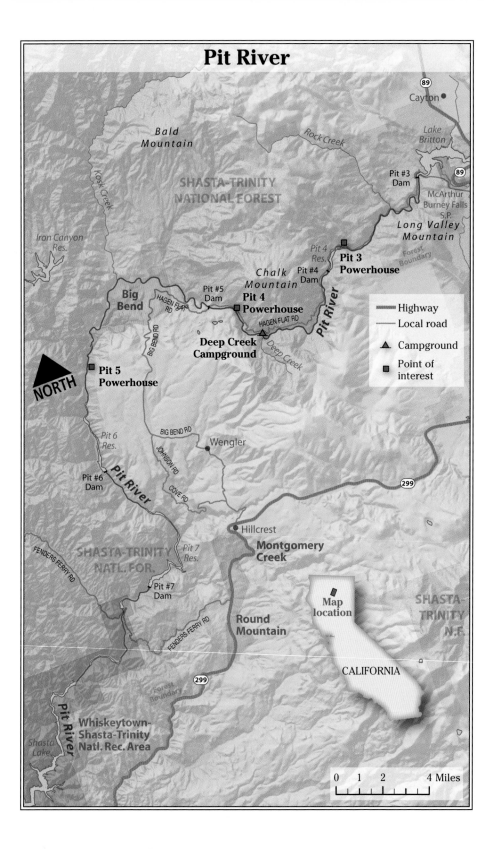

Pit River

CHAPTER 4

Pit River

Picture a rugged, brownish-green canyon hemmed in by rolling mountains richly adorned with thick timber. Out in the current, an angler is frozen perfectly still and wrapped in concentration like a great blue heron, rod parallel to the water and slightly elevated. His entire world and focus is the foot of fly line immediately above the surface of the water and the liquid way his leader tracks downstream with the current. At the slightest tap, hesitation, or suspicious twitch, the angler strikes. If it moves, it's a trout; if not, just another rock. Woops, he fell in . . . again.

As its name implies, this first-rate wild-trout fishery will chew up and spit out a wading angler just for the fun of it. But, in a quirky sort of way, it is this river's roughness that contributes to its terrific charm and appeal. You have to accept a few things about fishing the Pit River in advance before you get in, well, over your head.

The Pit is notorious for tough-going, extremely slippery wading, and most anglers who fish it end up swimming. You will likely lose flies as they get stuck in the cracks and crevices of the giant boulders that compose the river's substrate, but that's where the fish are. The canyon is lush with poison oak and there are, of course, those snakes. Nevertheless, the trade-off is a solid reputation for being the easiest place to catch wild trout in Shasta County. Anglers either love this place or hate it, but the Pit has a large and devoted following of fiercely loyal fans who would rather swim the Pit than stay dry almost anywhere else.

When anglers talk about the Pit, they are generally referring to the water downstream of Lake Britton, about 15 minutes northeast of Burney. Massive Lake Britton Dam, just northwest of Burney Falls State Park, is where the action begins. The Pit then flows through and past Pit 3 Powerhouse, under Pit 4 Dam, and through another powerhouse under Pit 5 Dam, skirting the town of Big Bend, and through yet another powerhouse. Most of the land adjacent to this year-round wild-trout fishery is owned by PG&E (Pacific Gas

Lake Britton Dam is where the Pit 3 section begins. For good reason, the pool below the dam is called "Glory Hole" and the run below it "Glory Run."

Wild, native Pit River rainbows come in many different varieties. Most are slightly dark with a few spots and white-tipped fins. Most trout are not huge, but some are.

and Electric) and the numbers given these various hydroelectric projects have been adopted by Pit River regulars.

In its distant upper reaches, the Pit isn't trout habitat due to decades of irrigation and cattle grazing that have turned it into a sluggish, low-gradient pasture stream. Prime trout habitat begins below Lake Britton Dam eight miles above Burney. The Pit 3, Pit 4, and Pit 5 projects came along between the 1920s and the 1950s, pockmarking the canyon with dams and powerhouses. The dams created reservoirs that collect sediments and stratify the water above by temperature. Cooler water bubbles out below, creating coldwater trout habitat. The water, so rich with life-supporting nutrients, leaves a shiny glaze on Pit River boulders. Wading is necessary to fish most of it, since stream banks are fairly brushy in most areas, and a wading staff is essential for keeping your balance as well as probing water depth.

Most of Pit 3 and 4, and part of Pit 5, can be accessed off Hagan Flat Road, which runs between Lake Britton Dam and the tiny town of Big Bend, offering limited access to over 20 miles of outstanding trout stream. Pit 3 is the most accessible and Pit 4 is the most remote. Since anglers have been loving this river for a long time, a good strategy is parking in any of the turnouts close to the river. There are many, especially in Pit 3. At every turnout, a path leads down to the river.

Since sections of Pit 4 and 5 are fairly remote, don't consider fishing these solo, and don't expect cell phone reception to call for help. Since there are around ten miles of Pit 4 to fish, it's certainly possible to spend days in this section without seeing another human soul. Even here there are a few turnouts along Hagan Flat Road and paths down to the river. Some hardy folks bushwhack to the river here, but I would not recommend it because of the poison oak and snakes.

Wading staffs are mandatory for a variety of reasons beyond stability while wading. On the paths down to the river there are frequently poison oak bushes or blackberry vines you won't want to make contact with, and you can swing them out of your way with a staff. The staff is also useful for staying on your feet down steep hills or tapping behind boulders or downed logs where you can't see. Since this is rattlesnake country, you should take appropriate cautionary measures.

Rather than cold and clear, the Pit is relatively warm and translucent. While not a deep river, wading the slippery boulder-strewn riffles can be physically taxing, especially if you're determined to stay on your feet. The Pit owes its reputation for slippery wading to the rich algae bloom in Lake Britton. The off-color water is a rich soup of fish food, an unlikely mix of pure springwater and stagnant frog water absolutely pregnant with organic sediment. What that means for the rest of us—don't even consider getting into the Pit without a wading staff. Studded wading boots help, too. Many anglers fall in despite these measures, and very often in the slow water right next to the bank.

Fishing the Pit River well requires the right frame of mind. First, you cannot fear the river. If you're terrified of falling in, you will lack the proper con-

The section of Pit 3 between Lake Britton Dam and the first ridge provides great fishing. Because it is so remote, fish this stretch with a friend.

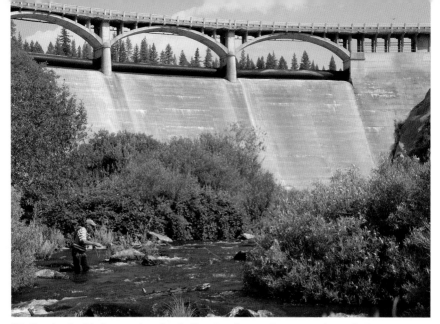

Wading in the Pit is notoriously challenging due to slippery rocks and almost opaque water. Fortunately the river is not deep, and your ego takes most of the beating here.

centration to fish it well. No one on record has ever drowned in the Pit, but almost everyone slips and falls in the water. Expect it. Savor it. It's part of the river's charm. Locals will claim, "If you don't fall in the Pit once in a while, you're just not doing it right." You can usually stand right back up after each little baptism, and only your ego is worse for wear.

The other noteworthy characteristic of the off-color water is that it does a fair job of hoodwinking anglers into assuming the water is deep, but the Pit is a fairly shallow river. The bottom is so uneven that you might very well step into a spot deeper than the top of your waders, but after your unexpected baptism the next step is often shallow again. Many Pit River regulars don't even bother with waders during the warmer months. What's the point? On the other hand, you don't want to fish it in November without bringing a nice warm change of clothes.

Pit 3

The most popular region of the Pit River is Pit 3, the special-regulations water. Pit 3 begins as a steady 150 cfs of cold water frothing out from beneath Lake Britton Dam and running six miles downstream to Pit 3 Powerhouse. Pit 3 has a two-fish limit, using only barbless artificial lures and flies, and only fish 18 inches or better may be kept. Almost everyone in Pit 3 practices catch-and-release. There are no special angling regulations in either Pit 4 or Pit 5, and anglers may harvest up to five trout using bait, lures, or flies.

Pit 3 is the coldest, most turbid, and most productive stretch of the Pit River. Algae blooms from the slower, warmer flows upstream give the water a distinctive greenish color that is apparently just the right recipe to produce intense populations of aquatic insects. If the trout have any complaints about the river's funky color, they are offset by its virtually unlimited food supply. Pit 3 is trout heaven.

Except for the long, steep trail from the road to the bottom of the dam, the next easy access to Pit 3 is three miles downstream at Rock Creek. The road from the dam into the canyon begins far up the ridge and gradually descends to river level. There are two ridges in this remote section with paths down to the water. By spotting cars ahead of time, anglers often fish "ridge to ridge" or "ridge to dam."

During the intensely hot summers from mid-July to mid-September, the water between the second ridge and Rock Creek becomes very warm, and fishing is better either upstream or down. Because it is cooler, Pit 3 offers the most consistent fishing available when air temperatures soar. From Rock Creek down to Pit 3 Powerhouse numerous turnouts along the road provide access to good fishing spots.

Pit 3 has another distinction that neither Pit 4 nor Pit 5 share. Trout are the dominant fish in all but the largest, slowest pools. Since Pits 4 and 5 are warmer than Pit 3, their pools harbor native rough-fish species like Sacramento suckers, northern pikeminnows, and hardheads in staggering numbers, but few trout. Pit 3 is cool enough for trout to do well in the pools, and they tend to be the largest fish.

For 60-plus years after the dam and powerhouse at Pit 3 were completed in 1925, the river contained no riffles, runs, or pools. In fact, there was no water either. The canyon remained bone-dry and every drop was diverted through massive pipes into the Pit 3 Powerhouse downstream. To a trout, this was like replacing normal habitat with a six-mile-long, fully enclosed water slide that dumped you off into a blender. California Trout and a tiny tributary named Rock Creek changed all that in 1987.

CalTrout, the California Department of Fish and Game, and the U.S. Fish and Wildlife Service teamed up and succeeded in mandating a minimum flow in Pit 3 of 150 cfs for the benefits of the native Pit River rainbows and the local bald eagle population. Rock Creek trickles into the Pit about three miles below the dam, and this is where trout in Pit 3 had historically spawned. When the faucet was turned back on in 1987, the players resisted the urge to dump hatchery fish into the river, and merely let the wild Pit River rainbows hanging on in Rock Creek repopulate the "new" stretch of stream.

Pit 4

If you are in good shape and prefer not seeing another angler all day long, Pit 4 was made for you. There is some easy access below Pit 4 Dam and some rough-camping areas, but below Pit 4 Dam the road takes another long ascent up and descent back down a ridge away from the river. Unless you hike up from the Pit 4 Powerhouse, the only access to the north side of the river is via rough paths down the slopes through poison-oak patches and rattlesnakes.

Guide Tom Peppas has been honing his nymphing skills on the river for many years and delights in sharing his knowledge and wry sense of humor.

Flows in Pit 4 are essentially the same as in Pit 3, but the water is slightly warmer and should be avoided during the hottest months. Overall, the stretch has fewer trout and more rough fish than Pit 3, but the trout are concentrated in the riffles and runs. The water here is somewhat clearer than in Pit 3.

The best access to Pit 4 is from the south side of the river. Drive downstream from the Pit 4 Dam for about eight miles until the road crosses over the Pit 5 Dam. Look for the sign on your left for Deep Creek Campground. The rough dirt road is about six miles long and requires slow going, even with four-wheel drive. The USDA Forest Service campground at the end is nice and provides great access to remote fishing spots upstream and down. This is an area frequented by black bears, especially at night, so take care to hang your food well away from your sleeping quarters.

Since the water temperatures downstream of Deep Creek Campground are the coolest in the Pit 4 system, it harbors a good trout population. The fishing here is as rewarding as it is physical. Bring a friend whenever fishing any of the Pit's remote sections.

Pit 5

Pit 5 has the warmest water, the fewest and largest trout, and the clearest water of any of the sections. It is just as rugged as every other Pit River reach, and the canyon is more open in its lower stretches. Flows beneath Pit 5 Dam

There is more to the Pit River than its relatively recent fame as a trout-fishing destination. The history of the area tells of a grim and bloody past. The territory surrounding the Pit 3, Pit 4, and Pit 5 projects had been home to two distinct bands of Pit River Indians for at least 7,000 years. The Ilmawi band occupied the lands surrounding Lake Britton to just downstream of the Pit 3 Dam. The second band, the Madesi, claimed the rest of the area downstream to the Pit's confluence with Montgomery Creek. Fish, including large Pacific salmon, played a crucial role in the Indians' diet and were captured using baskets, stone fish traps and weirs, spears, and even hooks and line.

Europeans first discovered the Pit River around the late 1820s. In 1827, Hudson's Bay Company trapper Peter Ogden led his party to the upper Pit (near the present-day town of Alturas) and named the river after large pits found along the game trails in that region. Used primarily to capture deer, they were pear-shaped with narrow openings at the top and sometimes up to 20 feet deep. The natives scattered the bottoms with sharpened deer and elk antlers—sometimes "sweetened" with rattlesnake venom—and covered the openings with vegetation.

Alexander McLeod (after whom the McCloud River is named) led the second Hudson's Bay expedition, following the river at least as far west as today's town of Fall River Mills. It was the third expedition led by John Work in 1832–1833 that had the first major impact on the Pit River Indians. Work's group camped on Hat Creek just south of the Pit River on August 29, 1833. According to Work's diary, "[S]ome Indians visited us and brought a few berries to trade, they received a few trifles and were sent off immediately. Where we were now, the natives bear a bad character." They woke the next morning to discover five of their horses had been shot with arrows. While Works didn't know it at the time, the Indians' offense had already been avenged, and then some.

Work's party infected the Indians with what was thought to be malaria, for which the natives had no immunity. Estimates suggest that the ensuing epidemic killed about 40 percent of the Pit River Indians. Twenty-three more years would pass before another "epidemic" of a more violent nature would take a further toll, the Lockhart's Ferry Massacre (see page 34) on the Pit River just below its confluence with Fall River. ∎

are limited to only 100 cfs. While the series of riffles below the dam are worth fishing and hold some huge trout, they also hold large numbers of rough fish. Below these riffles the water slows and warms, making it terrific rough-fish habitat, but poor for trout through the town of Big Bend and all the way downstream to Kosk Creek. Some of this water looks great, but don't waste your time.

From Big Bend, follow the signs toward Iron Canyon Reservoir. Kosk Creek is the first stream you cross, and you can park and follow the path down to the Pit River. By contributing its cold, clear flows, Kosk somehow transforms lower Pit 5 into terrific trout habitat that receives very little fishing pressure. You can also work up from the Pit 5 Powerhouse. Like all areas of the Pit, the going is physically taxing, so bring a friend.

Hatches and Strategies

Like most rivers, hatches on the Pit vary somewhat from year to year in timing and intensity. They also follow the same rough profile as the other major tributaries of Shasta Lake, the Upper Sacramento and McCloud rivers. But there are some important differences between these fisheries in how the fish respond to the naturals and your flies. One good, basic rule to follow is unless you see fish rising during the day, which is unlikely, fish nymphs.

The Pit has good news for you if you are into keeping things simple. Although fish sometimes prefer nymphs that closely match the natural insects during major hatches, almost any #12-18 general-purpose nymph will catch fish throughout most of the season. The most numerous bugs on the Pit are caddis, mainly *Brachycentrus* and *Hydropsyche*. Brown Birds Nests, Prince Nymphs, and Gold-Ribbed Hare's Ear are the bread-and-butter flies of the Pit River. When the fish become more selective, any of Mercer's Micro Mayflies or Morrish's Hotwire Caddis or Anato-May series (#16-18) will often get stubborn fish to respond.

Northern California is nymphing country. The typical high, bright sun seems to make trout less willing to take dry flies here than in other places. Most anglers start fishing nymphs unless they see actively rising fish.

The Pit River is open to angling year-round, but for even the hardiest among us, the first reasonable fishing is to the Golden Stonefly hatch in March and April. Call the local fly shops to check on river conditions before making the trip during the rainy spring season. In wet years there may still be water gushing over the dams, rendering the river not only unfishable, but a menace to even approach in some areas. There are a few relatively safe areas to fish in high water, and these are generally below the dams in places you can stand on rocks and fish without getting into the water. Any dark #6-12 nymph will match the Golden Stones if properly presented. I tend to prefer smaller #10-12 sizes during this hatch simply because even though these are smaller than the naturals, the fish will take them and you will snag bottom less frequently.

Epeorus mayflies appear as the days get warmer and compete with the caddis for the trout's attention during evening dry-fly time. A #12 Yellow Humpy is a good match for them, or a #12-16 Elk Hair Caddis works just as well in the evenings. The fish show little preference for *Epeorus* nymphs during the day, so stick with searching caddis or mayfly patterns in the summer.

During the summer, Pale Morning Duns ride the surface of the water, particularly in the evenings. Because PMDs are smaller insects, the trout have trouble spotting them in faster water. Look for fish rising to PMDs mainly in the runs and pools where they are more easily seen by fish. In July and August, fish crowd into and just below riffles and require more care in reviving before releasing.

Mid-September usually marks the end of the hot summer doldrums and *Isonychia* mayflies begin to appear in response to the cooler ambient temper-

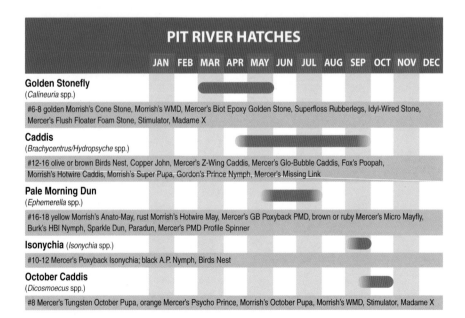

PIT RIVER HATCHES

	JAN	FEB	MAR	APR	MAY	JUN	JUL	AUG	SEP	OCT	NOV	DEC
Golden Stonefly (*Calineuria* spp.)			▇	▇								

#6-8 golden Morrish's Cone Stone, Morrish's WMD, Mercer's Biot Epoxy Golden Stone, Superfloss Rubberlegs, Idyl-Wired Stone, Mercer's Flush Floater Foam Stone, Stimulator, Madame X

Caddis (*Brachycentrus/Hydropsyche* spp.)						▇	▇	▇	▇			

#12-16 olive or brown Birds Nest, Copper John, Mercer's Z-Wing Caddis, Mercer's Glo-Bubble Caddis, Fox's Poopah, Morrish's Hotwire Caddis, Morrish's Super Pupa, Gordon's Prince Nymph, Mercer's Missing Link

Pale Morning Dun (*Ephemerella* spp.)						▇	▇					

#16-18 yellow Morrish's Anato-May, rust Morrish's Hotwire May, Mercer's GB Poxyback PMD, brown or ruby Mercer's Micro Mayfly, Burk's HBI Nymph, Sparkle Dun, Paradun, Mercer's PMD Profile Spinner

Isonychia (*Isonychia* spp.)									▇			

#10-12 Mercer's Poxyback Isonychia; black A.P. Nymph, Birds Nest

October Caddis (*Dicosmoecus* spp.)									▇	▇		

#8 Mercer's Tungsten October Pupa, orange Mercer's Psycho Prince, Morrish's October Pupa, Morrish's WMD, Stimulator, Madame X

Working nymphs on a short line in fast water requires keeping your fly line off the water and staying in close contact with your flies.

atures. These mayflies hatch and lay their eggs under cover of darkness, so forget about fishing dry flies. Were it not for their shucks stuck to midstream boulders, you might not even suspect they are there, but the fish know and are looking for them. October Caddis may not be present in quite the same numbers as in the Upper Sac and McCloud, but the fish will gladly scarf up both nymphs and dry flies, especially in the afternoons and evenings. Look for the adults bobbing up and down on the surface like yo-yos during the evenings while laying their eggs.

If you are not catching fish while nymphing the Pit, fly selection is often the least likely reason. Anglers either fail to get a true drag-free drift with their nymphs, or they don't recognize when a fish has taken their fly. This may sound fairly elementary, but none of these things are necessarily easy on the Pit. Having the right equipment and knowing how to use it will greatly improve your success. Because the water is cloudy and the daytime sun can be intense, polarized sunglasses and a hat with a brim are standard equipment. Fishing the Pit without a wading staff is like deciding to walk a tightrope without a safety net. Some anglers prefer metal staffs, which are commercially available, or they simply use old ski poles. Others prefer staffs made from wood. Many Pit River regulars also prefer studded wading boots, which will make a dousing slightly less likely. A 9-foot fly rod for 4- to 6-weight lines is perfect. The longer length will allow you to present a natural drift in a larger area, covering more water than with shorter rods.

Dick Galland owned Clearwater House on Hat Creek for many years before retiring. Galland has taught hundreds of anglers how to connect with Pit River trout. MARK TOMP-KINS PHOTO

Before plowing into the water take a moment before you get in to develop a strategy. Surveying the water you intend to fish will reveal slight differences in the water color. You will be able to see the river bottom in some areas, but not in others. Pit River trout are almost always sitting on the bottom in the deepest holes they can find. If you can clearly see the rocks on the river bottom, stand there, but don't fish there. Fish off into the water where you can't see the bottom, which is deeper. Deep spots will appear to have a darker color when you look at the surface. Work upstream or down, wading from one shallow area to another, but fishing into the deeper sections.

Nymphing University

Together with the McCloud and Upper Sacramento rivers, the Pit is where devoted nymph anglers go to hone their skills. But unlike the first two, the water clarity in the Pit is maybe a foot or two at best, and you can routinely get within a rod length of the fish if you're careful. Short-line nymphing, a technique not unlike pulling a string to attract cats, is in its prime here.

Carefully wade to within a rod length of where you suspect a trout may be, such as pockets of deeper water behind or upstream from rocks and other obstacles that carve out slightly deeper spots. With only about a foot of fly line extending beyond the tip of the rod, smack your nymph(s) into the water upstream, and with your rod only about a foot above the surface, drag your nymph downstream, almost. That is, you want to guide the nymph downstream at about the same speed as the current, but not faster. It's important not to allow slack line to develop between your rod tip and nymph or you will not see potential takes.

You don't need a floating strike indicator for this style of fishing. Many anglers opt for using a foot-long butt section of red Amnesia monofilament between their fly lines and tapered leaders. The red color is easy to focus on even against a backdrop of white water. If that monofilament stops, twitches, or does anything mildly unusual, "cross his eyes!" Many times, of course, it isn't a fish, but the worst thing an angler can do is start assuming it's just another rock. Very often it's a fish, and there are plenty of them in the Pit.

When you need to fish a bit farther out, high-stick nymphing comes into play. This is just simply pointing the rod up rather than at the water with as much as 6 feet of fly line beyond the tip of the rod. Some prefer to use floating strike indicators for this fishing, but the red Amnesia butt section works just as well. High-stick nymphing is the most productive technique with an 8- or 9-foot leader tapered to 5X or 6X. Because the water isn't clear, fluorocarbon leaders and tippets are not necessary. One or two medium-size split-shot fastened about 8 inches above the fly are about right for getting your nymph (or nymphs) down deep enough. If you're constantly getting caught on rocks, remove one shot.

The Pit is best-known for pocketwater. Locating the fish is never a problem, since there is at least one in front of and behind every boulder. MARK TOMPKINS PHOTO

Hold your rod up at a 45-degree angle so that your fly line traces an upstream "J." Move your rod downstream at about the same speed as the current, with the end of the fly line just above the water's surface. Watch the end of the fly line for the slightest tug or twitch or hesitation. Anglers are often amazed at how delicately Pit River trout can take a nymph. Plan on striking a time or two on almost every cast. You have nothing to lose by setting the hook. To the attentive angler, trout and snags look exactly the same on the Pit. Expect to get your nymphs hung up on submerged rocks fairly often. It's all part of the game. The common mistake is when you start believing each little twitch in your line is just another rock. It is vitally important that no matter how repeatedly you hang up, you must treat everything like a fish. Most trout are lost because they were never properly hooked in the first place. Ideally, you should drink about ten cups of espresso before nymphing the Pit River.

Morrish's Biotic Nymph (Black)

Hook:	#14-16 Tiemco 2457
Bead:	Black nickel
Weight:	.015 lead or lead-free wire
Thread:	Black 6/0 Danville
Tail:	Black pheasant-tail fibers
Rib:	Black Ultra Wire
Abdomen:	BWO turkey biots
Thorax:	Peacock herl
Wing Case:	BWO turkey biots
Legs:	Hungarian partridge fibers
Head:	BWO turkey biots

Morrish's Dirty Bird (Olive)

Hook:	#6-16 Tiemco 3761
Bead:	Black tungsten
Weight:	.015-.030 lead or lead-free wire
Thread:	Black 6/0 Danville
Tail:	Hungarian partridge shoulder feather fibers
Rib:	Copper wire
Abdomen:	Equal parts Golden Stone (#13) and Dragonfly Nymph Olive (#9) Whitlock SLF
Hackle:	Hungarian partridge feather
Wing Case:	Pearl Accent Flash
Legs:	Pearl Accent Flash
Head:	Dark Stone (#15) Whitlock SLF

Morrish's Anato-May (Peacock)

Hook: #8-16 Tiemco 3761
Bead: Black tungsten
Weight: .020-.030 lead or lead-free wire
Thread: Black 6/0 Danville
Tail: Natural pheasant-tail fibers
Rib: Copper wire
Abdomen: Peacock herl
Thorax: Peacock herl
Back: Root beer Krystal Flash
Wing Case: Root beer Krystal Flash
Legs: Root beer Krystal Flash
Head: Dark Stone (#15) Whitlock SLF

Mercer's Poxyback Isonychia

Hook: #12 Tiemco 200R
Thread: Camel 8/0 Uni-Thread
Tail: Brown ostrich herl tips
Rib: Fine copper wire
Carapace: Dark mottled turkey-tail slip and
            a strip of pearl Flashabou coated
            with 5-minute epoxy
Abdomen: Dark brown dubbing
Gills: Dark brown aftershaft feathers
            from base of dyed ring-necked
            pheasant breast feathers
Thorax: Same as abdomen
Wing Case: Same as carapace
Legs: Hen-back fibers
Head: Same as thorax

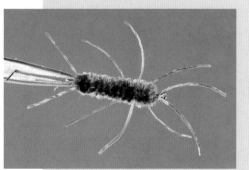

Superfloss Rubberlegs (Brown/Brown)

Hook: #4-8 Tiemco 5263
Thread: Dark brown 8/0 Uni-Thread
Tail: Light brown Super Floss
Body: Brown chenille
Legs: Same as tail
Antennae: Same as tail

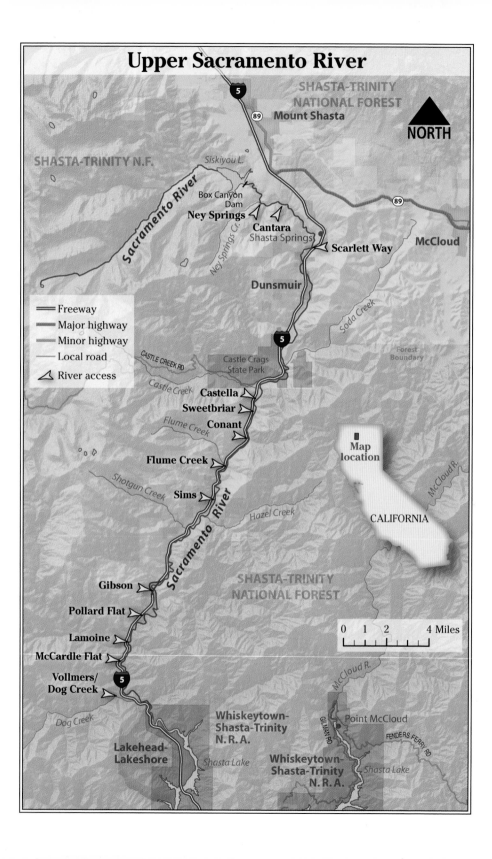

Upper Sacramento River

SHASTA-TRINITY NATIONAL FOREST

Mount Shasta

NORTH

SHASTA-TRINITY N.F.

Siskiyou L.

Sacramento River

Box Canyon Dam

Ney Springs

Ney Springs Cr.

Cantara

Shasta Springs

Scarlett Way

McCloud

Dunsmuir

Soda Creek

Forest Boundary

Freeway
Major highway
Minor highway
Local road
River access

CASTLE CREEK RD

Castle Creek

Castle Crags State Park

Castella

Sweetbriar

Conant

Flume Creek

Flume Creek

Sims

Shotgun Creek

Sacramento River

Hazel Creek

Map location

CALIFORNIA

McCloud R.

Gibson

Pollard Flat

Lamoine

McCardle Flat

Vollmers/ Dog Creek

SHASTA-TRINITY NATIONAL FOREST

0 1 2   4 Miles

Dog Creek

Lakehead-Lakeshore

Shasta Lake

Whiskeytown-Shasta-Trinity N.R.A.

GILMAN RD

Point McCloud

FENDERS FERRY RD

McCloud R.

Whiskeytown-Shasta-Trinity N.R.A.

Shasta Lake

CHAPTER 5

Upper Sacramento River

L ike a love affair, one great day of fishing can leave a star-struck angler
anticipating the next trip with a fervor bordering on lust. Over time there
are periods of both excitement and boredom, and all the while, if you
hang in there, you may form a lasting bond that etches every riffle, run, and
pool indelibly into your psyche.

There weren't any stars or fireworks when I first saw the Upper Sac, yet
decades later, I remember that day clearly. The river sparkled seductively in
the morning sunlight and the air was clean and fresh. There were large,
clumsy *Epeorus* mayflies on the water and a pod of rising fish visible at 12
o'clock. While I had concocted the "perfect" trout stream in my dreams many
times before, here it was running past my feet. A perky Yellow Humpy was
good enough to match the hatch, and I found myself connected to a river in
a way I never had before.

The Upper Sacramento River is the portion of river that flows from Lake
Siskiyou below Box Canyon Dam, 38 miles south to Shasta Lake. It starts as a
spring on the north side of the town of Mt. Shasta. Below Lake Siskiyou it
runs south toward the historic railroad town of Dunsmuir. More springs
refresh the river and add to its volume. Between Dunsmuir and Shasta Lake,
numerous tributaries swell the lower river until it's more than twice the volume of the upper. While most of the water comes from pure snowmelt, the
startling clarity of the water makes it look more like a spring creek.

The Sacramento was a famous fishing destination long before Shasta Dam
was completed in the 1940s, forming Shasta Lake and cleaving what had been
one river into two. Like many California rivers, it was once famous for boun-
teous runs of salmon and steelhead, but they were eventually traded for irrigation water and hydroelectric power. These horrendous changes certainly
altered the river, but they did not kill it. Neither did accidentally poisoning
every plant, bug, and fish in all but two miles of the river in the early 1990s do
it permanent harm. The ecosystem is so robust that life seems to be drawn
here. If you're a wild rainbow trout, this is a place where the living's easy.

The stretch directly upstream from Sims Campground offers great views of monstrous Mount Shasta. During periods of high sun the trout often seek the deepest water they can find.

If you can find deeper water adjacent to the bank, who needs to wade? Here the author high-sticks through a deep hole often loaded with hungry trout. ZACH O'BRIEN PHOTO

The Upper Sac personifies the image of a classic American trout stream, even though some of it flows right next to Interstate 5. A few stretches also pose the possibility of snagging a railroad locomotive on your backcast. The 14,000-foot, snow-covered volcanic bulk of Mount Shasta presides over the river's headwaters, while 38 miles downstream lies Shasta Lake, the largest man-made reservoir in California. Yet for all its visibility, notoriety, and easy access, fishing the Upper Sac somehow remains an intimate experience.

Fishing the Calendar

The Upper Sac is open to fishing all year long. Still, there are good times, bad times, and completely insane times to be here. Even during the prime times it pays to have a notion of what's going on in the stream and with the hatches. Also, as every ardent angler knows, you can have a slow day during the best months or hit a bonanza during an otherwise off month. But in general, the river sticks to well-established routines based on weather and the seasonable snowpack.

Early spring can be hit or miss, but good fishing is possible on almost any day. Beyond a wild trout's natural fussiness, mature fish are also dealing with spawning this time of year and much more water in the system from seasonal rains and melting snowmelt. One good tactic is to concentrate on the places where numerous tributaries flow into the river. Be careful not to fish the trib-

Due to the staggering clarity of the water, it makes sense to seek out water with a broken surface. In water this clear, trout are seldom found in shallow water.

utaries themselves, which may not be open to fishing. When flows are high, trout hold in different places than they do under normal conditions. Concentrate on softer water where it might be more comfortable for a trout to hang out and still be adjacent to seams that might funnel food. Many of these places are right along the bank.

During high springtime flows safety is more of a concern. You can't just wade across the river anymore. Access is limited to working up or down one side of the river, unless you're close to any of the numerous bridges across the river. I wouldn't consider fishing during high water without a wading staff, and an inflatable life vest isn't a bad idea either.

Prime time for fishing the Upper Sac is mid-June to mid-July, and then again during October. In most years, the water level from about May 1 to July 1 will drop a solid six feet as the last of the snowpack cycles through on its steady meander toward the Pacific. As the water drops and clears, access to more good fishing water opens up and the major summer caddis hatch activity kicks in. Although there are dry-fly opportunities occasionally on summer evenings, nymphing is the way to fish this river 90 percent of the time.

Due to the extreme clarity of the water during warmer months, successful anglers either learn to cast nymphs and strike indicators a good distance or work a short line in broken water or deeper runs where it's harder for trout to see above them. In a typical day of fishing it's a good strategy to nymph without a floating indicator when you can, and with one when you must. The nature of the fishery dictates that if I had to choose one way to do it, I would stick with the indicator, but change the depth often. But both techniques have their advantages.

The Upper Sac has plenty of deep water, and there are lots of places you can stand out of the water completely on large ledges or boulders and fish into the deep shadows. Getting deep enough, soon enough, in such places is difficult if you're worrying about sinking a floating indicator, so I often do without. I prefer to get close to these places, within about 15 feet where I can clearly watch the end of my line, and add as much lead to the leader as I think I need. People occasionally mock me for using six or eight split-shot, until they see the bend in my rod. Another good place to go without an indicator, often overlooked by nymph fishermen, is the heads of pools. Using standard nymphing techniques is all but useless in these areas because the nymphs never get the chance to sink to the fish's level before being whisked away by the faster current above.

A reasonable setup for this kind of fishing is a 9-foot leader tapered to 4X fluorocarbon. Tie on one or two nymphs (general caddis imitations work well) and anywhere from four to ten medium split-shot about 10 inches above the top fly. I wouldn't recommend trying to make a standard cast with it without a crash helmet, but it's perfect for this specific situation. With no more than 6 to 8 feet of fly line beyond the tip of your rod, drive the flies into the water hard as far upstream as you can above the drop-off. Give your flies a few seconds to sink, but then move your rod downstream quick enough to

Since the Cantara Incident that killed the river in the early '90s, the trout population has once again exploded. Now the river contains lots of trout and some good-size fish.

keep slack from entering the system between the rod tip and your flies. This takes a little practice, but it isn't rocket science either.

The trick is in learning how fast to move your rod downstream. If you move the rod too slowly, slack will creep into your system preventing you from seeing potential strikes. Too fast and all of a sudden you're dragging your nymphs downstream faster than the current, which may spook the fish. But with a little patience you will get in the zone and find that sweet spot that's somewhere in between. Due to the clarity of the water, don't expect to find fish in water shallower than about three feet.

While indicator fishing, try to remember to fish deep enough. I rarely fish with less than six feet between my nymphs and strike indicator. If you can be quick but delicate with setting the hook, dropping down from 4X to 5X or 6X fluorocarbon will get your nymphs down even faster.

While caddis are king during this June-July peak period, you have the advantage of the trout not having seen too many flies in recent memory. Matching the hatch might mean fishing any of a number of great caddis pupa imitations like #12-16 Mercer's Z-Wing Caddis, Fox's Poopah, or Morrish's Hotwire Caddis. But until the fish become more jaded you can also get away with fishing more general patterns like a brown Birds Nest, Copper John, or Gordon's Prince Nymph. Presentation is more important than exact imitation.

Sometime in July, depending on the specific year, fishing in the river stalls as ambient temperatures climb. If you can't sit on a streamside boulder with-

Elephant ears (also called Indian rhubarb) along the banks and in the middle of the stream provide cover for trout on bright, sunny days, and they stack up in the shadows immediately beneath them. These spots are often overlooked by anglers.

out flirting with third-degree burns, it's reasonable to assume swimming might be a better option than fishing. During this time the cooler water above Dunsmuir often fishes much better than down closer to Shasta Lake. But understand I speak in generalities. Sometimes the need to go fishing has nothing whatever to do with the probability of success, and good luck happens.

During the heat of July, August, and September, the best window for trout fishing seems to be just before dark, and you may get as much as an hour or as little as 15 minutes of dry-fly fishing at this time. Even though caddis are most abundant during the summer, mayflies offer the better dry-fly option, especially on July evenings. As soon as the sun is off the water, begin looking for noses. Dry-fly fishing in water this clear requires 12- to14-foot leaders and tippets tapered down to 6X, or even 7X if the fish are fussy. A #16-18 yellow Paradun or Mercer's PMD Profile Spinner will match the hatch nicely. Evening is also an excellent time to encounter snakes, so watch your step.

In the summer, if you really want to fish the Upper Sac during the day, consider fishing for bass. Since the chemical spill that radically affected the river in the early 1990s, the most abundant fish in the pools downstream from Sims are no longer trout. Alabama spotted bass move up from Shasta Lake during the summers to feed primarily on the river's abundant population of riffle sculpin.

On the east side of the river at Lamoine, a rock wall offers a stable platform from which you can look down into the water plunging to a depth of 20 or more feet and watch the bass cruise back and forth; I have spent many delightful hours playing tug-of-war with these fish. You have to swim across the pool to get to this spot. The best flies are streamers or leeches that have some kind of weight up front to get the fly down fast and produce that certain up-and-down jigging action that bass just seem to love. A Fox's Sleech, a noted steelhead pattern, is a great choice for this fishing. Upstream around Gibson or downstream around Dog Creek are also good places to fish for bass.

By the end of September the heat will begin to moderate, and the trout react to the better conditions. Granted, there can still be 110-degree days in October, but evening temperatures tend to be far cooler and the river gradually begins to fish better. The river's premier fall hatch is the October Caddis, and you can see the hatch in all its glory above Dunsmuir.

During the day the nymphs migrate to midstream rocks and crawl out to emerge in stonefly fashion. It's very common for bugs to become dislodged during this process and the trout are waiting for them. But of course, the real fun is fishing dry flies in the evenings. You can either target a rising fish, or work the likely places with short staccato casts. Trout will often hammer a dry fly as soon as it lands on the water. Keep a headlamp on your head and a container of powdered desiccant handy for quick and frequent application. This is fast fishing, and there is never enough of it.

Sometime in November the river begins to turn off again in response to cooler nighttime temperatures and the fact that most aquatic insects aren't

Golden Stones proliferate in many California streams and trout respond well to both nymph and dry-fly imitations during late spring and early summer.

hatching or active. It's fairly easy to be lulled into a false sense of security when you get one of those warm, sunny December days. I once fished a December day with three other guide friends with an accumulated total of over 100 years of fly-fishing experience among us. We did not move one trout that day. We even fished several sections that I had snorkeled with Department of Fish and Game counting fish. I knew how many trout were turning up their noses at us. Just be aware there are otherwise beautiful winter days when fishing seems like a great idea, but the fish don't think so.

Top to Bottom

Below Box Canyon Dam west of Mt. Shasta and north of Dunsmuir, the river is small and intimate. You can view the river by parking at the dam and hiking to an overlook just below, but without technical climbing gear, access would be nearly impossible. The first reasonable access is Ney Springs on the western side of the river. From here you can park and fish upstream or down. While the water is small, enough deep holes harbor good numbers of fish, some of them big. After the Cantara spill, the Department of Fish and Game used the stock from this stretch of river to jump-start the wild fish population. Compared with other sections of river sandwiched between I-5 and the railroad right of way, this section of stream sees little pressure, but it is also remote. When you fish it, bring a friend.

The next reasonable access downstream is the Cantara site, now owned by California Trout. You can view the notorious bridge from which the freight car fell in the 1990s and fish up- or downstream. The river is still rather small here.

Prospect Avenue access is found by following signs in north Dunsmuir. Hike the tracks up or down, understanding that if you go far enough downstream you will arrive at Mossbrae Falls, a popular fishing, picnicking, and photography spot. But it's easier to hike upstream from the Scarlett Way Bridge access below. You very rarely find people fishing this section even though you can clearly see trout when looking down from the railroad tracks.

Scarlett Way is a gated community on the river with a public parking access mostly used by Mossbrae Falls' visitors. There are some deeper stretches of river here and tossing a nymph under an indicator into the heads of pools is a great strategy. As popular as this area is for sightseers, hardly anyone fishes here.

Dunsmuir City Park is another good place to fish, as long as you don't mind hatchery fish. The lush greenery is accented by colorful flowerbeds, and

Any deep water on the Upper Sac is a prime area to fish nymphs under floating strike indicators. Here the author is working a long drift that started by casting into the head of the pool and drifting back into deep water. ZACH O'BRIEN PHOTO

After the Cantara Incident, new management strategies were implemented to satisfy, it was to be hoped, most major user groups. If you typically fish barbless and practice catch-and-release you only need worry about which sections of the river are open to fishing, and when. Frankly, regulations are fairly complex and warrant close scrutiny and awareness of precisely where you are at any given time.

From Box Canyon Dam above Ney Springs downstream to Scarlett Way Bridge, the river is open all year long, but restricted to barbless artificial lures or flies and a zero limit. This area enjoys the most restrictive regulations of all as a hedge against potential future disasters like the Cantara Incident.

The area from Scarlett Way Bridge downstream to Sweetbriar is open yearlong, but there are certain times you may keep fish, and others when you can't. Anglers are allowed to harvest up to five trout (presumably hatchery fish) from the last Saturday in April through November 15, and barbed bait, lures or flies may be used. After November 15 and before the last Saturday in April only barbless artificial lures or flies may be used, and all fish (presumably wild fish) must be released.

From Sweetbriar Bridge downstream to Shasta Lake you may harvest up to two fish from the last Saturday in April through November 15. After November 15 and before the last Saturday in April all fish must be returned to the water in good condition, and no bait or barbed hooks are allowed.

Some might describe these regulations as a victory for democracy and the spirit of compromise. Others might describe them as patently ridiculous, way too complex, and an infraction of Fish and Game regulations just waiting to happen. ■

Norman Rockwell could not capture any better rendering of the quaint goodness of a "small town" city park. As a compromise with a dedicated constituency of bait fishermen, the California Fish and Game Commission agreed to continue stocking a ten-mile stretch of river from Scarlett Way down to Sweetbriar. For many years before the spill almost the entire river was stocked with abandon. The City Park water is popular and scenic, but the fishing varies depending on when it was last stocked. Nevertheless, it is an excellent place for beginners or people intent on keeping fish. There are several other minor access points in downtown Dunsmuir.

Another popular spot is directly beneath the I-5 Bridge over the river. Once a rather seedy place where at least one transient was gunned down in recent years, the area has been transformed into a first-rate river access named Tauhindauli Park and Trail. The name commemorates a Wintu Indian man named Laktcharas Tauhindauli who worked at the Upper Soda Springs Resort in the latter 19th century. He later changed his name to one easier for whites to pronounce and spell, Grant Towendolly. A relative named Ted Towendolly was the first fly-fishing guide on the river. He is believed to have tutored Ted Fay, another beloved guide who owned the Ted Fay Fly Shop, which is still in operation in downtown Dunsmuir. If you go, the deep pool below the bridge is worth fishing.

Soda Creek access seems to attract more bait anglers in response to hatchery fish and the deep hole just above the bridge. The water downstream from here tends to be vacant of others, and offers amazing views of Castle Crags. Now a state park, the stunning rocks were the scene of the last battle between Indians and miners where the Indians still fought with bows and arrows. The name Castle Crags comes from the Spanish *La casa del Diablo*, "House of the Devil."

Castella is the next access going downstream, and much of this area is residential. But don't let the houses put you off. This is one of the richest sections of river and snorkel survey crews have observed 7,000 to 8,000 fish per mile in this area. Concentrate on nymphing the deeper runs.

Sweetbriar is an area of long-established cabins along the river and only a few places offer easy access. Water downstream from here receives no hatchery fish. If you can picture a river flowing through a sleepy residential neighborhood, maybe even a neighborhood from the 1960s, you've pretty much got a feel for Sweetbriar.

This plaque from Dunsmuir City Park honors Ted Fay, Upper Sacramento legend, and also speaks to the importance the area places on fly fishing this popular river.

Conant offers access to some deep pools and unofficial summertime swimming holes. This is also a fish-rich area worth spending a good bit of time and a particularly good evening dry-fly spot. Hiking the railroad tracks up- or downstream will reveal numerous paths leading down to the river where you are just as likely to find swimmers and picnickers as anglers. Some of the deeper pools popular with swimmers also hold sizable trout. When the sun is off the water and swimmers head back to their cars, trout will become more active.

Flume Creek, especially heading downstream, offers some great runs and pocketwater. If you head down far enough, you may encounter anglers fishing their way up from Sims. This is an area with a few broader runs and some of the deeper water opposite the railroad tracks holds good fish. Working a long line and keeping your presentation in the deepest water possible for as long as possible is a good tactic. Anglers with good line-handling skills have a leg up.

Sims fishing access is worth more vivid description. The bridge over the river leading to Sims Campground affords a stellar view on the upstream side of Mount Shasta towering over the area. Just downstream is the historic CCC footbridge. Both span an area of the river known as Sims Flat, a popular but difficult dry-fly venue. Looking upstream there is a pool next to an old bridge abutment. There is always a pod of fish in the tail of this pool. Fish down the deeper eastern side of the river. There are also good riffles and runs down below; this is an area where you are very likely to have company, but it's a good, long hike down to the next access, so chances are good you can get away from the crowd.

Much of the Gibson access is deeper water, full of fish, but requiring different skills. Here it's important to be able to get a good, long drift with each cast. Usually this means quartering upstream, mending and feeding line downstream as far as you dare. Some of this area is west of the river, some east. I-5 crosses Gibson in two places.

The Pollard Flat access has been improved in the last few years and now provides restrooms and picnic tables. There is exceptional water both upstream and down, but I like downstream better. Hike the tracks downstream over two railroad bridges. Below the second bridge is a wonderful section of riffles and deeper runs. I've had a few of my better Upper Sac days in this area. Upstream from the parking access holds fond memories of a large black bear that came lumbering down the hill on the far side for a late evening drink of water. Feeling far enough away and certain the bear hadn't seen me, I yelled "Hey Mr. Bear" at the top of my lungs and watched the bruin do a classic double-take before almost flying back up the hill and out of sight.

Downstream from Pollard Flat is the Lamoine river access. Bypass the big pool you come to first thing (unless you want bass) and fish the deep run just upstream. Many 20-inch-plus trout call this water home. Even though some-

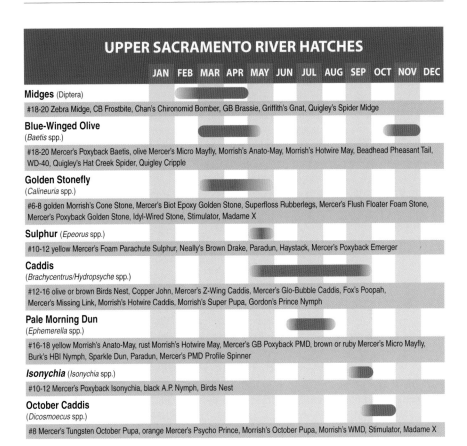

UPPER SACRAMENTO RIVER HATCHES

	JAN	FEB	MAR	APR	MAY	JUN	JUL	AUG	SEP	OCT	NOV	DEC

Midges (Diptera)

#18-20 Zebra Midge, CB Frostbite, Chan's Chironomid Bomber, GB Brassie, Griffith's Gnat, Quigley's Spider Midge

Blue-Winged Olive
(*Baetis* spp.)

#18-20 Mercer's Poxyback Baetis, olive Mercer's Micro Mayfly, Morrish's Anato-May, Morrish's Hotwire May, Beadhead Pheasant Tail, WD-40, Quigley's Hat Creek Spider, Quigley Cripple

Golden Stonefly
(*Calineuria* spp.)

#6-8 golden Morrish's Cone Stone, Mercer's Biot Epoxy Golden Stone, Superfloss Rubberlegs, Mercer's Flush Floater Foam Stone, Mercer's Poxyback Golden Stone, Idyl-Wired Stone, Stimulator, Madame X

Sulphur (*Epeorus* spp.)

#10-12 yellow Mercer's Foam Parachute Sulphur, Neally's Brown Drake, Paradun, Haystack, Mercer's Poxyback Emerger

Caddis
(*Brachycentrus/Hydropsyche* spp.)

#12-16 olive or brown Birds Nest, Copper John, Mercer's Z-Wing Caddis, Mercer's Glo-Bubble Caddis, Fox's Poopah, Mercer's Missing Link, Morrish's Hotwire Caddis, Morrish's Super Pupa, Gordon's Prince Nymph

Pale Morning Dun
(*Ephemerella* spp.)

#16-18 yellow Morrish's Anato-May, rust Morrish's Hotwire May, Mercer's GB Poxyback PMD, brown or ruby Mercer's Micro Mayfly, Burk's HBI Nymph, Sparkle Dun, Paradun, Mercer's PMD Profile Spinner

Isonychia (*Isonychia* spp.)

#10-12 Mercer's Poxyback Isonychia, black A.P. Nymph, Birds Nest

October Caddis
(*Dicosmoecus* spp.)

#8 Mercer's Tungsten October Pupa, orange Mercer's Psycho Prince, Morrish's October Pupa, Morrish's WMD, Stimulator, Madame X

what deep, on a sunny day you can see them through the clear water. Downstream from the big bass pool there is more excellent water, but not all of it is easy to get to. Access where you can depending on the flows, but deep water, steep grades, and lots of blackberry vines often limit your options in getting to fish the other side.

McCardle Flat is where I've done most of my dry-fly fishing on the Upper Sac. Much of the year it isn't quite as good as water farther upstream, but I was living in Redding at the time and it was the closest really good dry-fly fishing spot.

The lowest access to the river above Shasta Lake is Vollmers, generally known to anglers as Dog Creek. Here you can park on either side of the river. The confluence pool where Dog Creek enters is a great spot, but during warm months you might have to share the water with tubers. There is great water both up- and downstream. The farther downstream you go the more likely the water is to become deep, still, and warm. After all, depending on water levels, you are now all but fishing Shasta Lake. This is great bass water.

The Cantara Incident

The day remains etched in my mind as if it were yesterday. I was living in Redding and working for California Trout at the time. Early that morning, July 15, 1991, the clerk at my health club asked "Did you hear what happened to the Upper Sac?" I had not. He attempted to sum up what had occurred the night before, and I dropped my bag and headed for the lobby pay phone where I ended up spending most of the day.

At 9:50 PM the night before a Southern Pacific Railroad car carrying 19,000 gallons of an herbicide called metam sodium did a belly flop off the Cantara Bridge into the river north of Dunsmuir. Gradually this creeping death leached its way downstream killing every plant, bug, and fish in its wake. This turned into the largest inland hazardous substance spill in California history.

Desperate situations call for creative solutions, and many potential fixes were debated before allowing an experiment with a previously untried technique. Since the poison stopped in its tracks when it hit the wall of still water that is Shasta Lake, they decided to attack it there. Air was pumped through hoses to a depth beneath the poison, since contact with air broke the substance down, leaving only nontoxic materials in its place. The experiment was deemed a success and the emergency was over. Lawyers seemed to circle the river like a flock of buzzards. But there was still the matter of what to do with a dead river. For obvious reasons, the river was closed to fishing until further notice.

While Southern Pacific Railroad worked with the people and businesses who would surely take a massive economic hit, California Department of Fish and Game (DFG) was charged with the ultimate responsibility of managing the river's recovery. Debate over what to do with the river began almost immediately and suggestions ran from merely restocking fish in the river and calling it good to leaving the river alone and letting nature take its course. Cooler heads prevailed and DFG decided a largely natural solution was best. For the most part, the river would be allowed to heal naturally.

Although the tragedy did not occur during spawning time when mature fish would have been in the tributaries rather than the main stem of the river, there were still native fish in the tributaries and in the two miles of river above the spill. It was reasoned that aquatic insects and fish from these areas would eventually repopulate the entire river, and they did. Forty-seven wild trout were captured from above the spill and spawned at the Mt. Shasta Fish Hatchery. The wild fish didn't take to the artificial environment of the hatchery as well as scientists hoped and many died. However, about 7,000 fingerlings survived and were returned to their river. A similar reseeding program was accomplished for the native sculpin, the most abundant fish in the river. The brood stock of native fish was used to "jump-start" the recovery, and were stocked in sections of the river farthest away from tributaries.

In a backward sort of way the Cantara Incident actually focused much-needed attention on the river and helped scientists learn more about the river

A good technique when nymphing is to let your flies swing up to the surface at the end of each drift. Trout that may have ignored your drifting flies sometimes prefer the motion of a swinging fly. ZACH O'BRIEN PHOTO

than they had previously known. The traditional ways to estimate fish populations in rivers are snorkel surveys and electrofishing, both only capable of giving ballpark guesses. After the spill scientists actually got to collect and count fish corpses and truly know what was in the river.

It turns out that the river harbored more than 6,000 trout per mile, less in some sections and more in others. No one had guessed the river was this rich, placing it near the top of a short list of California streams capable of sustaining such populations. Despite the untold millions of hatchery trout that were added to native stocks since the 1930s, hatchery fish only composed about 15 percent of what was in the river. Genetic studies also revealed that very little spawning between hatchery fish and native stocks occurred, less than 1 percent, meaning the purity of the native population was surprisingly intact. These insights into a previously misunderstood river helped lay the foundations for new, more enlightened approaches to managing the fishery.

Morrish's Pickpocket (Black)

Hook: #12-18 Tiemco 3761
Bead: Black nickel
Weight: 015-.025 lead or lead-free wire
Thread: Black 6/0 Danville
Tail: Black pheasant-tail fibers
Abdomen: Black Ultra Wire
Back: Black goose biots
Thorax: Black Ice Dub
Wing Case: Black goose biots
Legs: Black Krystal Flash

Morrish's Anato-May (Hare's Ear)

Hook: #8-16 Tiemco 3761
Bead: Black tungsten
Weight: .020-.030 lead or lead-free wire
Thread: Black 6/0 Danville
Tail: Natural pheasant-tail fibers
Rib: Copper wire
Abdomen: Smoky beige Scintilla dubbing
Thorax: Smoky beige Scintilla dubbing
Back: Root beer Krystal Flash
Wing Case: Root beer Krystal Flash
Legs: Root beer Krystal Flash
Head: Dark Stone (#15) Whitlock SLF

Morrish October Caddis

Hook: #8 Tiemco 100
Thread: Coffee 6/0 Danville
Body: Orange foam colored with burnt
            umber pen
Hackle: Brown and medium ginger
Wing: Natural cow elk
Head: Tan foam

Foam Parachute Sulphur

Hook:	#14-20 Tiemco 100
Thread:	Tan 8/0 Uni-Thread
Tail:	Ginger hackle fibers, split
Rib:	Pearl Flashabou
Abdomen:	Hendrickson pink Super Fine
Thorax:	Thin strip of pink foam
Post:	White calf tail
Hackle:	Ginger

Andy Puyan's A.P. Nymph (Black)

Hook:	#10-18 Tiemco 3761
Thread:	Black 6/0 Uni-Thread
Tail:	Dark moose
Rib:	Copper wire
Body:	Black Hare-Tron
Wing Case:	Dark moose
Thorax:	Same as body
Legs:	Same as wing case
Head:	Same as body

Cal Bird's Birds Nest (Black)

Hook:	#8-16 Tiemco 3761
Thread:	Black 8/0 Uni-Thread
Tail:	Black wood-duck fibers
Rib:	Copper wire
Abdomen:	Black Australian opossum
Legs:	Black wood-duck fibers
Thorax:	Same as abdomen

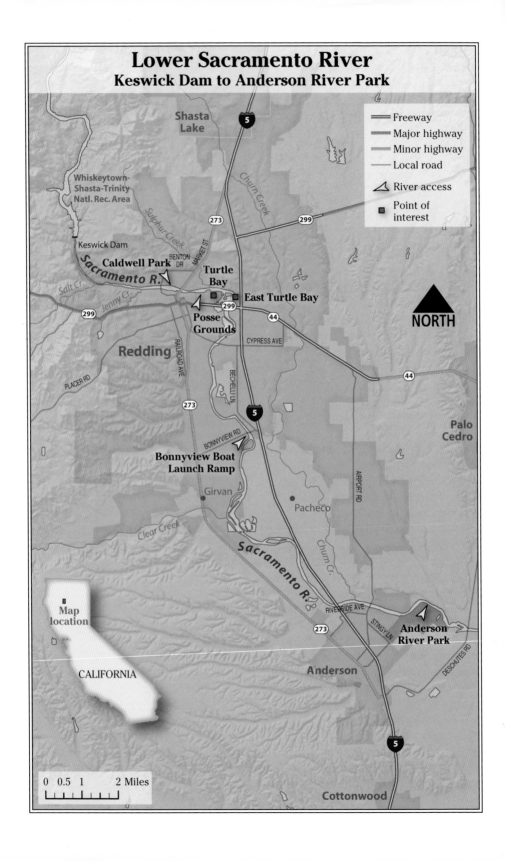

Lower Sacramento River
Keswick Dam to Anderson River Park

Shasta Lake

Whiskeytown-
Shasta-Trinity
Natl. Rec. Area

Keswick Dam

Caldwell Park

BENTON DR

Turtle Bay

East Turtle Bay

Posse Grounds

Redding

Churn Creek

Sulphur Creek

Salt Cr.

Jenny Cr.

MARKET ST

RAILROAD AVE

BECHELLI LN

CYPRESS AVE

PLACER RD

Sacramento R.

Bonnyview Boat Launch Ramp

BONNYVIEW RD

Girvan

Clear Creek

Pacheco

AIRPORT RD

Churn Cr.

Palo Cedro

44

Sacramento R.

RIVERSIDE AVE

STINGY LN

Anderson River Park

DESCHUTES RD

Map location

CALIFORNIA

Anderson

Cottonwood

	Freeway
	Major highway
	Minor highway
	Local road
◁	River access
◾	Point of interest

NORTH

0   0.5   1   2 Miles

CHAPTER 6

Lower Sacramento River

The Lower Sacramento River is renowned as one of the best wild-trout fisheries in the western United States, and with good reason. Despite the fact that it flows through northern California's largest city, and guides and their clients work the river relentlessly almost every day of the year, the fishing holds up. Amazingly, the combined flows of the Upper Sac, McCloud, and Pit rivers conspire to achieve an angling experience that is often better than any of its single parts.

The Sacramento River begins as a spring bubbling out of the flanks of massive Mount Shasta, 70 miles to the north. Several dams interrupt its flows, Box Canyon Dam creating Lake Siskiyou above and Shasta Dam forming Shasta Lake below, creating two very different Sacramento Rivers. The upper section, between Box Canyon Dam and Shasta Lake, is known as the Upper Sac. The lower part, from Keswick Dam downstream, is called the Lower Sac. Although these rivers contain some of the same water, the Upper and Lower Sac are as different as day and night.

Even when the water is low in the cooler months before the rains begin, the Lower Sac is a big, brawling river. Summer flows, mid-May through mid-September, range from 12,000 to 15,000 cubic feet per second (cfs) making drifting all but mandatory. Winter flows, mid-September through mid-May, are typically in the 3,000 to 4,000 cfs range, and open up almost unlimited opportunities for wading. Even at low flows, however, the Lower Sac is a massive stream where safety should be taken seriously.

In particularly wet spring conditions the Bureau of Reclamation will occasionally "dump" water from Shasta Lake upstream to keep Shasta Dam from overflowing. These situations usually don't last for long, but the system is able to handle 79,000 cfs for sustained periods, and you don't want to get anywhere near the river unless you're looking for a cheap ticket to San Francisco Bay. A call to any of the local fly shops can provide an update on river conditions.

Scenery along the Lower Sac is varied. In Redding you are within sight of houses, restaurants, and office buildings. The area below Redding is more rural with great views and natural beauty. MARK THAU PHOTO

Guide Vanessa Cummings-Downs about to release another rainbow. Due to the river's large size, it rarely feels crowded—even when a lot of people are fishing.

The wild rainbow trout thrive in the controlled water temperatures below Shasta Dam. There are anadromous fish yearlong, mainly king salmon, and several of these runs are state and federally listed endangered species. It is illegal to fish for salmon above Deschutes Bridge south of Redding, but their dislodged eggs become a major component of the trout diet during the fall.

In addition to stable water temperatures, the Lower Sac is an absolute bug factory. One entomologist estimated approximately 2,500 aquatic insects per square foot of river bottom. While the river is simply too big and broad for biologists to use any of the traditional fish-counting methods used to manage other fisheries, no one disputes that the trout population in the river seems healthy and immense. Creel census data from the 1990s estimates the average trout landed in these waters is better than 16 inches, and individual fish are often a lot larger than that.

Even biologists have a hard time telling big resident trout from steelhead. While some anglers claim they can tell a large Lower Sac rainbow from a steelhead, the only credible way to tell is by looking at a scale under a microscope to determine if the fish has been to the salt. So that's exactly what we did. Working as a consultant, I helped California Department of Fish and Game, Region I, perform a scale-sample survey of fish landed in the Redding area. The goal was to ascertain what percentage of the trout, especially the larger specimens caught and released in the Redding area, were actually steelhead.

A number of Sacramento River guides, most with The Fly Shop in Redding, enthusiastically collected over a hundred scale samples from trout caught in the Lower Sac. These were viewed under a microscope to determine how many had actually been to salt water. It turns out that not one of them had. The general consensus was that very few steelhead actually make it up the Sacramento River as far as Redding. The good news is that resident trout in this area may still attain steelhead dimensions.

Day-in, day-out, drifting the river is the most efficient way to fish year-round, since covering a lot of water is by far the best strategy. There is so much good habitat, fish aren't pressured into frequenting specific areas of the river in order to survive. There is food for them everywhere. Because Lower Sac rainbows move around a lot, wading anglers are forced to concentrate on relatively small areas that may or may not hold fish. A spot that fishes well one day may produce nothing the next. In fact, even if there are good numbers of fish in a given area, someone may have pounded that water just before you arrived. If you're not catching fish in likely looking places, move on. Because the fishing can be so good, these fish see a fair number of drift boats and anglers almost every day, and the fish become selective and move around. The better spots are worked over thoroughly by one group, and as soon as they drift downstream another boat might slip in to take its place. You can catch lots of fish and some very large ones, but it isn't necessarily easy fishing.

Common sights and sounds along the river include abundant cottonwood and oak trees, ubiquitous blackberry and manzanita bushes, along with spectacular mountain vistas of Mount Shasta, Lassen Peak, and Shasta Bally. Most days you will see many varieties of ducks, great blue herons, egrets, Canada geese, belted kingfishers, killdeers, swallows, ospreys, and occasionally bald eagles. With all this beauty surrounding the river you almost don't notice that massive I-5 runs right next to the river in several areas. Even here, at the pinnacle of California's big-water, big wild-trout fishing experience, there remains that unexplainable West Coast love affair with the automobile. Because it is an urban fishery, do not leave valuables in your unattended vehicle.

Lower Sac Hatches

Pick up any rock or stick out of the river and you will be astounded by the number of aquatic insects clinging to it. Generally speaking, the Lower Sac owes much of its richness to a fabulous abundance of macroinvertebrates. Due to the river's vastness and length, it's a good bet that almost every aquatic insect species is present somewhere.

Since the primary engine that powers aquatic insect activity is the sun, the bug activity is lowest during the rainy months of December, January, and February. On some early spring days when the rain is a fine mist and Blue-Winged Olives will hatch in enough abundance to capture the trouts' attention, #18-20 Pheasant Tail Nymphs, Copper Johns, Poxyback Baetis produce well. For midges try #18-20 Zebra Midges, Brassies, or Mercer's Midgelings.

Drift boats are commonly used to fish the Lower Sac during warmer months when the flows are high and the wading limited. MARK THAU PHOTO

Occasionally trout rise in slack-water areas where dry flies might work well. Typically these dry-fly opportunities are fleeting, because if it starts raining too hard the fish can no longer see the tiny flies. Still, I have had some memorable afternoons with tiny dry flies and large trout south of Redding and especially around Anderson River Park.

The caddisfly hatches on the river are among the most intense I've seen anywhere. March and April are usually good times for the *Brachycentrus* that hatch with such abundance they virtually blanket the surface of the water. This hatch sometimes produces so many billions of caddisflies that their decaying carcasses form a thick, sludgy mudlike substance along the banks of the river.

Under such circumstances an angler can't help but wonder why a trout would take an imitation, specifically *his or her* imitation, when there are an unlimited number of naturals all around. Your only choices are to change nothing and expect different results (definition of insanity?), or to do something different. Trying a slightly larger or smaller fly will often turn the trick and snatch you away from the very jaws of madness. Just to see a hatch and trout rise of this intensity at least once in your life will make a lasting impression.

Over the summer the species of caddis will change, favoring the *Hydropsyche* over the *Brachycentrus,* but all this means to the angler is a slight color change from patterns favoring an olive cast to ones more that are more brownish in hue. Truth is, it's not a bad idea to have both green and brown caddis

Most of the fishing on the Lower Sac is with nymphs, and a fly box with many kinds of patterns offers a definite advantage. The abundance and diversity of the river's rich aquatic insect population make it a special fishery.

nymphs ranging in size from #12-16. While the vast majority of the fishing is nymph fishing, there can be opportunities for dry-fly fishing, especially in the evenings. Any dry caddis pattern like the Elk Hair Caddis in #14-16 will work if fished well.

While the water is typically around 60 degrees most of the summer, the air is often over 110 degrees during July, August, and September. The river does provide some relief by reducing the heat by around 5 degrees close to the water, but it's still toasty. Summertime anglers often fish the river from drift boats wearing only shorts, T-shirts, and flip-flops and manage to stay comfortable. Standing in the water without waders is almost unthinkable any other time of the year, but on hot summer days it works. Bring lots of water to drink, polarized sunglasses, sunscreen, and a hat with a brim.

During fall and winter the river fills with huge spawning king salmon, and their contribution to the trout diet cannot be overlooked. These are low-water months for the river, and giant salmon can be plainly seen actively digging redds and spawning. Greedy egg-sucking trout pile up behind salmon redds and gobble dislodged eggs with great enthusiasm. These trout often become so gorged on salmon eggs that they spew from the trout's gullet while anglers are trying to release them. These trout put on a lot of weight during salmon season, and all that protein seems to turn them an even brighter shade of crimson.

Finding what color egg pattern trout prefer on any given day takes patience and willingness to experiment. Only the trout know why the color that worked so well yesterday is shunned today. Single egg patterns vary in color from chartreuse and champagne to shades of orange and pink. One good bet is a #12 Pettis' Unreal Egg. Not only does it fool the fish, but the fly is pretty much bulletproof. Another good idea is to present one egg pattern to the fish along with a caddis or mayfly nymph as a dropper. Searching patterns such as #14-16 Prince Nymphs, Gold-Ribbed Hare's Ears, Zug Bugs, or even a few larger stonefly patterns can work well at times, as can swinging streamers and leech patterns.

Wading anglers seek shallow riffles and drop-offs to concentrate their efforts. From a drift boat you can fish these, but also take advantage of fishing all the medium-velocity flows from 6 to 10 feet deep. Guides will often try to position their boats in this zone as much as possible, avoiding deeper or shallower water. The key is to maintain a natural drift and keep your flies in the water working for you.

Having the right fly is important, but not nearly as important as getting the proper drift. These fish have seen it all and are much more likely to take a fly not matching the hatch. Fish feed on the surface on occasion, but day-in and day-out the successful anglers will be fishing nymphs under a floating strike indicator.

Big Water Gear

The most common mistake first-time Lower Sac anglers make is showing up undergunned. Sure, you can catch fish with a 9-foot, 5-weight, but you won't be able to fish as efficiently or confidently as with a stouter rig. Remember, this is big water with big fish in it. Your next cast could produce the fish of a lifetime. Most regular Lower Sac anglers prefer a fairly stiff 6- or 7-weight rod. My favorite outfit for this river is a 9 1/2-foot 6-weight loaded on a quality reel with a smooth drag. Trout in most northern California streams can be handled without a reel that has a disk drag, but not those in the Lower Sac. Trout here are capable of tearing all the line off a reel.

Just as it pays to go a bit heavier with rod and reel, the terminal tackle most often used here isn't kid stuff either. Your needs are going to be different working from a drift boat as opposed to wade-fishing, so your leader setup should be different as well. When fishing from a drift boat, a good nymphing rig begins with a 2-foot section of 30-pound-test mono to which a yarn strike indicator is fastened. Next comes an 8-foot section of 3X fluorocarbon to which the top fly is fastened. Since good 3X fluorocarbon is about 9-pound-test, here is where I cheat a little. I intentionally tie an overhand knot in the tippet about a foot above the top fly. This is to prevent the two or three medium split-shot I use to sink the rig from sliding down on the top fly. Using more 3X fluorocarbon tied to the hook bend of the top fly, I hang a second nymph about 2 feet below the first. The entire rig is about 12 feet long with two nymphs, lots of weight, and a big fluffy indicator that can float a battleship. True, this is not a picnic to cast. But from a drift boat you

Summer evenings are a great time to find rising trout on the river. When the weather is hot fish will still take a well-presented dry once the sun is off the water. MARK THAU PHOTO

really don't need to do much more than an occasional roll cast along with continual mending.

Leaders for wade-fishing tend to be less complex because they need to cast easily without getting constantly tangled. I rarely go over 9 to 10 feet in length while wading, and start with a standard 9-foot 3X fluorocarbon leader right out of the package. From there I fasten my indicator up close to the thickest part of the leader. I add split-shot as explained above, then my first fly, followed by my second fly about two feet below. The main difference in the rig I use when wading is that I find that a fully tapered leader (one piece of mono tapered from thick to thin) turns over better while casting. It doesn't sink my flies as quickly as the drift-boat setup, but neither does it tangle nearly as often while casting.

While not perfect, I can still cast 30 to 40 feet upstream with this setup. While it drifts back toward me, I take up line to prevent too much slack from entering the system. I mend the line as the indicator passes just below me, and then feed all the line back out below me just like the Fall River Twitch (see page 30). With the right rod and reasonable line-handling skills, even a relative novice can achieve a 60- to 80-foot drift. On the Lower Sac you want to cover as much water as possible. Needless to say, anglers who lack good casting and line-handling skills are at a disadvantage on this huge river.

Above the ACID

While the Sacramento qualifies as the longest river in California, the spectacular trout fishing begins below Keswick Dam just above Redding. The upper three miles is deep, dark, and cold above the Anderson-Cottonwood Irrigation Dam (ACID) framed on either side by the Sacramento River Trail. In low-water months you can wade the river in a couple of spots to access shallow riffles that don't get fished very often.

You can launch at the Caldwell Park boat-launch ramp, motor upstream, and fish your way back down. There are no launch facilities below Keswick Dam. This upper stretch doesn't get fished as much as the downstream sections and a lot of it is deep. Still, if you have a boat and motor, it can produce excellent fishing with very little competition. The lower part of this drift just upstream from Caldwell Park can also be good. The water isn't as deep as up above, and the likely spots for trout to hold are more obvious. But be careful. If you're in a drift boat and manage to get yourself downstream of the boat-launch ramp without a motor, you're in serious trouble.

For anglers inclined to do a little hiking, there are several good riffles off the Sacramento River Trail on the river's north side. Since motorized vehicles are prohibited on the River Trail, some anglers ride mountain bikes in.

Posse Grounds to Bonnyview

Behind the Redding Convention Center on Auditorium Drive are corrals, horses, stables, and, somewhat surprisingly, a parking lot and boat-launch ramp. The Posse Grounds is not far below the ACID (dam) and is one of the most popular places to begin floating the river. It's often a busy place on summer mornings and evenings. This float will take you right down through the middle of Redding and is just as exceptional for the fishing as it is for the urban scenery.

You will see mansions, office buildings, and several bridges including Redding's flagship Sundial Bridge. A work of art in itself, this massive pedestrian walkway connects Turtle Bay Museum to the gardens and hiking trails on the river's north side. As strangely urban as this drift is, the water is gorgeous and provides good fishing both for floating and wading. It can also be crowded, but there are almost always fish to be had in this area 12 months a year.

There is certainly enough good fishing water to spend all day fishing this section, or it can also work for half a day depending on your speed. The river takes a broad bend to the south at Turtle Bay. Pay attention to the 4- to 9-foot-deep water around the islands on the inside of the bend, focusing on anything that can funnel food to the fish such as structure and changes in depth.

Below the CA 299 bridge, but above the Cypress Street bridge, East Turtle Bay provides good fishing around the several islands located here. Look for the Bonnyview boat-launch ramp on the west side immediately below

ANGLING REGULATIONS

The Lower Sac is open to fishing 365 days per year, but that doesn't mean you necessarily ought to rush right out there on any given day. At high water, wading access is severely limited and sometimes dangerous. Drifting is more reliable, but occasional high springtime flows can make it less of a fishing trip and more of a white-knuckle thrill ride. Even at low flows the river can be dangerous for drift boats, and the river is constantly changing.

Barbless hooks are required regardless of your method of take (bait fishing is also allowed in the Lower Sac). There is some very complicated verbiage in the angling regulations about keeping hatchery trout and steelhead. If you intend to keep fish, check the angling regulations and know exactly where you are on the river. There are four different specific time slots when keeping hatchery fish is permissible, assuming you can tell a hatchery trout or steelhead from a native. The only hatchery fish in the Lower Sacramento River system migrate in from tributaries, and the astronomically low chances of ever hooking a "one in a million" hatchery fish are so low, further comment here is a waste of space. If you plan to "take only photographs and leave only footprints," just debarb your hooks and don't worry about the regs. ∎

Bonnyview boat-launch ramp is a well-used, centrally located launch site with good fishing only minutes away. Boats and rafts of all kinds launch here.

South Bonnyview Bridge in a big, flat area with views of office buildings and cars on the bridge upstream.

Bonnyview to Anderson River Park

While not quite as urban as the Posse Grounds float, plan on being within easy view of many palatial homes with a few more remote sections creeping in as the landscape begins to become more rural. Clear Creek, a major spawning tributary for trout, steelhead, and salmon comes in from the west around a series of islands and makes the river immediately upstream and downstream all the more productive. This is also a popular wading area that can be accessed behind Cascade Park on the west side. From I-5 take the South Bonnyview exit on the south side of Redding and turn left on CA 273. Take another left on Girvan and look for the park on your right. You can't see the river from the park, but follow any of the several trails through the trees behind the park a short distance to the water.

When the flows are high during the summer, boats have the option of weaving in and out of several islands where Clear Creek enters the river. Because the islands provide habitat for both insects and fish, these are good areas to either float or wade.

Anderson River Park to Balls Ferry

As the river continues downstream it begins to lose even more of the urban quality it has up above. There are occasional homes, parks, restaurants, and bridges to remind you civilization is not far away—even a short stretch of I-5 running beside the river—but then the river becomes quieter.

There is a full-fledged boat-launch ramp at Anderson River Park as well as ample bank access to some good water both above and below the sweeping right-hand turn the river takes. The Anderson River Park (west) side of the river offers good fishing for floating or wading anglers. The east side of the river also fishes well around this bend, but private property makes this water impractical for wading anglers to get to. It fishes well from a boat, especially in the evenings.

The next bridge below Anderson River Park is Deschutes Road. Above this bridge it is illegal to fish for salmon, but the river downstream supports a popular salmon fishery. All anglers fishing for trout downstream from the Deschutes Road bridge are required to carry a Steelhead Report Card along with their fishing license; steelhead frequent this water during fall and winter months. The card is required on all California streams where steelhead may be present, even though most anglers lack specific knowledge on how to tell a steelhead from a resident trout. The state attempts to track harvested and released steelhead in hopes of better managing these resources.

It's important for anglers wading in the Lower Sac to avoid wading on top of redds. Salmon spawn in the gravels and bury their fertilized eggs just

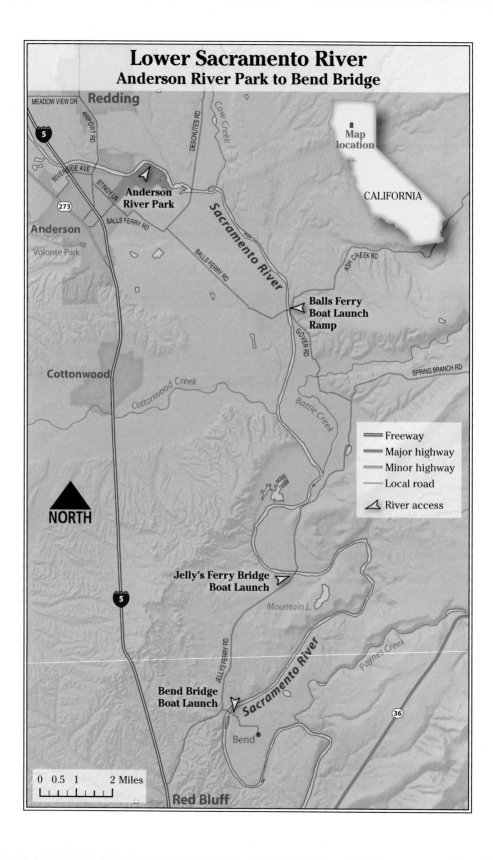

Lower Sacramento River
Anderson River Park to Bend Bridge

MEADOW VIEW DR

Redding

5

AIRPORT RD

RIVERSIDE AVE

STINGY LN

273

DESCHUTES RD

COW Creek

Map location

CALIFORNIA

Anderson River Park

Sacramento River

BALLS FERRY RD

Anderson

Volonte Park

BALLS FERRY RD

ASH CREEK RD

Balls Ferry Boat Launch Ramp

Cottonwood

Cottonwood Creek

GOVER RD

SPRING BRANCH RD

Battle Creek

Freeway

Major highway

Minor highway

Local road

River access

NORTH

Jelly's Ferry Bridge Boat Launch

Mountain L.

5

JELLY'S FERRY RD

Sacramento River

Paynes Creek

Bend Bridge Boat Launch

36

Bend

Sacramento River

0 0.5 1   2 Miles

Red Bluff

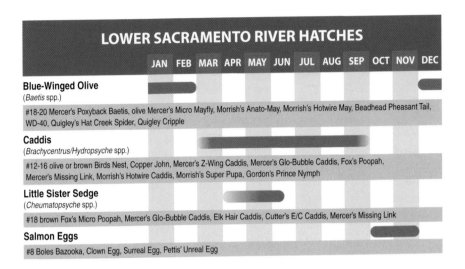

LOWER SACRAMENTO RIVER HATCHES

	JAN	FEB	MAR	APR	MAY	JUN	JUL	AUG	SEP	OCT	NOV	DEC

Blue-Winged Olive
(*Baetis* spp.)

#18-20 Mercer's Poxyback Baetis, olive Mercer's Micro Mayfly, Morrish's Anato-May, Morrish's Hotwire May, Beadhead Pheasant Tail, WD-40, Quigley's Hat Creek Spider, Quigley Cripple

Caddis
(*Brachycentrus/Hydropsyche* spp.)

#12-16 olive or brown Birds Nest, Copper John, Mercer's Z-Wing Caddis, Mercer's Glo-Bubble Caddis, Fox's Poopah, Mercer's Missing Link, Morrish's Hotwire Caddis, Morrish's Super Pupa, Gordon's Prince Nymph

Little Sister Sedge
(*Cheumatopsyche* spp.)

#18 brown Fox's Micro Poopah, Mercer's Glo-Bubble Caddis, Elk Hair Caddis, Cutter's E/C Caddis, Mercer's Missing Link

Salmon Eggs

#8 Boles Bazooka, Clown Egg, Surreal Egg, Pettis' Unreal Egg

below the surface. Anglers are easily drawn to these areas because of the pods of rainbow trout holding downstream in hopes of intercepting dislodged salmon eggs. What these anglers do not realize is that they are literally squishing hundreds and thousands of would-be adult salmon. These fish have a hard enough time making it to adulthood, and many of these runs are listed as endangered species. They do the trout population of the Sacramento River nothing but good, providing food in the form of dislodged eggs and nutrients and minerals critically important to aquatic insects as their bodies decompose. Do not tramp on the salmon redds.

Downstream from Anderson the river becomes even more rural, and in many places you could easily forget you are in our nation's most populous state. There is rugged natural beauty, mountain landscapes, and plenty of sky above you. During the lower flows of winter, you can go hours without seeing another person below Anderson.

The Deschutes Road bridge crosses the river and just below are several islands as well as the mouth of Cow Creek. Concentrate on areas below riffles, ledges, drop-offs, and seams. Remember whether floating or wading to cover as much likely looking water as possible. The farther downstream from Redding you go, the fewer people you are likely to see, and the more deer along the river and bald eagles overhead.

Extending the Trout Fishery

Thanks to more precise temperature controls at Shasta Dam, this region between Redding and Red Bluff has recently become much better trout habitat. In the 1990s a temperature control device (TCD) was added to Shasta Dam above Redding to allow the precise control of water temperatures downstream for the benefit of salmon and steelhead.

Not only has the TCD helped habitat for anadromous fish, but there has also been a side-door benefit for the trout fishery. While there is some debate on whether the trout are bigger or more abundant than before, everyone seems to agree on one thing. Because the water is now colder during certain times of the year, the trout fishery has been extended farther downstream.

Balls Ferry boat-launch ramp, the next access downstream from Anderson River Park, used to be about as low as any fly-fishing guide cared to drift his or her clients. Most agreed that the water below was warmer and less productive trout habitat. Today anglers are experimenting with drifts far below Redding trying to determine how much farther the good fishing has been extended. The drift from Jellys Ferry Road to the Bend boat-launch ramp above Red Bluff may be the most beautiful stretch of the entire river I've seen, and the fishing is great.

At some point on its journey downstream the river does become warmer and other species tend to dominate the habitat. Alabama spotted bass and smallmouth bass, so plentiful in Shasta Lake above, also inhabit warmer, slower sections of the Lower Sac, even within Redding's city limits. During summer's warmer months I've had the rare pleasure of spending numerous days landing tough rainbows in the river proper, and then discovering sun-drenched weedy sloughs also willing to provide 30 or 40 bass to the day's total. Below the town of Red Bluff the river even supports a terrific shad run during June and July.

Keswick Reservoir

The Lower Sacramento River wild-trout fishery begins at Keswick Dam 3 miles above Redding and extends downstream for at least 25 miles. Keswick Reservoir is the 9 miles of water above Keswick Dam, between Keswick and Shasta dams.

Just about everything about Keswick is a bit strange, so it should come as no shock that this amazing fishery was more or less created accidentally. Prior to the installation of the temperature control device on Shasta Dam, and then the tragedy of the 9/11 terrorist attack, it wasn't much of a fishery.

First, the TCD on Shasta Dam improved water quality and habitat. Secondly, the terrorist attack referred to as 9/11 caused federal authorities to shore up security efforts around large dams that might make enticing terrorist targets. More than anything else it was these things that created a "new" wild-trout fishery.

When I first started fishing Keswick it was a much different place than it is today. In the late 1980s flows beneath Shasta Dam were warmer, rendering the flows beneath better habitat for Sacramento suckers and pikeminnows than for trout. First, the TCD improved water quality, tipping the habitat preference balance in favor of the trout. Then the presence of security patrols monitoring the dams made being in this once rather seedy area one of the safest places around. Today you can't spend much time at Keswick without seeing

Guide Brooke Matteson grins big with this typical Lower Sac rainbow. Studies show the average size of fish landed here is over 16 inches.

at least one of the several security agencies patrolling the area, and no one may drive across Shasta Dam without having first been cleared by security.

Being this close to Shasta Dam, Keswick's flows are the coldest and most stable in the Lower Sacramento River system. They usually fluctuate between about 48 and 50 degrees year-round. The water and flows in Keswick are also either rising or falling constantly. Amazingly, the fish have adapted. The daily de-watering of vast areas has made it tough for mayflies and caddisflies to thrive here, but midges do just fine, and they have become the cornerstone of the trout diet.

Though it is technically a reservoir, Keswick fishes like a vast, slow-moving river. But because of the fluctuating flows, it isn't the place you'd want to bring your boat. There is only one boat-launch ramp about a mile above Keswick Dam, so to fish the best water you would have to motor upstream at least seven miles. Secondly, there are tons of rock gardens in Keswick both above and just beneath the water's surface, and I have seen these all but destroy motorized boats making their way upstream. Strangely, while I have seen some boats in Keswick over the years, I have never seen anyone in a boat catch a fish here.

Keswick is, however, a superb float-tube fishery. Lots of folks groan when I tell them this, and many would much rather bring their pontoon boats. Don't do it. Pontoon boats work well on the river below Keswick Dam but not up here. The most efficient way to fish Keswick is to fish/float downstream, then get out of the water and hike back to your vehicle with your float tube strapped to your back.

Pontoon boats don't work for two reasons. First, some of the best fishing spots on Keswick are small just like some of the best spots to fish in rivers are small. Pontoons are just not as maneuverable as float tubes to wiggle in and out of these tight places. Secondly, even if you have a wheel for rolling your pontoon boat, there is still the need to wrestle it through the brush and up to the trail (at least 100 vertical feet) leading back to where you started. Friends who've insisted on not taking my advice have always wished they had.

While it seems crazy to fish moving water from a float tube, it works well in this unique situation. First, whatever is happening to the water levels, a float tube will keep you above it all, even if you bump into a few rocks. The water is moving, but it isn't fast. The main current sticks close to the middle of the reservoir, which is deep and not terrific fishing water anyway. The fishing is along the edges, sometimes a foot or two off the bank. Three to six feet of water is the secret, wherever that is. You may begin the day fishing the slowly moving water along the bank, but if the water is dropping you may have to switch to fishing farther out.

The best rig for fishing Keswick is a 9-foot leader tapered to 4X fluorocarbon, a small floating strike indicator about 5 feet above a #12 brown Birds Nest nymph tied with a tungsten bead. These fish don't see a lot of flies, and in a good day of fishing Keswick you might expect to catch and release 20 pounds of wild trout.

In the spirit of not wanting to take all the fun out of discovering this place, get a Shasta Dam permit and explore Keswick yourself. As of this writing permits have been temporarily suspended while forest fire damage to an outlying area is addressed. Google "Shasta Dam Permit" for the latest information. Keswick Reservoir is open to angling year-round. There is a five-fish limit and all angling methods are allowed. The only months Keswick is not productive are December and January, although August and September can be awfully hot with hiking back to your car in 110-degree heat and no shade.

Morrish's Super Pupa (Olive)

Hook:	Tiemco 2457 (#8-12); Tiemco 2487 (#14-16)
Bead:	Black nickel
Weight:	.015-.025 lead or lead-free wire
Thread:	Black 6/0 Danville
Rib:	Copper wire
Abdomen:	Equal parts of olive and caddis green Hare-Tron
Back:	Olive and black Flashabou Accent
Wing Case:	Same as back
Legs:	Brown Hungarian partridge fibers
Head:	Black Hare's Ear Plus

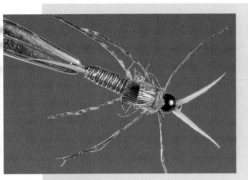

Morrish's WMD (Golden Stone)

Hook: #6-8 Tiemco 5263
Bead: Black nickel
Weight: .025-.030 lead or lead-free wire
Thread: Dark brown 6/0 Danville
Tail: Olive-brown goose biots
Antennae: Olive-brown goose biots
Abdomen: Gold and olive Ultra Wire (large)
Back: Gray 1/8" Scud Back
Thorax: Golden brown Ice Dub
Wing Case: Dark turkey shorts, coated and folded
Legs: Brown Lumaflex
Head: Golden brown Ice Dub

Fox's Poopah (Cinnamon)

Hook: #12-18 Tiemco 3769
Bead: Copper
Thread: Camel 8/0 Uni-Thread
Tail/ Cinnamon Caddis
Overbody: Vernille
Rib: Gold wire
Underbody: Pearl tinsel
Legs: Brown partridge or hen-back fibers
Head: Brown ostrich
Antennae: Lemon wood-duck fibers

Fox's Poopah (Olive)

Hook: #12-18 Tiemco 3769
Bead: Copper
Thread: Olive 8/0 Uni-Thread
Tail/ Olive Vernille
Overbody:
Rib: Gold wire
Underbody: Pearl tinsel
Legs: Brown partridge or hen-back fibers
Head: Black ostrich
Antennae: Lemon wood-duck fibers

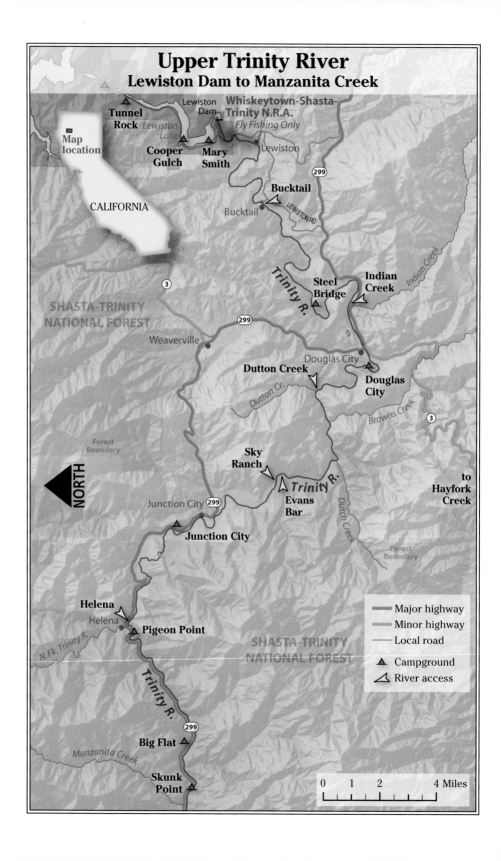

Upper Trinity River
Lewiston Dam to Manzanita Creek

Tunnel Rock

Lewiston Dam

Lewiston Lake

Whiskeytown-Shasta-Trinity N.R.A.
Fly Fishing Only

Map location

Cooper Gulch

Mary Smith

Lewiston

CALIFORNIA

Bucktail

Bucktail

LEWISTON RD

Trinity R.

Steel Bridge

Indian Creek

Indian Creek

SHASTA-TRINITY NATIONAL FOREST

Weaverville

Douglas City

Dutton Creek

Dutton Cr.

Douglas City

Browns Creek

Forest Boundary

Sky Ranch

Trinity R.

to Hayfork Creek

Junction City

Evans Bar

Dutch Creek

NORTH

Junction City

Forest Boundary

Helena

Helena

Pigeon Point

N. Fk. Trinity R.

Trinity R.

SHASTA-TRINITY NATIONAL FOREST

Major highway
Minor highway
Local road
Campground
River access

Big Flat

Manzanita Creek

Skunk Point

0   1   2   4 Miles

CHAPTER 7

Trinity River

ar and away the most popular steelhead stream in California, the Trinity
often threads between hundreds of GORE-TEX covered legs in a weekend while being gently stroked by the smooth sides of drift boats. Trinity anglers share a passion that, to some, borders on insanity. While the Trinity
can fish very much like a normal trout stream, there are also opportunities for
what lots of stalwart steelheaders live for—freezing to death while not catching fish hour after hour.

The Trinity is born in the remote Salmon-Trinity Alps due west of Mount
Shasta. It gathers steam from the Trinity Divide and heads south to first create Trinity Lake famous for smallmouth bass. Below Trinity Dam is Lewiston
Lake, one of northern California's renowned stillwater fisheries. Below Lewiston Dam the water bubbles cold and clean and is a full-fledged steelhead
river. From top to bottom it runs 150 miles to where it flows into the Klamath
near Weitchpec.

Steelhead runs vary from year to year. Some years many more steelhead
return to the river than others. Word gets out quickly on the strength of the
run, and this helps determine how crowded the river might be on a given
year. Some of the most pleasant fishing actually occurs during years with a
lower fish count. The ability to fish the water you want, in the way you want,
accounts for a lot of satisfaction, even if you don't catch as many fish.

The character of the Trinity makes it easy for anglers to love. First, there
is so much river to fish and access is almost unlimited. Wading anglers generally have an easy time in most places, and floating the river is a genuine joy.
The illusion that you're just fishing an intimate trout stream is complete until
your indicator dips beneath the surface and the giant shock wave hits your
fly rod full force. In fact, fishing the Trinity is a lot like fishing an average trout
stream. Trout, however, don't pull like Polaris submarines, and when you
realize you've connected yourself to a steelhead there's an instinctive moment
of fear and excitement as you wonder "who's got whom?"

111

Bright autumn days drifting the Trinity River are hard to beat. Gorgeous weather seems contrary to most people's idea of steelhead fishing, but you can find it on the Trinity.
MARK THAU PHOTO

The steelhead run is different every year, but generally speaking the Trinity just keeps getting better and better.

Is it any wonder that steelhead fishing is some of the most addictive fly fishing there is? Because of the Trinity River there are legions of anglers, most of them not crazy, who fish far more in the cold, wet season than during the balmy days of summer. What inspires anglers to get up at "0-dark-thirty"; brave rain, snow, or sleet to put themselves in a dark, foggy, frigid scene for hours on end; and later get all misty about that steelhead they *almost* caught while already laying plans for their next trip? It's either madness, or steelhead fishing, or both.

While there are brown trout throughout the Trinity River system, they are fewer in number than other species, but some of the biggest. The first brown trout eggs came to California from Michigan in 1893 or 1894 and were received by the Fort Gaston Hatchery on the Trinity River near Willow Creek. This facility operated on the grounds of a former military reservation between 1889 and 1898. It's unclear exactly where the very first brown trout were stocked in California, but the Trinity River would be a logical choice. Some of the Trinity's brown trout stay in the river year-round, and others migrate to the ocean and back like steelhead and take on their huge dimensions. Brown trout are taken every year in the upper stretch, and some of them go over ten pounds.

Steelhead is what this river is all about, and an average fish will run about four pounds, with plenty of smaller and larger ones thrown in. Mike Mercer elevated his celebrity when he hooked and landed a 15-pound Trinity steelhead on a one-weight fly rod. It was a dark fish, he said, well colored up, and

The heads of pools are great places to find resting steelhead. The pools themselves are best worked from a boat and should not be ignored.

he caught it sight-fishing in the upper section. These are the opportunities steelhead anglers live for and talk about in hushed tones in front of campfires for years to come.

Runs vary from year to year in terms of the number of steelhead and percentages of wild fish versus hatchery fish in the river. When the run is strong, word spreads quickly. In some ways it's almost better for the run to be off slightly so the river doesn't become so crowded. The winter of 2007–2008 was an epic year with high steelhead numbers in the system with corresponding numbers of anglers determined to hook them. An informal consensus among the guides who know this river well suggests the ratio of hatchery to wild fish was about 70 percent hatchery steelhead versus 30 percent wild. There were so many steelhead in the river that fishing for them was almost easy.

The 2008–2009 season had many fewer fish, as well as anglers. On weekdays you could almost forget how popular this fishery is. Because of the lower fish counts, anglers had to work harder to hook fewer fish, but at least the maddening crowds were held at bay. Since the wild steelhead population is somewhat stable, it's mostly the hatchery population that varies. During the 2008–2009 winter the ratio of hatchery fish to wild fish was more like 60–40.

Upper River

The highest concentration of fish, and anglers, can be found from Lewiston Dam downstream to Junction City and the river's confluence with the North Fork. At times, especially on weekends from October through December, this section of river can take on a carnival atmosphere, and it almost seems like there isn't a single run, riffle, or pool without eager fishermen camped out on it. This can be frustrating, and drifting anglers describe how the river can seem more like a parade route. There are one hundred guide permits issued on the Trinity each year, and you can only hope they all don't show up at the same time in the same places.

On the other hand, this isn't an accidental phenomenon. When the fish are in, this is usually the place to be if you don't mind a little company. The habit of anglers to show up in notoriously productive places while it's still dark and dredge the same water for hours without letting anyone else have a chance is fairly typical. Of course, the river is not always crowded, and most think it's worth the risk of not being able to fish exactly where you want. If the river isn't crowded, the best strategy of all is to move around and fish a lot of different water. Joyously, there are some days when the crowds stay home. Due to the great clarity of the water, the Trinity offers good opportunities for sight-fishing.

Some popular upper drifts include Lewiston to Bucktail, Bucktail to Steel Bridge, Steel Bridge to Indian Creek, Indian Creek to Dutton Creek, Dutton Creek to Evans Bar, Evans Bar to Sky Ranch, and Sky Ranch to Junction City Campground. The upper water is fine for drift boats or pontoon boats. This is the smallest water in the system, beautiful and intimate.

Guide Jay Cockrum working a run with a light Spey rod. Much of the river looks more like a trout stream than a steelhead river, and the steelhead prefer the same places as trout.

The area just below Lewiston Dam is popular in May when the hatchery releases the steelhead smolts for their journey to the ocean. This water has an amazing number of fish in it. The smolts run from about 8 to 12 inches, but what they lack in size they more than make up for in spunk. They won't let you forget they are steelhead, however small. This is outrageous fishing and a great place to bring kids or anyone else who needs to "catch" rather than merely "fish." It's not uncommon to get more than one grab per cast, and there are also a few adult steelhead hanging around in this water along with outsized resident and anadromous brown trout to spice things up. Rather than setting the hook on something you think is a foot long, you may come to realize it's really a yard long.

This upper section of the river is rich in places to launch and remove boats, as well as good places to camp. There is a campground about every five miles, and virtually unlimited bank access for wading anglers. While wading the river does not allow you to cover as much water, fish do move in and out of particular areas. If you are restricted to wading, it's usually a good strategy to try to hit at least two or three different locations in a day's fishing. Even if you move only a few miles, it's different water and new fish each time. This will often increase your catch rate versus anglers who insist on camping on a short stretch of water all day long.

Once in a while everything comes together. Guide Dax Messet hoists a big Trinity steelhead on a sunny day. Could life get any better than this?

Most of the water in the Trinity can hold steelhead, at least some of the time. This makes covering a lot of water in a day of fishing even more important.

Middle River

Many smaller tributaries flow into the river, and a few major ones. The farther downstream you go, the more water there is, but this happens in a gradual and friendly manner on the Trinity. The best fishing is really just a matter of where the crowds are and which parts of the river are convenient to get to on a given day. Sometimes having a piece of water to yourself is just as important as catching fish. Not far below Junction City is Helena, where the North Fork Trinity flows in.

Below Helena is Pigeon Point, which is a popular place to take out when drifting the river because it marks the beginning of Pigeon Point Run, a popular white-water rafting venue. While there is some good fishing water in this section as there is throughout the Trinity, there are numerous fairly technical rapids and drops including Hell Hole, a good ten-foot drop more like a waterfall than a rapid. Anglers are better left to probe this area by driving west on CA 299 and using the many turnouts for wading access to this section.

The lower you go on the river, the bigger the flows and the fewer the anglers. There is plenty of good swing water between Del Loma and Willow Creek and from Willow Creek down to Hoopa. It can be good fishing down low even during September and October, intercepting fish headed for the upper river.

If you're planning to fish the Trinity for a few days, it might be worth taking a side trip and fishing Hayfork Creek, an underfished gem with plenty of

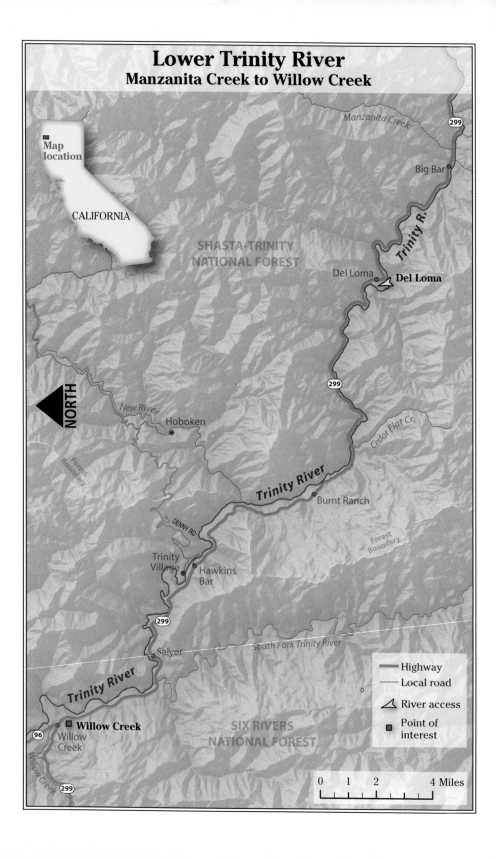

Lower Trinity River
Manzanita Creek to Willow Creek

Map location

CALIFORNIA

NORTH

Manzanita Creek

299

Big Bar

Trinity R.

SHASTA-TRINITY
NATIONAL FOREST

Del Loma

Del Loma

299

Cedar Flat Cr.

New River

Hoboken

Forest Boundary

Trinity River

Burnt Ranch

Forest Boundary

DENNY RD

Trinity Village

Hawkins Bar

299

Salyer

South Fork Trinity River

Trinity River

96

Willow Creek

Willow Creek

299

Willow Creek

SIX RIVERS
NATIONAL FOREST

	Highway
	Local road
	River access
	Point of interest

0   1   2   4 Miles

All manner of flies are likely to take Trinity steelhead, even traditional trout nymphs. Some of the best have rubber legs or marabou that imparts motion to the fly.

wild steelhead in it. Veer south on CA 3 just before Douglas City and pass through the town of Hayfork. Between Hayfork and Hyampom, CA 3 parallels Hayfork Creek for at least 20 miles, much of which is remote canyon. This section is perfect for summer camping trips and summer steelhead fishing. The terrain is fairly rough, but if you live for adventure, this is a great side trip and you may not see another soul.

Tactics and Techniques

There are two deadly ways to fish the Trinity. The first is to fish it with nymphs under floating indicators, only with stouter rods, strike indicators, and tippets. While these steelhead will eat smaller nymphs just like trout, most anglers use heavier and larger hooks so fish can be released quickly without straightening out the hooks. Steelhead hold in all the same places a big trout would. Look for water from two to six feet deep, and the Trinity has a lot of it.

Most anglers agree that during October these fish are looking for nymphs. Pattern choice is an individual thing with fish accepting a wide variety of flies. Perhaps a good guideline would be to use any #10 nymph with a beadhead. Prince Nymphs, PT Nymphs, Morrish's Cone Stone, Mercer's GB Biot Golden Stone, Mercer's Superfloss Rubberlegs are all reasonable choices. But like in most trout fishing, the choice of nymph pattern is not as important as how well it is presented to the fish. The only other skill needed is the ability to interpret what the strike indicator is doing and setting the hook when necessary. Experienced anglers know that an indicator doesn't necessarily need to be jerked under water to mean you've got one, even if it's a steelhead.

To some, "bobber fishing" for steelhead is sacrilegious. A more dignified angler would call it indicator nymphing. But no one denies how effective the technique is on the Trinity. Good leader setups for this technique are 9-foot

Guide Jay Cockrum covers the water with a light Spey rod. When a steelhead takes a swung fly, you feel the jolt.

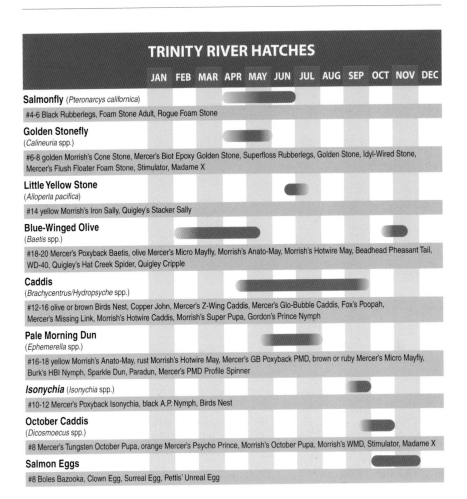

TRINITY RIVER HATCHES

	JAN	FEB	MAR	APR	MAY	JUN	JUL	AUG	SEP	OCT	NOV	DEC
Salmonfly (*Pteronarcys californica*)					███	███						
#4-6 Black Rubberlegs, Foam Stone Adult, Rogue Foam Stone												
Golden Stonefly (*Calineuria* spp.)					██	██						
#6-8 golden Morrish's Cone Stone, Mercer's Biot Epoxy Golden Stone, Superfloss Rubberlegs, Golden Stone, Idyl-Wired Stone, Mercer's Flush Floater Foam Stone, Stimulator, Madame X												
Little Yellow Stone (*Alloperla pacifica*)						██						
#14 yellow Morrish's Iron Sally, Quigley's Stacker Sally												
Blue-Winged Olive (*Baetis* spp.)			███	███	███						██	
#18-20 Mercer's Poxyback Baetis, olive Mercer's Micro Mayfly, Morrish's Anato-May, Morrish's Hotwire May, Beadhead Pheasant Tail, WD-40, Quigley's Hat Creek Spider, Quigley Cripple												
Caddis (*Brachycentrus/Hydropsyche* spp.)					███	███	███					
#12-16 olive or brown Birds Nest, Copper John, Mercer's Z-Wing Caddis, Mercer's Glo-Bubble Caddis, Fox's Poopah, Mercer's Missing Link, Morrish's Hotwire Caddis, Morrish's Super Pupa, Gordon's Prince Nymph												
Pale Morning Dun (*Ephemerella* spp.)						██	██					
#16-18 yellow Morrish's Anato-May, rust Morrish's Hotwire May, Mercer's GB Poxyback PMD, brown or ruby Mercer's Micro Mayfly, Burk's HBI Nymph, Sparkle Dun, Paradun, Mercer's PMD Profile Spinner												
Isonychia (*Isonychia* spp.)										██		
#10-12 Mercer's Poxyback Isonychia, black A.P. Nymph, Birds Nest												
October Caddis (*Dicosmoecus* spp.)									██	██		
#8 Mercer's Tungsten October Pupa, orange Mercer's Psycho Prince, Morrish's October Pupa, Morrish's WMD, Stimulator, Madame X												
Salmon Eggs										███	███	
#8 Boles Bazooka, Clown Egg, Surreal Egg, Pettis' Unreal Egg												

leaders tapered to 2X. Suspend one or two flies about 6 feet beneath a floating indicator big enough to float them easily. When working to visible fish that have seen a lot of flies, drop down to 3X, but no lower. Another variation doesn't employ a store-bought leader at all. Start with a 2¹/2- to 3-foot section of 15-pound-test mono. Form a perfection loop at the end of this section, and make a loop-to-loop connection with a 3- or 4-foot piece of 1X mono. Tie a 2X to 3X tippet to the 1X section using a surgeon's knot and you're good to go. Some Trinity River guides recommend fluorocarbon; others say it doesn't matter.

The other technique that continues to be growing in popularity is what might be called ultralight Spey casting. Ideal Spey rods for the Trinity run from 12 feet for a 5-weight line to 12¹/2 feet for a 6-weight line. These long, light rods allow all the advantages of Spey fishing—longer casts, the fly in the water more, without the hassle of needing a backcast. If only because Spey

Public wading access to the Trinity is fairly easy, but the best way to find success is in drifting the river and covering more water. Pontoon boats and drift boats are widely used on this fairly easy float.

anglers have their flies in the water so much more than anglers using single-handed rods, the efficiency of the technique cannot be denied. Nor can the toll it takes on Trinity River steelhead. It's a little bit fancy, but well worth the effort if you have the skill. Spey fishing has one other advantage to indicator nymphing. You can actually *feel* the take rather than react to a visual stimulus. There is something primal about being able to feel the grab.

Morrish's October Pupa

Hook:	#6-8 Tiemco 5263
Bead:	Black nickel
Weight:	.035 lead or lead-free wire
Thread:	Black 6/0 Danville
Rib:	Amber Vinyl Rib
Abdomen:	Scintilla dubbing #34
Hackle:	Hungarian partridge feather
Wing:	Brown dyed grizzly hen cape feathers
Wing Case:	Pearl Flashabou Accent
Antennae:	Natural pheasant-tail fibers
Head:	Hot orange Hareline Dubbing and Dark Stone (#15) Whitlock SLF

Morrish's WMD (October Caddis Pupa)

Hook:	#6-8 Tiemco 5263
Bead:	Black nickel
Weight:	.025-.035 lead or lead-free wire
Thread:	Dark brown 6/0 Danville
Antennae:	Natural pheasant-tail fibers
Abdomen:	Ginger and amber Ultra Wire (large)
Back:	Gray 1/8" Scud Back (double thickness)
Thorax:	Golden brown Ice Dub
Wing Case:	UV Minnow Belly
Wings:	Natural Brahma hen saddle
Hackle:	Natural gray and brown Hungarian partridge
Collar:	Golden brown Ice Dub
Head:	UV black Ice Dub

Pettis' Unreal Egg

Hook:	#8-12 Tiemco 2487
Thread:	Flaming pink 6/0 Uni-Thread
Body:	Orange or pink hot glue
Shell:	Glo Bug Yarn

Fox's Sleech

Hook:	#2 Gamakatsu Octopus (trailer) and #2 Mustad 3406
Bead:	Spirit River Bright Bead
Weight:	15 wraps of .035 lead or lead-free wire
Thread:	Black 140-denier Ultra-Thread
Tail:	Zonker cut rabbit
Body:	Polar Chenille
String:	30-pound Cortland Micron Backing
Collar:	Schlappen

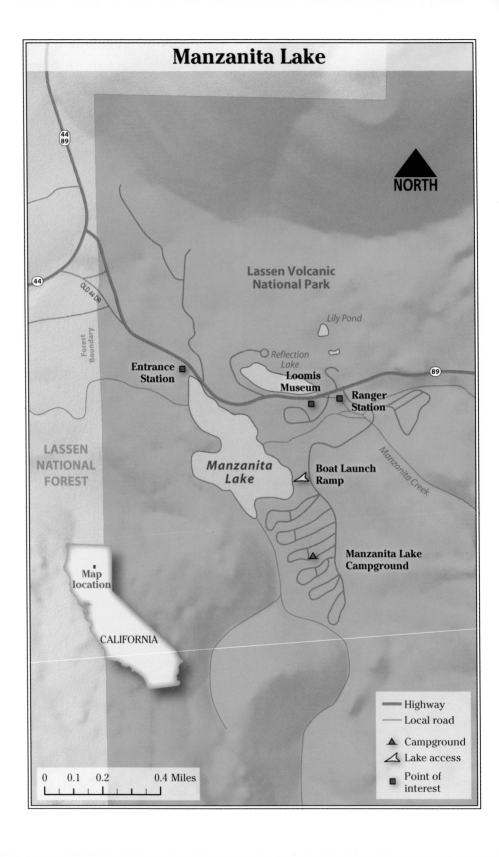

Manzanita Lake

NORTH

Lassen Volcanic
National Park

Lily Pond

Reflection
Lake

**Entrance
Station**

**Loomis
Museum**

**Ranger
Station**

*Manzanita
Lake*

**Boat Launch
Ramp**

Manzanita Creek

**Manzanita Lake
Campground**

LASSEN
NATIONAL
FOREST

Forest
Boundary

OLD 44 DR

44

44
89

89

Map
location

CALIFORNIA

0   0.1   0.2   0.4 Miles

Highway
Local road
Campground
Lake access
Point of
interest

CHAPTER 8

Manzanita Lake

I f it were suddenly my job to fashion the "perfect" trout lake, it would look a lot like Manzanita Lake. Adjacent to the north entrance to Lassen Volcanic National Park about 50 miles east of Redding, Manzanita has clear water, lavish weed growth, dense hatches throughout the season, and huge wild fish in an environment so stunningly beautiful you could easily forget to bring your fly rod and not even care.

Manzanita Lake sits squarely at the foot of 10, 357-foot Lassen Peak, which reflects off the water like a glistening gem. Fishing in the shadow of a massive volcano is a lot like having someone looking over your shoulder while you fish. You get kind of comfortable with it being there. You see it when you look up; you see its reflection on the water when you look down. Between 1914 and 1917, Lassen erupted more than 150 times producing pyroclastic flows and a 7-mile-high mushroom cloud that spewed volcanic ash more than 500 miles away. President Theodore Roosevelt designated Lassen a national park in 1916 for its significance as an active volcanic landscape. Sometime after that, anglers designated Manzanita Lake a remarkable place to fish.

First and foremost, there don't seem to be any small fish. The lake is a virtual food factory, so trout grow large fairly quickly. Dinnertime seems to be more or less a perpetual state. Hatches can be intense and the trout eat almost constantly, except of course when they don't. Like wild trout everywhere there are times when, even in the midst of a seemingly endless food supply, lockjaw prevails.

Managed by the National Park Service as a trophy trout fishery, Manzanita Lake is strictly catch-and-release fishing with single, barbless hooks. No motors are allowed on boats, so rowing, kicking, or wading are your only options. In other words, it's a mecca for fly anglers. Deer commonly graze all around the lake and Canada geese, ospreys, bald eagles, belted kingfishers, Steller's jays, buffleheads, coots, mallards, and double-crested cormorants can be seen on almost any day.

125

On a clear day Lassen Peak is easy to see above and in the reflection on the surface of the lake. When California burns, as it often does during the summer, smoke from fires can look like fog, masking the view.

Manzanita Lake is rightly called beautiful and scenic, but referring to it as "natural" would not be completely accurate. At first the lake was smaller than it is today. Most anglers never even notice the eight-foot earthen dam built at the outflow of Manzanita Creek in 1911. Actually, thanks to that dam, Manzanita Creek has formed a different outflow from the northeast corner of the lake.

In the 1990s a motion was made to reconstruct the dam at Manzanita to protect the unsuspecting world from the supposed perils of a 1,000-year flood event. Fortunately it was recognized for what it was; the U.S. Army Corp of Engineers having to invent needless projects to spend money burning a hole in their pockets. The character of this charming and challenging fishery was preserved.

If you choose to camp at Lassen Park there are plenty of activities for the nonanglers in your family. The park offers seven campgrounds, the most popular is very close to Manzanita. Be forewarned. Even in the dead of summer

Manzanita Lake is small enough to fish easily from a float tube, but most anglers prefer pontoon boats or small prams. You can stalk trout in shallow water by wading carefully and quietly.

it gets very cold at this elevation in the middle of the night. You can take the trail to the top of Lassen Peak, the climb taking roughly two hours for the physically fit. You can also visit bubbling mud pots, steaming fumaroles, and boiling springs.

Ice Out

Depending on the weather and snowpack, access to the lake usually begins as early as May or as late as July. Since the lake rests at close to 6,000 feet elevation, some years it remains snow- and icebound later than others. Fortunately it is close to the north entrance to Lassen Park and fairly close to busy CA 44, which is usually kept clear. Still, if the short drive from the north park entrance to the lake is not plowed, access remains almost impossible. It's not unusual for there to be 20 feet of snow on the road. Once access is opened up, the early fishing can be fairly easy for wild rainbows and browns averaging 15 to 17 inches. It's wise, however, not to get used to it. After the first month or so, the trout aren't as easily fooled and things become more interesting.

Bobbing around in a float tube can be a chilly proposition when there is still snow on the ground, but the great fishing can help you forget that you lost feeling in your toes hours ago. A pontoon boat or small pram is a better bet when the water is like ice. Just after ice-out, there are abundant midge hatches, and you may notice trout sipping clusters on the surface, especially in the area near where Manzanita Creek, the lake's spawning tributary, flows

Getting to Manzanita Lake is easy. It's a little more than an hour east of Redding on CA 44. Turn in at this sign, and you will see the lake just beyond the guard shack.

The shallower water between the willow "islands" and the bank are excellent places to fish, but remember to use stealth in both your approach and casting style.

in. Signs posted around the inflow indicate how close you may fish to the stream, and park rangers are watching. Go long by lengthening your leader to 12 to 15 feet and 6X or 7X tippets. A #16-18 Griffith's Gnat or Quigley's Spider Midge delicately presented will often do the trick. Some anglers have a hard time with these light tippets setting the hook on large trout, and a light touch needs to be cultivated.

When the fish aren't showing on the surface, you still have several good options. While some people turn their noses up at "bobber fishing," hanging a nymph under a floating strike indicator is an absolutely deadly lake-fishing technique. I like the little painted Styrofoam indicators that are fastened to your leader with a toothpick. These are buoyant enough to suspend two nymphs and a small split-shot without catching too much air when it's time to recast. I also use 5X to 6X fluorocarbon tippets for my nymphing simply because I land a much higher percentage of fish with these stouter lines. Good midge nymphs include the #16-18 Chironomid Pupa, Ascending Midge Pupa, or Brassies, but the fish will take almost any good mayfly nymph provided it's small enough.

Anglers who like fishing sinking lines with leech or Woolly Bugger patterns often find success this time of the year because the vegetation that will grow up and stick to their flies later in the year is pleasantly absent. Later in the year plant growth makes using these lines a nuisance, but trolling a Type III Uniform Sink line very slowly just after ice-out can be a killer technique.

While geologists estimate that Manzanita Lake was formed about 300 years ago, a notorious Atsugewi Indian called Old Shavehead claimed to be the first man to ever see it in the 1800s.

The same year as Lockhart's Ferry Massacre (see the Pit River chapter, page 34), conflicts between Indians and the growing contingency of immigrants seemed to peak. The first white homesteader to the area, a Scotsman named Sam Burney, was brutally murdered that year, and witnesses arrived on the scene as three Indians were caught carting away some of his possessions. Two of the three were shot on the spot; but the third, the man who came to be known as Shavehead, managed to escape.

While many of the incoming settlers were sworn to shoot Shavehead on sight, they could never catch him. Finally he was apprehended, possibly by missionaries, who were determined to turn Shavehead into a "good Indian" before sending him off to a reservation. Shavehead was first taken to Sacramento to show him just how many whites were moving into the area. Then he was taken to San Francisco where his head was shaved to take away some of his "magic." From there he was put on a boat and transported to one of the islands off the northern California coast where Indians at the time were being detained. One day Shavehead and a few others climbed to the highest point on the island and, when looking east, recognized Mount Shasta off in the distance. Suddenly the Indians knew where they were and somehow managed to escape the island in short order. After his escape from captivity, Shavehead became the most wanted and feared Indian in California.

Perhaps he mellowed with age. Perhaps he gave up his violent ways in response to the seemingly endless supply of whites moving into his domain and the shrinking numbers of his people, who had no immunity to white man's diseases. In any case, Shavehead was eventually forgotten. By the late 1890s he found himself alone, the last surviving member of the once-great Atsugewi tribe. As an old man he lived along the south shore of Manzanita Lake, claiming it was fishless before he threw some rainbow trout from Hat Creek into it. He eventually made his living by capturing trout from Manzanita Creek and selling them to ranchers' wives around the town of Viola. He had somehow procured a wagon and mule and was known to alternate layers of trout and snow on his wagon to keep his catch fresh while making regular rounds.

One day he arrived at a ranch in Viola obviously very ill. The rancher tried to bring him inside, but he refused to go into a white man's house. The rancher then built him a lean-to against a fence, and the Indian took shelter there and accepted some food. That is where Shavehead died in the year 1900, the last of the Atsugewi. ∎

Until the water warms a bit the takes might not be the "big grab" you might expect later in the season. You may only feel a sluggishness at the end of your line like you've hung yourself up in weeds. Set the hook and hold on!

Summer *Callibaetis*

As the weather warms, midges will slowly give way to the big summer *Callibaetis* hatch that runs for several months. Trout can be seen taking both midges at the surface around the shallow edges of the lake as well as big *Callibaetis* spinners lying flat on the water. By June, the *Callibaetis* hatch will really begin catching the fish's attention, and they will only get more selective as the season progresses. The first *Callibaetis* to hatch are fairly big bugs (#12-14), while later in the season the individual insects become smaller (#16-18). A #12 Mercer's Profile Spinner or CDC Callibaetis Spinner at the end of a 12- to 15-foot 6X leader will catch fish if cast into a likely area and then watched closely. A good tactic is to cast as close as you can get to the many willows sprouting out of the water. Fish love to cruise the edges of these looking for food, especially along the eastern shore of the lake. Anglers experienced with this type of fishing know as soon as you glance over at that interesting bird or to take in the volcano, you're likely to get a hit.

Rainbows and browns cruise the shorelines on summer afternoons looking for **Callibaetis** *spinners. Figure out from which direction the wind is blowing, and cast into the bank on the opposite shore.*

Callibaetis spinners routinely are blown into the eastern shore of the lake by winds coming in from the west, providing great summertime fishing.

Too many anglers fish "stillwaters" as if they were really still. They usually aren't, at least not completely. Even on glassy lakes like Manzanita, breezes, feeder streams, and out-flows create tiny microcurrents in the water that can drag your fly like a nun pinching a kid's earlobe on the way to the principal's office. Pay attention to what's going on with your line, mend accordingly, and never let the line between your rod tip and fly get too straight. Keep a bit of slack in there. Lakes are best fished as if they were spring creeks in slow motion.

The bread-and-butter technique that accounts for most fish landed on most days is to fish one or two nymphs under a floating strike indicator. Good nymphs include Mike Mercer's Poxyback Callibaetis Nymph or a #12 brown Birds Nest. I prefer my own version of this pattern, the O'Brien Birds Nest, because it has a tungsten bead eliminating the need for split-shot to sink the fly.

The main hatch begins around lunchtime; earlier in the early season, later as the season progresses. For those who enjoy nymph fishing, there are days when you never need to change tactics. Sometimes nymphs produce well throughout the day. There are other times, however, when the trout will become selective and can drive you absolutely crazy until you figure things out. Keep changing things until you start catching fish.

Stalking the Shallows

Anglers love to come to Manzanita for the sight-fishing. The south and west-ern edges of the lake contain sandy silt-covered flats where you can wade while looking for wary trout cruising the shallows. Cruising trout are easy to spot with polarized sunglasses against the light-colored bottom. They move around slowly in water one to two feet deep and may take flies on the bot-tom, in the film, or on the surface. They are easy to spook, but learning how not to spook them is much of the fun and challenge.

When you spot a fish, resist the urge to get your fly in the water right away. Take some time to watch where the fish is going and what it's taking. Don't make any sudden or big movements because the fish can surely see you as well as you can see it. You will probably notice the fish is working a pre-dictable pattern, usually in a big oval or triangle. Try to predict where the fish will go and cast to an area you expect the fish to be. This is tough but com-pletely absorbing fishing, making any fish you catch a bonus.

If a fish is working the bottom I like to use beadhead nymphs that roughly look like a *Callibaetis*. With beadhead flies you don't have to worry about using split-shot to get your fly to the bottom. Once you've got an idea of the fish's feeding pattern, cast your fly to the farthest corner of his "beat" so you don't spook the fish. Now just wait as motionlessly as a great blue heron and watch. If you see the fish pick up your fly, try to wait one nanosecond before setting the hook. You don't want to pull the fly away before the fish has actually taken it. If your nymph is sitting on the bottom, a slight twitch will often bring it to the fish's attention.

Lesser-Known Hatches

In addition to the summer *Callibaetis* hatch, two other midsummer hatches are worthy of note. Undoubtedly first named by some pithy Brit, the Capering Sedge hatch has been Americanized to become known in northern California as the Motorboat Caddis hatch. (I'm surprised it didn't end up as the "Motorboat Caddis, *Dude*.")

Generally in late June and early July, and right at dark, the *Phryganea californica* pupae abandon their weedy homes and swim to the surface at breakneck speed. Upon emergence, the adults scuttle across the surface like little motorboats, creating a V-wake behind them. Whether the trout key in on the emerging pupa or the posthatching adult, the key to this hatch is motion.

Terrestrials compose an important part of the trout diet here, especially on summer afternoons. If you see rising fish in the middle of the lake, but no insects on the water, the fish may well be taking ants and beetles.

The most popular method is to use a #8-10 Goddard Caddis and just drag it behind your boat, pontoon boat, or float tube, imitating the wake made by the natural. Truthfully, choice of fly pattern is secondary to the motion you give the fly. Don't worry about fishing beyond the time you can actually see your fly, either. Since you are fishing a tight line, you will certainly *feel* the strikes, making 3X or larger fluorocarbon tippets necessary.

Even when the Motorboat Caddis are not hatching, sometimes the most effective technique of the day is merely dragging a dry fly behind your float tube. Friends sometimes scoff at me until they realize that I'm catching fish while they're not. I think the fish get so keyed into the motion produced by these big bugs that eventually anything moving on the surface is viewed as food. As long as it floats, fly pattern is irrelevant. Just keep it moving slowly at the surface and try not to break your tippet when a fish strikes.

The other midseason hatch often baffles anglers who aren't really aware of what's going on. At higher elevations it's common to get afternoon winds blowing in from the west. When the trout continue rising despite the wind, many anglers make the mistake of thinking the trout are still taking *Callibaetis* mayflies. Very often the trout have actually switched to flying ants and black beetles being blown into the water by the wind. The ants are fairly large, but they have a low profile in the rippled water and are very difficult to see. Even anglers who take the time to observe what the fish are taking are often frustrated. The fish seem to be rising to an invisible hatch. Try a big, floating terrestrial like a #10-12 Foam Beetle or Parachute Ant.

Angler Ed Volpe with a Manzanita Lake brown. Lassen Peak in the background is an active volcano that erupted almost a century ago.

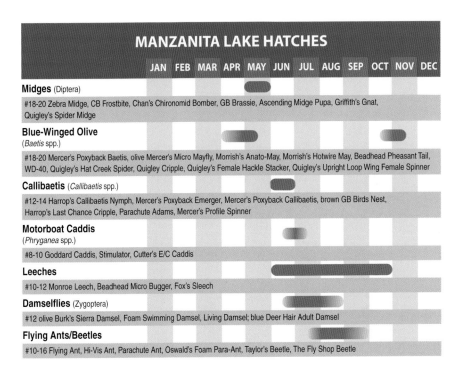

MANZANITA LAKE HATCHES

	JAN	FEB	MAR	APR	MAY	JUN	JUL	AUG	SEP	OCT	NOV	DEC

Midges (Diptera)
#18-20 Zebra Midge, CB Frostbite, Chan's Chironomid Bomber, GB Brassie, Ascending Midge Pupa, Griffith's Gnat, Quigley's Spider Midge

Blue-Winged Olive
(*Baetis* spp.)
#18-20 Mercer's Poxyback Baetis, olive Mercer's Micro Mayfly, Morrish's Anato-May, Morrish's Hotwire May, Beadhead Pheasant Tail, WD-40, Quigley's Hat Creek Spider, Quigley Cripple, Quigley's Female Hackle Stacker, Quigley's Upright Loop Wing Female Spinner

Callibaetis (*Callibaetis* spp.)
#12-14 Harrop's Callibaetis Nymph, Mercer's Poxyback Emerger, Mercer's Poxyback Callibaetis, brown GB Birds Nest, Harrop's Last Chance Cripple, Parachute Adams, Mercer's Profile Spinner

Motorboat Caddis
(*Phryganea* spp.)
#8-10 Goddard Caddis, Stimulator, Cutter's E/C Caddis

Leeches
#10-12 Monroe Leech, Beadhead Micro Bugger, Fox's Sleech

Damselflies (Zygoptera)
#12 olive Burk's Sierra Damsel, Foam Swimming Damsel, Living Damsel; blue Deer Hair Adult Damsel

Flying Ants/Beetles
#10-16 Flying Ant, Hi-Vis Ant, Parachute Ant, Oswald's Foam Para-Ant, Taylor's Beetle, The Fly Shop Beetle

Damselflies can also be a major food source for these fish at times. For some reason I've had my best damselfly action in the northeast corner of the lake. Adult damsels will often cruise a foot above the water, and you can see aggressive fish trying for them. A deer hair or foam adult damsel pattern thrown into the general vicinity of these fish will often induce strikes.

Late Summer and Fall

At this elevation, the big hatches of summer eventually run their course and dwindle by September. Fortunately the fish remember what to feed on, mainly *Callibaetis* mayflies in their various forms, and you can still catch fish. As fall approaches, Manzanita Lake's brown trout population gets ever more aggressive.

There is some speculation about whether there are more wild rainbows or browns in Manzanita Lake, and the answer is no one knows for sure. In the past a solid 80 percent of the catch was rainbow trout, but a case could be made that the browns were just more selective and harder to fool. In recent years more brown trout are being caught at Manzanita, so they are either becoming more abundant or less selective. Fortunately most anglers could care less whether they land large wild rainbows or large wild brown trout. It's all good.

With the cooling temperatures of fall, smaller mayflies like *Baetis* and midges again become more important to the fish, and finer tippets are in

Adult damselfly imitations work well on gusty afternoons when the wind is blowing the low-flying naturals to the water. At this time, trout watch for opportunities to grab a big, blue mouthful.

order. The days are getting shorter, and the most productive fishing tends to be in the afternoon. By now the weeds are not as robust as they were mid-summer, but they aren't as sparse as they were at ice-out. Sinking-line streamer tactics work well this time of year, but you can't fish as deep as you might have after ice-out. Try using a slow sinking line like an Intermediate or Type II Uniform Sink and stripping leeches or Woolly Buggers. While you will still catch an occasional rainbow, you will notice more browns coming to hand and the strikes will be much more aggressive than earlier in the year.

Weather is always a concern this time of the year. Float-tubers wear extra layers under their waders, and the possibility of rain increases. The nighttime temperatures may dip into the single digits, and the mornings are frosty. Fishing is usually done for the year around Halloween.

Equipment

It's hard to beat a 9-foot, 5-weight rod for this fishing. The length is great for when you need to cast a bit farther so the fish can't eyeball you. The 5-weight can be delicate enough without sacrificing strength to handle big fish that love nothing better than burying themselves deep in the weeds. You could also get by with a 4- or 6-weight rod. For nymph fishing I like 9-foot leaders tapered to 5X or 6X fluorocarbon. For dry-fly fishing you will need 12- to 15-

Fish are drawn to Manzanita's numerous willow "islands" for both cover and food.

foot leaders tapered to 6X or 7X. These fish learn the difference between 5X and 7X.

Pontoon boats work great and are popular at Manzanita because they allow you to easily access the entire lake in a day's fishing. Float tubes also work well, but they have to work a little harder to cover as much ground. Small prams are probably the most comfortable to fish from throughout the year. Lacking any of the above, consider wading. There is a good trail looping around the lake from which to scan potential good fishing spots. Favorite wading areas include the south and western sides of the lake where there are abundant flats between the shores and several brushy islands. Sunscreen, polarized sunglasses, and a hat with a brim are also necessary items.

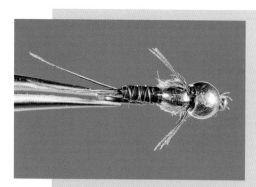

Mercer's Micro Mayfly (Brown)

Hook:	#14-20 Tiemco 921
Bead:	Copper
Thread:	Camel 8/0 Uni-Thread
Tail:	Natural pheasant-tail fibers
Abdomen:	Stripped peacock herl
Rib:	Silver wire (fine)
Wing Case:	Golden brown mottled turkey tail and pearl Flashabou coated with 5-minute epoxy
Thorax:	Mahogany brown Super Fine
Legs:	Same as tail
Head:	Same as thorax

Cal Bird's Birds Nest (Tan)

Hook:	#8-16 Tiemco 3761
Thread:	Gray 8/0 Uni-Thread
Tail:	Wood-duck fibers
Rib:	Copper wire
Abdomen:	Tan Australian opossum
Legs:	Wood-duck fibers
Thorax:	Same as abdomen

O'Brien Birds Nest

Hook: #12-16 Tiemco 2302
Bead: Gold tungsten
Thread: Brown 8/0 Uni-Thread
Tail: Teal or widgeon
Body: Chocolate brown Hare-Tron
          and natural Australian opossum
          fur, blended
Rib: Copper wire
Wing: Teal or widgeon
Collar: Same as body

Oswald's Foam Para-Ant

Hook: #10-16 Tiemco 100
Thread: Black 6/0
Abdomen: Black Fly Foam tied back and
          folded forward
Thorax: Same as abdomen, only tied
          forward and folded back
Post: Yellow Fly Foam
Hackle: Brown

Griffith's Gnat

Hook: #14-20 Tiemco 101
Thread: Black 6/0 Uni-Thread
Body: Peacock herl
Rib: Gold wire
Hackle: Grizzly tied in at back and
          palmered forward

This Yuba rainbow took a Sloan's Persuader, an excellent all-around imitation of stone-flies and hoppers.

FLY FISHING

MID-SACRAMENTO REGION

Mid-Sacramento Fly Shops and Guides

American River

American Fly Fishing Co.
3523 Fair Oaks Blvd.
Sacramento, CA 95864
(800) 410-1222
americanflyfishingtravel.com

Bill Lowe
Bill Lowe's Guide Service
(916) 966-0999
billloweflyguide.com

Damien Forsythe
Hooked Up Anglers
506 Arlene Drive
Roseville, CA 95678
(916) 207-2428
hookedupanglers.com

Fly Fishing Specialties
6412 Tupelo Dr. (Suite C)
Citrus Heights, CA 95621
(916) 722-1055
flyfishingspecialties.com

Kiene's Fly Shop
2654 Marconi Avenue
Sacramento, CA 95821
(916) 486-9958
kiene.com

Yuba River

American Fly Fishing Co.
3523 Fair Oaks Blvd.
Sacramento, CA 95864
(800) 410-1222
americanflyfishingtravel.com

(continued)

I-80 is an artery connecting the tremendous mass of humanity to an oasis of solitude, natural beauty, and challenge. That urban fisheries exist at all is miraculous, but the fact they usually remain uncrowded in America's most populous state renders them that much more extraordinary. But believe it. These three rivers—the American, Yuba, and Truckee—offer three very different angling experiences, meaning your chances of finding water that suits your style of fishing are quite good. Of course, there are far more exotic and famous fisheries the world over, and they will always be there. The beauty of these mid-Sacramento streams is that you can fish them for even part of a day without sacrificing time you really don't have or your children's college funds. They all contain big wild fish that require commitment and skill to catch consistently.

The American River cleaves the state capital of Sacramento, and tens of thousands of people drive along it or over it every day without even noticing. They've seen the river so much they don't really see it anymore, and this just might be a good thing. Though the surface rarely changes, there is much going on beneath the surface. Steelhead, stripers, and shad enter the river to spawn. Steelhead have always used this water, but the shad and stripers brought from the East Coast have also been here for over a century and have found their place.

Yuba River (continued)

Bill Lowe
Bill Lowe's Guide Service
(916) 966-0999
billloweflyguide.com

Cary Jellison
G & J Outdoor Enterprises
300 Daniels Drive
Auburn, CA 95603
(530) 885-1492
gandjoutdoors.com

Damien Forsythe
Hooked Up Anglers
506 Arlene Drive
Roseville, CA 95678
(916) 207-2428
hookedupanglers.com

Kiene's Fly Shop
2654 Marconi Avenue
Sacramento, CA 95821
(916) 486-9958
kiene.com

Sam Craig
Norcal Guide Service
7038 Sicard Flat Road
Browns Valley, CA 95918
(530) 639-1102

Truckee River

Alpine Fly Fishing
Jim Crouse
P.O. Box 10465
South Lake Tahoe,
CA 96158
(530) 542-0759
alpine-flyfishing.com

**California School
of Flyfishing**
Ralph & Lisa Cutter
P.O. Box 8212
Truckee, CA 96162
flyline.com

(continued)

Guide Bill Lowe shows off a buck shad just landed by friend Bruce Tiger.

Traffic and crime and population and even the workings of state government are foreign to the fish, as maybe we wish they were to you and me. Perhaps that's the attraction: the ability to spend time in fishing, surrounded by the natural innocence of wild creatures in a world that occasionally seems to have gone off the deep end.

The Yuba is somehow so close, tucked away just east of Marysville, and yet it seems so far away. Maybe it's a matter of "out of sight, out of mind," but this remarkable fishery gets very little fishing pressure and grows wild trout sometimes mistaken for steelhead. The fact that anglers need to float the river to do it justice weeds out most people, but it is not a difficult or technical float. Some of the scenery along the river reveals the extent to which man is willing to alter the environment in search of gold.

The Truckee reminds me of the Upper Sac and Pit rivers in that there is so much of it, and with a little hiking you can always find water to have all to yourself. Its proximity to the casinos and bright lights of Reno almost seems absurd, and yet there it is as if to suggest that wildlife comes in many different forms. In places the ancient railroad along the river speaks of a time when frontiers were being connected and Chinese laborers chiseled huge blocks of sandstone to form foundations. Nearby the Donner Party focused attention on the hardships facing the area's numerous groups of emigrants. Huge cutthroat trout resided in the stream and elk and grizzly bears roamed the alpine landscapes.

Much has changed since those days, but hopefully we've learned some things. We've realized that even in the face of man's ineptitude or greed, nature has remarkable restorative abilities. We've learned that without staunch and vigilant advocacy, history is destined to repeat itself, and it takes many years to bring an ecosystem back.

Truckee River (continued)

Four Seasons Fly Fishing
P.O. Box 10731
Truckee, CA 96162
(530) 386-0525
flyfishingtruckee-tahoe.com

Orvis
13945 S. Virginia Street
Summit Sierra Shopping Center, Suite 640
Reno, NV 89511
(775) 850-2272
orvis.com/reno

Reno Fly Shop
294 East Moana Lane, #14
Reno, NV 89502
(775) 825-FISH
renoflyshop.com

Stillwater Guide Service
Chris Wharton
Reno, NV 89502
(775) 851-1558
chris@out4trout.com

Thy Rod & Thy Staff
Frank Pisciotta
P.O. Box 10038
Truckee, CA 96162
(530) 587-7333
cyberfly.com

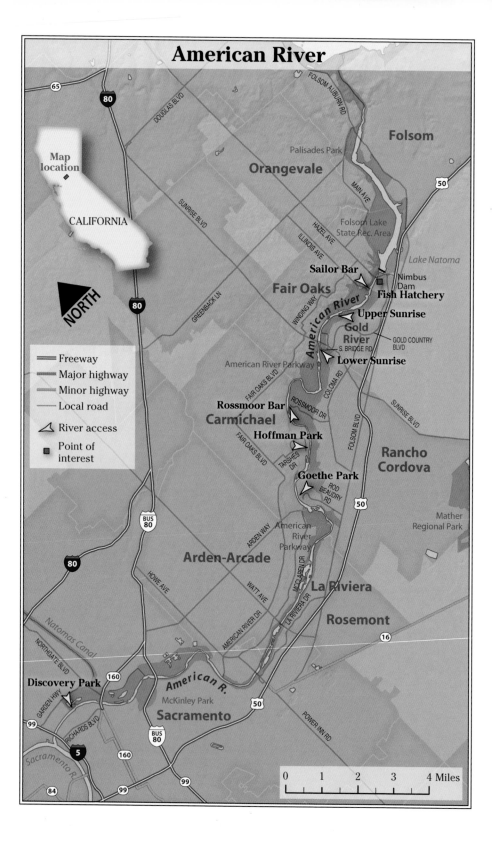

American River

Map location

CALIFORNIA

NORTH

Freeway
Major highway
Minor highway
Local road
River access
Point of interest

Folsom

Orangevale

Palisades Park

Folsom Lake
State Rec. Area

Lake Natoma

Fair Oaks

Sailor Bar

Nimbus Dam

Fish Hatchery

American River

Upper Sunrise

Gold River

GOLD COUNTRY BLVD

S. BRIDGE RD.

Lower Sunrise

American River Parkway

Rossmoor Bar

Carmichael

Hoffman Park

Rancho Cordova

Goethe Park

ROD BEAUDRY RD

Mather Regional Park

Arden-Arcade

American River Parkway

La Riviera

Rosemont

Discovery Park

American R.

McKinley Park

Sacramento

Natomas Canal

Sacramento R.

0   1   2   3   4 Miles

CHAPTER 9

American River

Before January 1848, the American was just another California river that happened to flow past Sutter's Mill. Gold changed all that and turned the river, and many others, literally inside out. Today the American is still rich in beauty, wealthy in friends, and prosperous in great fishing opportunities within casting distance of the Golden State's capital. Treasure, of course, is recognized in the eye of the beholder. But where else can you find shad, stripers, and steelhead that provide year-round good fishing so close to half a million people who, most days, would never suspect those fish are even there?

While three forks of the American are interrupted behind Folsom Dam northeast of Sacramento, the river below meanders through a largely urban landscape including Arnold Schwarzenegger's backyard on its 23-mile trek to the Sacramento River. Most upper sections of the American are open year-long, so there is never a good reason not to fish it.

The other distinguishing feature of this extraordinary river that flows straight through a major metropolitan area is that it is vapor clear. The wading is also easy in most places as it flows over even rocks and few drop-offs. Opportunities for sight-fishing are good for steelhead, shad, and striped bass. Floating the river with polarized sunglasses on sunny days will allow you to see for yourself just how many fish inhabit this water. Beyond the three species described here, the river also hosts good populations of Chinook salmon, largemouth bass, and even catfish. Regardless of the particular fish you're after, you will need a Bay-Delta Sport Fishing Enhancement Stamp in addition to a typical California fishing license.

Cool Weather Steelhead

The run of steelhead with the biggest fish, both wild and hatchery, reaches the American sometime in December. This is prime time for connecting with fish averaging 5 to 12 pounds, and the fishing can be great through April.

The scenic beauty of the American is never more evident than on a summer evening. It's easy to forget the river runs through downtown Sacramento.

These winter months are often rainy in northern California, but seldom cold. The Nimbus Hatchery began stocking the river with the Eel River strain of steelhead by the early 1960s. Flows in the river depend on the amount of rain the area has had, or hasn't had, and the snowpack in the mountains up above. Recent years have been dry; producing low-water winters for the American and flows as low as 1,000 cubic feet per second (cfs). Wet years might see winter flows of 5,000 to 6,000 cfs.

The best way to fish the American is by drifting the river, only because you have a better chance to cover more water. The river is amazingly accessible, with much of the river corridor devoted to greenbelt and numerous launch sites. The upper part of the good fishing is just below the fish weir below Nimbus Dam. On the north side of the river across the river from Nimbus Hatchery is the Sailor Bar River Access from which you can launch a boat.

Upstream from the launch is a morass of humanity, according to guide Bill Lowe, ". . . a lot of hardware fishermen and a great place to go if you want to get into a fight." There is a moveable weir system below Nimbus Dam and lots of gear fishermen competing for the fish that get stopped there. "If you go up there with a fly rod," chuckled Lowe, "you *are* going to get into a fight."

So, wanting to leave the drama behind, a good 4- to 5-mile drift through good water is Sailor Bar to Rossmoor Bar, giving anglers access to a lot of good swing water. The American is ideally suited to Spey fishing, which is taking a solid hold here. The most popular section is from Sailor Bar down to

Access to the American is easy for both wading and floating anglers. Either way works, but anglers with boats have more options and are better able to get away from the crowds.

Big steelhead like this are in the river much of the year, but few people pursue them. Angler Perry Sims shows off this deeply colored fish. SEAN MORAN PHOTO

Howe Avenue. Another great drift is from Upper Sunrise on the south side of the river to the Gristmill ramp.

The drift from Howe down to Discovery Park where the American meets the Sacramento is long, and the water is slower and generally better suited to striped-bass fishing. There are several good steelhead spots down here, and if you have a powerboat you can fish down through them several times and then motor back up to Howe.

The American is classic, big-river Spey water with plenty of room to lay down long casts. Good rods for this fishing are 13- to 14-footers for 7- to 9-weight lines. Skagit sink tips work best for their great casting qualities and sink rate options. While some American River regulars may consider a 9-weight to be overkill, 18- to 20-pound steelhead are landed here every year. Big, black articulated leech patterns are deadly, and a #6 Fox's Sleech or Sauk River Special is hard to beat. Short, 1X fluorocarbon tippets are effective for this fishing.

American River water is strikingly clear, so there is always a good chance of sight-fishing to steelhead and generally seeing what's in the river at any given time. Tailouts and runs below riffles are likely places to find fish, as are deeper slots. Since most of the spawning takes place in the riffles, give the wild fish a break and pass by these areas. Fishing above and below these spawners, however, is fair game. Ideal water is shallow, from two to four feet deep, and a Type III sinking tip is a great all-around choice. Other runs of smaller steelhead enter the river in the fall and spring, but they aren't as big and don't attract nearly as much attention from anglers. The steelhead seem more like resident trout, averaging from 12 to 20 inches. Of course, there are some larger ones, too.

Before the Spey-fishing craze took over, indicator nymphing with single-handed fly rods worked very well on the American, and that hasn't changed. Fly rods for 7- to 9-weight lines are good tools with floating lines and 9-foot leaders tapered to 1X fluorocarbon. Like steelhead everywhere, these fish will gladly eat egg patterns, and a few favorites include #8 Pettis' Unreal Egg, Single Eggs, and Surreal Eggs.

Shad

Perhaps no one alive today really cares if American shad or brook trout were the first fish imported to California, but the competition is neck and neck since both species were brought to California about the same time in the

Not even native to the West Coast, shad were introduced to California over a century ago, and they've prospered. Bucks like this show up in the catch first, followed by the larger females later.

1870s. Both East Coast species have found a home in California for over 100 years and they prosper in their relative ecosystems. But judging from the number of anglers sometimes lined up for the evening shad grab during lazy Sacramento summer evenings, these hard-fighting fish are a local favorite. Perhaps because steelhead fishing is a cool-weather proposition, it never gets as crowded as the summer steelhead grab. Anglers are prone to take up spots along the river's edge and practice casting, or simply wait for the twilight magic hour of fishing every evening.

Shad fishing is best when the light is low, and there are two periods of insane fishing every day. The first starts about 5:30 AM. Few fly anglers are willing to get up this early. The other really good time starts about 7 PM until dark. The timing of their grab is truly a sight to behold, and it's actually more interesting to be within sight of a couple of other anglers. The truth is, when you see one bent rod, you are likely to see others. It really seems like the fish are tuned in to some kind of underwater whistle or siren. All of a sudden they start hitting—all of them, at once. It's one of nature's miraculous mysteries.

Shad are not selective to fly pattern, although some anglers apparently disagree. Suffice it to say, they don't seem to be too picky in the American River. Shad patterns seem to be many, and every devotee has his own favorite one or two. Guide friends have hooked these fish on bare hooks, so if clients have cherished, secret shad patterns, there is no problem with indulging them. Virtually any bright shad pattern with bead eyes and chartreuse, hot pink, fluorescent orange, or white on the body or tail on a #6 hook seem to work equally well.

Like a lot of anadromous fish, shad do not eat when they enter fresh water to spawn. They smack a fly in a territorial response because they are really irritable at certain particular times. What is important to shad is the depth of your fly and, to some degree, its motion. The best method for catching shad is swinging flies at the proper depth. Shad start deep and move into shallower water as they approach the "magic times" early and late in the day. Of course, you can catch shad at almost any time, providing you put your fly in their face.

Beginning around 5 PM you might expect to begin catching fish using fast sinking lines like a Teeny 300 in water as deep as six feet. As the sun sinks lower in the sky the fish will gradually move into shallower water, say four feet, which is easier to fish effectively. Good lines for shallower water times are Teeny 200s and Type III sinking tips. As the shad grab heats up and the sun is all but gone during the last 20 minutes of light, anglers do well with a floating fly line, a slightly longer leader, and a weighted fly. Shad are not leader shy. A straight piece of 8-pound test mono will work fine, and leaders generally don't need to be longer than six feet. Most often the grab will occur when the fly line straightens out at the bottom of the drift, the time referred to as "the hangdown." Some shad guides confess if they could get their clients to let their flies just hang down in the current, sooner or later they would begin catching fish.

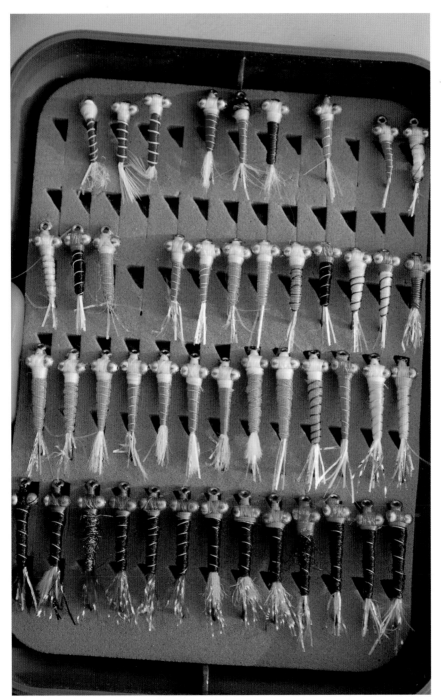

Guides agree when it comes to American River shad. Fly pattern and color matters very little, but bright, easy-to-see flies are the norm.

The first fish to show are the bucks, males that are around half the size of the hens, then the females. Males typically run from 1 to 2$^{1}/_{2}$ pounds, while the females go 3 to 5 pounds. Shad and steelhead seem to prefer the same kinds of water. Look for moving water that isn't too fast. Look for seams and fish the softer side of them. Try to position your rod so that the line comes straight (the hangdown) right in the seam line, and wait a moment before your next cast. Morning fishing, if you care to get up that early, usually starts with a bang and slows down gradually. In the evening the opposite is true. The grab is a gradual thing until everyone starts hooking up, ending with a bang.

You can fish for shad with just about any fly rod, but stouter ones make the most sense from two perspectives. First, the longer you play the fish the worse shape it will be in when netted. The fish has a much greater chance of survival when fought quickly and released as soon as possible. Secondly, an angler with a 6- or 7-weight rod can fight, land, and hook another fish while the guy with the 4-weight is still fighting his first fish. Ideal rods for American River shad run 9 or 9$^{1}/_{2}$ feet long for 6- or 7-weight lines.

Striped Bass

Maybe the shad were lonely for their East Coast brethren, but striped bass also came from that other coast some time after shad were imported. The striper fishery in the American has been improving in recent years and these

Most of the stripers in the American aren't nearly this big, but the possibility of hooking one like this keeps people coming back. JOHN SHERMAN PHOTO

The stripers follow the main pulse of shad up the American and will gladly eat them if they get a chance, but they are officially there to spawn. Shad-fishing anglers also have shots at catching stripers on the fly.

great fish are attracting more fly anglers than ever. The average American River striper runs from 5 to 12 pounds, but anglers land fish in the 16- to 20-pound class every year. American River stripers have been known to weigh 40 pounds.

While there seem to be some striped bass in the river year-round, the major push of fish entering the American from the delta comes in April or May. Striper season is the longest season of all, and good fishing can be expected all the way through October. The stripers follow the main pulse of shad up the American and will gladly eat them if they get a chance, but they are officially there to spawn. They vacate the American River again in November and December and head back down to the Delta.

Single-handed 8- and 9-weight rods work well in horsing these sluggers away from snags and toward a waiting net. The best lines for this fishing are 300- to 350-grain sinking tips for throwing large baitfish imitations like Clousers, Deceivers, and Flashtail Whistlers. Unlike shad, which apparently could care less about what fly pattern you dangle in front of their noses, stripers are a bit more finicky. Different color combinations attract more strikes on certain days. Good fly color combinations include chartreuse and white, green and white, blue and white, and during May and June when the suckers are spawning, yellow and white. Most fish are taken on large flies, #1/0-2/0, but there is hardly ever a need to go smaller than #2.

Bass are going to frequent different parts of the river than either steelhead or shad. The lower, slower water, especially sections of the water from Howe Avenue downstream to Discovery Park, is better bass habitat than much of the water upstream. But there are bass throughout the river. Bass prefer to hang out around structure, so look for things in the water that might attract them. Bass are motivated by hunger, and they love nothing better than to lie in some hidden place to ambush prey. I like to think of all bass as catlike in behavior and motivation. Bass like to eat, but they like it even better if they are able to see their prey before they are seen and then pounce on it from some hidden place.

Once your fly is in the water, things are different from the way you merely point the rod at the water and let the current move the fly. In striper fishing, you have to impart the illusion of life to your streamer. Rather than "fishing the water" as in some other types of fishing, in striper fishing you are fishing specific spots. Decide in advance where you think the bass may be—frequently the shady side of snags, trees, boulders, and root wads in the water—then make your cast to show your fly to that spot. Once your fly hits the water, whether it's on target or not, fish out that cast. First, give your fly a few counts to sink, then begin a *strip, strip, strip, pause* retrieve, varying both the length of your strips and the length of your pauses until you find what the bass want. Point the rod toward your fly and touch the tip to the surface of the water. Generally speaking, the warmer it is, the faster you can strip. The colder it is, the slower you have to go. But always experiment and let the fish determine what they want.

While somewhat different from the bass that live their entire lives in fresh water, stripers have some other things in common with their relatives. The best times to fish for stripers are dawn and almost dark. The evenings can be particularly good as the ambient temperatures are usually still mild. It's not uncommon to be coming in from an evening of shad fishing to see huge boils out in the current as a big striper gulps a meal, perhaps a shad. There's nothing wrong with bringing a heavier rod, a box of big streamers, and just going after them for an hour or so. Stripers often stick to the deeper water during hot, high-sun summer days, but as soon as the sun is off the water they enter shallower water prowling for food.

We tend to love chasing fish in remote, rugged, and beautiful areas. On the other hand, we sometimes overlook the fishing wealth in our own backyards. If more city-dwellers took advantage of the unbelievable fishing at their doorsteps, the far-off places might not have the same allure. The good news is you don't have to wait to inherit a fortune to find good fishing close by.

Dan Blanton's Flashtail Whistler

Lefty's Deceiver

Clouser's Deep Minnow

Dan Blanton's Flashtail Whistler

Hook:	#2-1/0 Mustad 34185S jig hook
Thread:	White single-strand flat floss
Eyes:	Bead chain
Tail:	White bucktail with multicolored Krystal Flash and silver and pearl Flashabou
Body:	Wrapped red chenille
Collar:	Red hackle

Lefty's Deceiver

Hook:	#4-1/0 Mustad 34007 or 34011
Thread:	White 6/0 Danville
Tail:	White saltwater saddle hackles (6 to 8) tied at hook bend
Flash:	Rainbow and/or pearl Krystal Flash trimmed to different lengths
Wing:	Two clumps of white bucktail on the sides, one clump of chartreuse bucktail on top
Throat:	Red Flashabou or red Accent Flash
Head:	Thread and painted eyes, coated with cement, epoxy, or Softex

Clouser's Deep Minnow

Hook:	#6-1/0 Mustad 3406B
Thread:	White 6/0 Danville
Eyes:	Lead or nonlead painted dumbbell eyes coated with epoxy, Softex, or head cement
Tail:	Holographic Flashabou
Body:	Olive and white bucktail

Yuba River

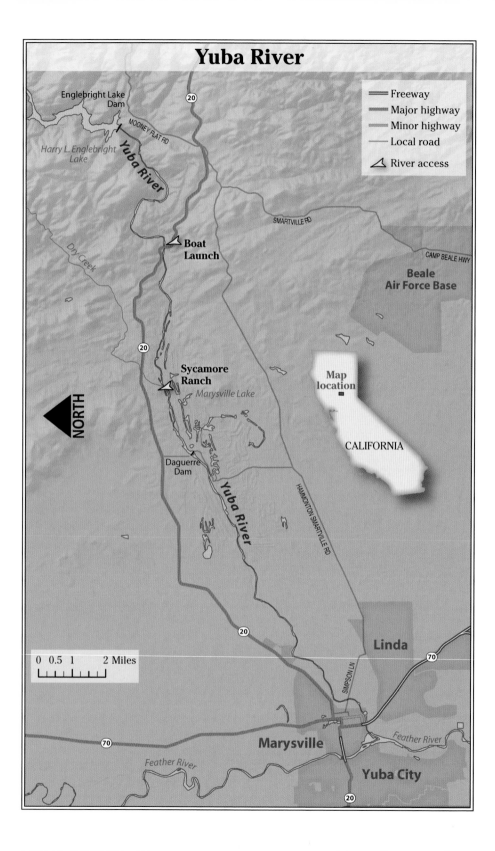

CHAPTER 10

Yuba River

The Yuba is a remarkable wild-rainbow-trout fishery, partly because it is so close to major population centers, and partly because it exists in the first place. In northern California it isn't uncommon to observe century-old scars on the landscape perpetrated at the hands of mindless zealots with a lust for gold. The only thing more unbelievable than man's ability to pillage the environment is nature's ability to somehow, in the end, bring it back again. The Yuba is a success story.

Northeast of Sacramento, the Yuba flows cold and clear beneath Engle-bright Dam through a treacherous white-water canyon section beneath the CA 20 bridge, through the Yuba Gold Field, and into the Feather River in the twin cities of Marysville and Yuba City. Wading access is limited, a lot of work, and not the best way to fish this river. The Yuba was made for drifting, and while there is really only one drift available, most devotees have come to cherish it.

The fish, wild rainbows and a few hatchery strays from waters above and below, are truly noteworthy. Where they came from in the first place is an item of speculation, but anyone who has hooked one of these fish knows them to be stout, highly acrobatic fighters. Historic fish-stocking records are sketchy, but there is a good probability the river was stocked with hatchery fish at some point. Maybe a few survived and maybe they didn't. Other possibilities include fish that may have washed over Englebright Dam at high water or swum up from the Feather River below, as a few hatchery fish still do.

Anglers impressed with the Yuba's large wild fish have made the case that some of these are actually steelhead. But DNA tests routinely show they are just magnificent resident trout. Average Yuba River rainbows run 14 to 16 inches, and there are plenty of larger fish with significant girths. A Bay-Delta Sport Fishing Enhancement Stamp is required on the Yuba in addition to a California fishing license.

Drama runs high when you hook a big Yuba River trout and feel its power. These fish often take to the air with repeated jumps, and landing them is by no means certain.

There is only one reasonable access for drifting the river, and this is by far the best way to fish the Yuba. CA 20 crosses over the river, and there is a rough place to launch a drift boat or pontoon boat on the south side, immediately upstream. From here you drift down to the take out at Sycamore Ranch, and they will charge you a few dollars for the privilege. It's a good deal and the drift is fairly mellow. Despite the lack of public launch facilities, most days you will have the water nearly to yourself and at times it almost seems private. The river cascades through rolling hills and scrub oak landscapes, around islands, and then into the great historic mining area.

The really striking thing about this landscape is the Yuba Gold Field section, which is almost the entire drift. The water is so clear it's easy to imagine it isn't even there while it rushes over a fairly even cobble bottom. But drifting here is more like taking a boat down Fifth Avenue in New York City, towering skyscrapers draping you in shadows. Only there are no skyscrapers on the Yuba, but 100-foot-tall mountains of ancient dredge tailings on either side of the river. The effect is much the same.

My first time down the Yuba I caught myself gawking at these unbelievable rock piles, the likes of which I have never seen on any other river, instead of paying attention to my dry fly. It's an odd mix; such robust wild trout in

Sloan's Persuader, like some of the other best flies for matching the Yuba's big bugs, floats high, is durable, and is easy to see.

Before Englebright Dam was finished in 1941, the Yuba hosted both king salmon and steelhead runs. While the mining all but slaughtered these runs, anadromous fish have been coming back slowly. The dam was built for a couple of reasons like to provide hydroelectric power and to control potential flooding, but also to catch mining leftovers like mercury from poisoning more of the system. Though the dam cut off salmon and steelhead spawning grounds upstream, the salmon, at least, hang on.

Built upstream of Englebright Dam, the New Bullards Bar Dam was finished in 1969, and a side benefit of the newer structure was to provide cooler water to enter Englebright. The cooler water temperatures resulting from this dam are lauded as major steps in maintaining and enhancing the Yuba River fishery downstream.

Barring unforeseen circumstances, the Yuba River wild-trout fishery seems destined to keep getting better and better. Protected as it is by limited access and special angling regulations, it seems secure for the foreseeable future. While other streams like the Trinity, Truckee, and Upper Sacramento rivers were dealt a pretty raw hand in the olden days, no other stream that I know of has endured what the Yuba did, or has come back in such grand style. ■

such an unlikely place. Hydraulic mining came to the Yuba in the late 19th century where, at least for a while, they used "water cannons" to melt the natural stream banks into oblivion. This was eventually outlawed, but not before the river bed was raised some 80 feet above where it started.

Miraculously, once you get over looking at the strange landscape and pondering the big questions about man's motivations and values, you see the river for what it is today. It is an absolutely beautiful, medium-size trout stream that could go toe-to-toe with almost any famous rivers that don't happen to flow through such wretchedness. And if you're coming from the Bay Area or Sacramento, the river is a lot closer than having to drive to Shasta, Trinity, or Siskiyou Counties. But without a drift boat or pontoon boat, access to the river is severely limited. On the other hand, with them I can't think of many rivers so ideally suited for a good float. There are sections of river that can be easily waded, and others where you will need to drop anchor and fish from the boat to get to the best water. The key to success on the Yuba is to fish a lot of different water in a day.

The Yuba seems to break the mold as far as other great Northern California wild-trout streams is concerned. If I didn't know better, I would swear wild trout living in water this clear would be nervous; would hardly ever take dries with a high sun overhead, and would best be approached by deep nymphing tactics. Yuba trout will take nymphs readily, but they take dries just as willingly during all times of the day.

Hatches and Strategies

While there are aquatic insects of many kinds and sizes in the Yuba, the presence of two major hatches and one summer terrestrial allows anglers to fish fairly large dry flies here with amazing success. Sloan's Persuader matches the January *Skwala* stonefly hatch, the May–June Golden Stonefly hatch, as well as the August–September hoppers that are thick along the river. Dave Sloan, the fly originator, lives in the Sacramento area and fishes and guides the Yuba frequently. The fly is easy to see on the water, and when you tie it to your leader.

A good setup for dry flies on the Yuba is a 9-foot, 5-weight fly rod and floating line. Despite the clear water you can get away with $7 1/2$-foot leaders tapered to 3X to 5X fluorocarbon, especially fishing larger dry flies. Despite the almost negative density of fluorocarbon, Sloan's Persuader is buoyant enough to stay on top. During those times when nothing large is hatching, anglers drop down to 5X and lengthen their leaders to 9 feet, more for the sake of achieving a more natural drift than the fishes' aversion to stouter tip-

Stonefly patterns, both nymphs and dry flies, are important to Yuba River trout throughout much of the year.

pets. Another potential reason why the fish aren't more leader shy is that the Yuba just doesn't get that much fishing pressure.

The *Skwala* stoneflies of early spring usually last into March, and despite the typical spring rains, the temperatures may reach into the 60s. While the *Skwalas* are still around, several other species seem to proliferate on the river all at the same time. There are typically Blue-Winged Olives in the early morning followed by March Browns a little later. By noon it's time to fish *Skwalas* again while waiting for the afternoon Pale Morning Duns (PMDs) to come off.

As the river continues to warm, PMDs, Little Yellow Stones, Golden Stones, and several species of caddisflies become more important. It's a good idea to have a variety of dry flies with you, since once your boat pulls into the river at CA 20, you're committed to float all the way through until the take out at Sycamore Ranch.

Yuba River trout often sit fairly close to the bank, even in fairly shallow water. This makes them excellent targets for a well-placed hopper pattern, such as a Persuader. Guide Bill Lowe prepares to net a big rainbow for a client.

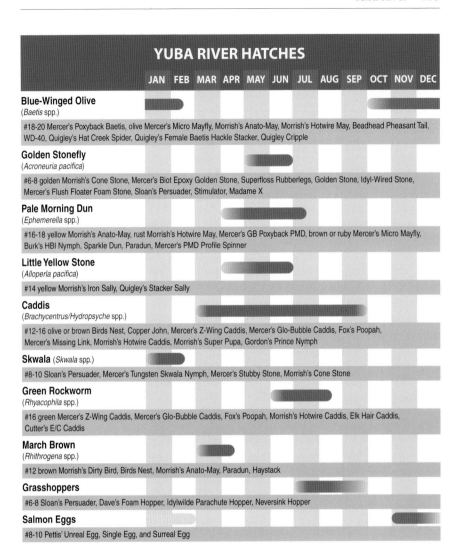

YUBA RIVER HATCHES

	JAN	FEB	MAR	APR	MAY	JUN	JUL	AUG	SEP	OCT	NOV	DEC

Blue-Winged Olive
(*Baetis* spp.)

#18-20 Mercer's Poxyback Baetis, olive Mercer's Micro Mayfly, Morrish's Anato-May, Morrish's Hotwire May, Beadhead Pheasant Tail, WD-40, Quigley's Hat Creek Spider, Quigley's Female Baetis Hackle Stacker, Quigley Cripple

Golden Stonefly
(*Acroneuria pacifica*)

#6-8 golden Morrish's Cone Stone, Mercer's Biot Epoxy Golden Stone, Superfloss Rubberlegs, Golden Stone, Idyl-Wired Stone, Mercer's Flush Floater Foam Stone, Sloan's Persuader, Stimulator, Madame X

Pale Morning Dun
(*Ephemerella* spp.)

#16-18 yellow Morrish's Anato-May, rust Morrish's Hotwire May, Mercer's GB Poxyback PMD, brown or ruby Mercer's Micro Mayfly, Burk's HBI Nymph, Sparkle Dun, Paradun, Mercer's PMD Profile Spinner

Little Yellow Stone
(*Alloperla pacifica*)

#14 yellow Morrish's Iron Sally, Quigley's Stacker Sally

Caddis
(*Brachycentrus/Hydropsyche* spp.)

#12-16 olive or brown Birds Nest, Copper John, Mercer's Z-Wing Caddis, Mercer's Glo-Bubble Caddis, Fox's Poopah, Mercer's Missing Link, Morrish's Hotwire Caddis, Morrish's Super Pupa, Gordon's Prince Nymph

Skwala (*Skwala* spp.)

#8-10 Sloan's Persuader, Mercer's Tungsten Skwala Nymph, Mercer's Stubby Stone, Morrish's Cone Stone

Green Rockworm
(*Rhyacophila* spp.)

#16 green Mercer's Z-Wing Caddis, Mercer's Glo-Bubble Caddis, Fox's Poopah, Morrish's Hotwire Caddis, Elk Hair Caddis, Cutter's E/C Caddis

March Brown
(*Rhithrogena* spp.)

#12 brown Morrish's Dirty Bird, Birds Nest, Morrish's Anato-May, Paradun, Haystack

Grasshoppers

#6-8 Sloan's Persuader, Dave's Foam Hopper, Idylwilde Parachute Hopper, Neversink Hopper

Salmon Eggs

#8-10 Pettis' Unreal Egg, Single Egg, and Surreal Egg

Yuba River trout often sit fairly close to the bank, even in fairly shallow water. This makes them excellent targets for a well-placed hopper pattern, and once again the Persuader is the first fly I reach for. Hopper fishing may be one of the few dry-fly techniques where it is perfectly reasonable to land your bug hard, *splat,* on the water, but that doesn't mean you don't need a good presentation. Other great hopper patterns include #6-8 Dave's Foam Hopper, Idylwilde Parachute Hopper, and the Neversink Hopper.

The trick to getting a good drift with a dry fly is to hoard just a little slack fly line between the tip of your rod and your fly. Basically, any time your line goes out straight as a poker, your fly begins to skate in an unnatural manner. The effect this has on the trout can vary between merely making them suspi-

While not the major draw to the Yuba, the river does have a shad run in late June–early July.

cious to scaring the hell out of them and sending them fleeing for their lives. You want your fly to drift, not swim.

Working from a boat you are looking for seams, pockets, drop-offs, eddies, and areas next to grassy banks, especially if they have overhanging vegetation. Always be on the lookout for rises, which are not all that easy to see in faster water sections. It took me a bit of time before I realized how delicately a trout can grab a dry in fast water.

During the hottest days of summer, the hatches evaporate during the middle of the day. The best times to fish midsummer are early and late in the day. Fish will hang around midstream gravel bars in the mornings, but also places where seams come together and deeper water along the edges. When flows are high, fish are attracted to the slower water and areas offering relief from the current. Target any areas that may trap or funnel food. Fish are almost always rising once the sun is off the water.

In the fall, Blue-Winged Olives come back with the cooler, shorter days, and it's back to tiny dries and squinting to see big trout sipping these miniscule tidbits, if you want to fish on the surface. However, the best action occurs when king salmon enter the river for their annual spawning run from late September through November. This is the time of year Yuba trout throw caution to the wind and eat like unruly swine. Almost any good single egg pattern will take fish, but many locals prefer a #8-10 Pettis' Unreal Egg. What I love about the pattern is that it's fun to tie and almost bulletproof.

Wading anglers should be extremely careful not to wade on salmon redds, or even in areas where salmon may have deposited eggs beneath the gravel. Careless or uninformed fishermen do more harm to anadromous fish than most people realize. Since all things in ecosystems are tied together, you cannot damage one part of a stream without also doing harm to others, like the wild trout.

River Flows and Regulations

The Yuba is open to fishing yearlong, but flows in the river can vary greatly depending on how much water is in the system. It's prudent to have a sense

Dropping a beadhead nymph off of a large, buoyant dry is an excellent strategy for covering the Yuba's water from a boat.

of what's going on with the flows before contemplating a float trip. No two years are exactly the same, but here are some general guidelines based on 2000–2007 flows.

January and February are somewhat stable, and flows average about 2,500 cubic feet per second (cfs). March through May are typically the wettest months, so flows hit their annual peaks during this time. Flows will vary between 3,000 cfs and 4,500 cfs. During summers the river begins a slow drawing down period where flows drop to 2,500 cfs, then 2,200 cfs, then 1,800 cfs. In September the flows dive to 800 cfs and remain in this range until December, when they once again rise to 2,000 cfs and repeat the annual cycle. If you're fishing from a boat, all of these flows are manageable. The higher flows of early spring mean less opportunity for wading, while the low flows of fall open up that possibility again.

Angling regulations for the Yuba are perfectly suited to catch-and-release-oriented fly anglers. There is no bait allowed on the river, and anglers must use barbless hooks year-round. The water between Englebright Dam and the CA 20 bridge is completely catch-and-release. Some of this water is fishable, but access is very limited and much of the water is wild white-water. From the CA 20 bridge downstream to Daguerre Point Dam, one hatchery trout or steelhead may be harvested. From Daguerre Point Dam downstream to the confluence with the Feather River, various combinations of hatchery fish and salmon may be harvested, but you had better read the regulations carefully and know exactly where you are before you go. The lower river is not as conducive to fly fishing as the CA 20 bridge to Sycamore Ranch stretch is, and so it is better left for the gear anglers.

Fox's Poopah (Cinnamon)

Hook:	#12-18 Tiemco 3769
Bead:	Copper
Thread:	Camel 8/0 Uni-Thread
Tail/ Overbody:	Cinnamon Caddis Vernille
Rib:	Gold wire
Underbody:	Pearl tinsel
Legs:	Brown partridge or hen-back fibers
Head:	Brown ostrich
Antennae:	Lemon wood-duck fibers

Morrish's Iron Sally

Hook:	#14-16 Tiemco 3761
Bead:	Gold
Weight:	.015 lead or lead-free wire
Thread:	Beige 6/0 Danville
Tail:	Gold goose biots
Abdomen:	Gold Ultra Wire
Back:	Black Flashabou Accent
Thorax:	Fox Squirrel Nymph (#2) Whitlock SLF
Wing Case:	White-tipped turkey tail, coated with flexible lacquer
Legs:	Black Flashabou Accent
Antennae:	Gold goose biots

Mercer's Tungsten Skwala Nymph

Hook:	#10-12 Tiemco 2302
Bead:	Black tungsten
Thread:	Olive 8/0 Uni-Thread
Tail:	Olive turkey biot tips
Rib:	Gold wire
Carapace:	Mottled olive Thin Skin
Abdomen:	Z-Wing Mercer's Buggy Nymph Dubbing
Thorax:	Same as abdomen
Wing Case:	Same as carapace
Legs:	Black/olive Sili Legs
Antennae:	Ring-necked-pheasant-tail fibers

Mercer's TB Swing Nymph

Hook:	#10-18 Tiemco 3761
Bead:	Black tungsten
Thread:	Camel 8/0 Uni-Thread
Rib:	Pearl Flashabou
Abdomen:	Camel 8/0 Uni-Thread coated with Softex
Thorax:	Peacock herl; bead is veiled with UV brown Ice Dub
Wing:	Brown Z-lon
Hackle:	Brown partridge

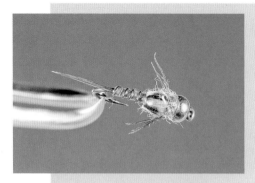

Mercer's Micro Mayfly (Olive)

Hook: #14-20 Tiemco 921
Bead: Copper
Thread: Olive 8/0 Uni-Thread
Tail: Natural pheasant-tail fibers
Abdomen: Stripped peacock herl
Rib: Silver wire (fine)
Wing Case: Golden brown mottled turkey tail
           and pearl Flashabou coated with
           5-minute epoxy
Thorax: BWO Super Fine
Legs: Same as tail
Head: Same as thorax

Mercer's Micro Mayfly (Ruby)

Hook: #14-20 Tiemco 3769
Bead: Copper
Thread: Camel 8/0 Uni-Thread
Tail: Natural ring-necked-pheasant-tail
           fibers
Rib: Silver Ultra Wire (small)
Abdomen: Red Flashabou
Wing Case: Golden brown mottled turkey tail
           and pearl Flashabou coated with
           5-minute epoxy
Thorax: Lava brown Buggy Nymph Dubbing
Legs: Same as tail

Sloan's Persuader (Tan)

Hook: #6-10 Tiemco 2312
Thread: Camel 6/0 Uni-Thread
Abdomen: Golden tan Antron Sparkle Dubbing,
           tan Fly Foam (2mm) over the top
Post: White Foam Parachute Posts (large),
           tan and orange Fly Foam (2mm)
Underwing: Black Aire-Foam Pre-Cut
           Stonefly/Caddis Wings
Wing: Natural moose body hair
Overwing: Fl. chartreuse Para Post Wings
Hackle: Grizzly Metz Magnum Saddle
           Hackle
Legs: Tan Barred Rubber Legs with a
           drop of Zap-A-Gap
Thorax: Golden tan Antron Sparkle Dubbing

Mercer's Poxyback PMD

Hook:	#14-18 Tiemco 2302
Bead:	Gold
Thread:	Camel 8/0 Uni-Thread
Tail:	Dyed yellow ring-necked-pheasant-tail fibers
Rib:	Pearl Flashabou
Carapace:	Dark mottled turkey tail
Abdomen:	PMD Mercer's Buggy Nymph Dubbing
Thorax:	Same as abdomen
Gills:	Cream/gray marabou clumps
Wing Case:	Dark mottled turkey tail, coated with 5-minute epoxy
Legs:	Same as tail
Head:	Same as thorax

Morrish's Hotwire Caddis (Tan)

Hook:	#12-16 Tiemco 2457
Bead:	Black nickel
Weight:	.015 lead or lead-free wire
Thread:	Black 6/0 Danville
Abdomen:	Tan Ultra Wire
Back:	Black Flashabou Accent
Wing Case:	Rust goose biots and pearl Flashabou Accent
Legs:	Brown Hungarian partridge fibers
Head:	Dark Stone (#15) Whitlock SLF

Morrish's Hotwire Caddis (Olive)

Hook:	#12-16 Tiemco 2457
Bead:	Black nickel
Weight:	.015 lead or lead-free wire
Thread:	Black 6/0 Danville
Abdomen:	Olive Ultra Wire
Back:	Black Flashabou Accent
Wing Case:	Rust goose biots and pearl Flashabou Accent
Legs:	Brown Hungarian partridge fibers
Head:	Dark Stone (#15) Whitlock SLF

Truckee River

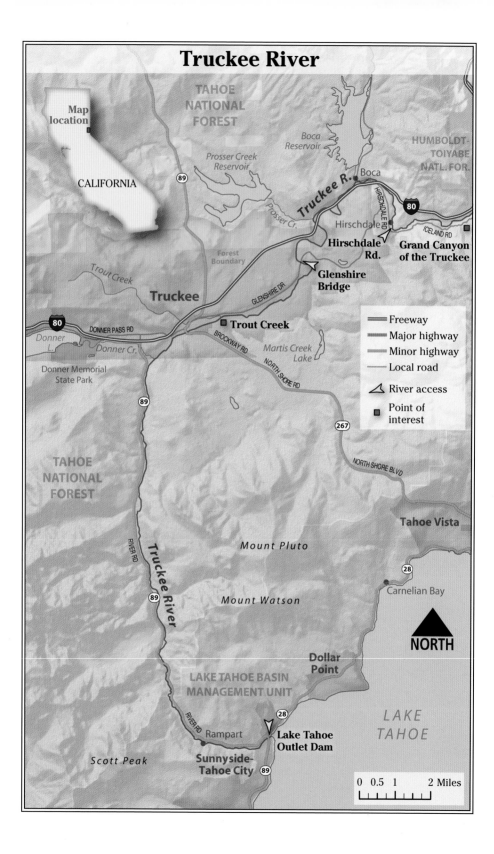

Map location

CALIFORNIA

TAHOE NATIONAL FOREST

Boca Reservoir

Prosser Creek Reservoir

HUMBOLDT-TOIYABE NATL. FOR.

Boca

Truckee R.

HIRSCHDALE RD

Prosser Cr.

Hirschdale

ICELAND RD

Hirschdale Rd.

Grand Canyon of the Truckee

Forest Boundary

GLENSHIRE DR

Glenshire Bridge

Trout Creek

Truckee

DONNER PASS RD

Donner L.

Donner Cr.

BROCKWAY RD

Trout Creek

Martis Creek Lake

NORTH SHORE RD

Donner Memorial State Park

267

89

NORTH SHORE BLVD

TAHOE NATIONAL FOREST

Tahoe Vista

28

Mount Pluto

Carnelian Bay

RIVER RD

Truckee River

89

Mount Watson

NORTH

Dollar Point

LAKE TAHOE BASIN MANAGEMENT UNIT

28

LAKE TAHOE

RIVER RD

Rampart

Lake Tahoe Outlet Dam

Scott Peak

Sunnyside-Tahoe City

89

	Freeway
	Major highway
	Minor highway
	Local road
◁	River access
■	Point of interest

0 0.5 1   2 Miles

CHAPTER 11

Truckee River

I've often wondered if the reason the Truckee is such a popular river to fish is because it is so visible. A section of it parallels I-80 between Sacramento and Reno, Nevada, and commuters on this always-hectic freeway undoubtedly look at it, and look at it, and look at it. Sooner or later it becomes an itch that just has to be scratched. And once you give in to the river, it gets under your skin and sticks.

The Truckee, for all its visibility, is not an easy place to catch fish. It's not a great river for beginners who need to spend a certain amount of time "catching" for the fly-fishing bug to take root. But it's no accident the river is a magnet for those more accomplished anglers who appreciate a challenge and a chance to test their skills against wild trout in a setting so close to the epicenter of California's rich history.

Draining Lake Tahoe and heading northeast from California into Nevada, the Truckee has been through a lot, and promises a lot. The landscape invokes images of the Donner Party, raucous mining camps, Chinese laborers chiseling a railroad bed out of sheer rock, and a mythical Ben Cartwright saddling up on the Ponderosa Ranch, which isn't too far from here.

In earlier times the Truckee became renowned for Lahontan cutthroat trout in the 10- and even 20-pound class. Today the cutts are struggling to regain their foothold, but the primary fish in the river are wild browns and rainbows, with the occasional whitefish thrown in so fewer anglers actually go home skunked.

Anglers who know the river expect to catch fish, but not always a lot of fish. There are big fish in the river, especially browns, but these are caught barely often enough to keep anglers coming back and stories circulating in the fly-fishing community. But any fish landed here is generally seen as a gift, and appreciated well beyond the status of what more gullible fish ever achieve.

Upper River

The Truckee is upside down. The river first flows from the northwest corner of massive Lake Tahoe and then takes a northerly meander next to CA 89 and Squaw Valley Ski Park. It flows virtually due north until it bends in a north-

California's typical bright blue sky seems to make deeper water more attractive to trout during midday. Smart anglers will seek out these places, which appear darker when observed through polarized sunglasses.

Choosing the right water is important on the Truckee. Here Guide Jay Cockrum high-sticks through a deep run, which is excellent holding water.

easterly direction just below I-80 and the town of Truckee. Most fly anglers know this as the "bait section" with fewer fish, but some big ones. This water, from 1,000 feet below the Lake Tahoe Outlet Dam to the river's confluence with Trout Creek east of town, carries a five-fish limit, any method of take provision. You generally see fewer fly anglers in this section, but the fishing can still be pretty good. The water within the city limits of Truckee is especially ignored by most anglers and, perhaps as a result, can be fairly productive.

My experience on other rivers within the limits of metropolitan areas, except the Sacramento River, is that anglers often assume fishing can't be good close to town. This is like the gorgeous woman who every man assumes must be dating someone, so she ends up sitting in front of the TV much of the time while lesser beauties get dates. Give the river in Truckee a try, and you may be surprised. There seem to be more brown trout in this section, if only because rainbows are more easily harvested than browns, and the bait-fishing community tend to harvest what they catch. Most anglers agree there are probably more browns than rainbows in the entire river, but they are caught less frequently.

Lower River and Canyon

From Trout Creek the river flows generally northeast following I-80 (actually vice versa) for about 20 miles to the Nevada border. The water between Truckee and the Grand Canyon of the Truckee below the border with Nevada is the most popular fly-fishing section. All of the water from Trout

The Glenshire Bridge area is popular with anglers and has a parking lot and picnic tables.

Creek to the Nevada border calls for barbless artificial hooks and catch-and-release fishing depending on the time of the year. There are generally more fish below Trout Creek, but they are not necessarily easy to catch.

Glenshire Bridge is a popular fishing area with a large parking area and picnic tables. Upstream from here is private water where hatchery rainbows are stocked periodically. Some anglers will wade up into this section being careful to stay below the high-water mark, but this can be a sketchy strategy. Others float down through this water in pontoon boats, which is also legal, but I often wonder why people go to so much effort to catch planted fish. For me, the reward of fishing the Truckee in the first place is testing your skills against wild fish in a gorgeous environment.

The river downstream from Trout Creek to the Nevada state line is defined both by special angling regulations and the popular nature of the water. The water is open to angling year-round, but two trout may be harvested from the last Saturday in May through November 15. After November 15 and before the last Saturday in April, catch-and-release fishing is required. You must use barbless artificial lures or flies from Trout Creek down yearlong. Bait is not allowed below Trout Creek.

Much of this is classic pocketwater, and the key to success is to fish it thoroughly and well. In sunny California this usually means fishing with one or two nymphs under a strike indicator with enough weight to get them down to the fish's level. Another good strategy is covering a lot of water by focusing on places likely to hold fish and spending the most time in the best spots such as heads of pools, deep runs, pocketwater, and seams. Always look for

TRUCKEE RIVER HATCHES

	JAN	FEB	MAR	APR	MAY	JUN	JUL	AUG	SEP	OCT	NOV	DEC
Blue-Winged Olive (*Baetis* spp.)					■	■				■	■	
Golden Stonefly (*Calineuria* spp.)				■	■							
Pale Morning Dun (*Ephemerella* spp.)					■	■	■					
Caddis (*Brachycentrus/Hydropsyche* spp.)						■	■	■				
March Brown (*Rhithrogena* spp.)				■	■							
Sulphur (*Epeorus* spp.)					■							
Trico (*Tricorythodes* spp.)							■	■				
Little Yellow Stone (*Isoperla* spp.)							■	■				
Mahogany Dun (*Paraleptophlebia* spp.)									■	■		
Green Rockworm (*Rhyacophila* spp.)						■	■					
October Caddis (*Dicosmoecus* spp.)										■		
Scuds (*Gammarus* spp.)					■	■	■	■	■	■		

Blue-Winged Olive (*Baetis* spp.)
#18-20 Mercer's Poxyback Baetis, olive Mercer's Micro Mayfly, Morrish's Anato-May, Morrish's Hotwire May, Beadhead Pheasant Tail, WD-40, Quigley's Hat Creek Spider, Quigley Cripple

Golden Stonefly (*Calineuria* spp.)
#6-8 golden Morrish's Cone Stone, Mercer's Biot Epoxy Golden Stone, Superfloss Rubberlegs, Golden Stone, Idyl-Wired Stone, Mercer's Flush Floater Foam Stone, Stimulator, Madame X

Pale Morning Dun (*Ephemerella* spp.)
#16-18 yellow Morrish's Anato-May, rust Morrish's Hotwire May, Mercer's GB Poxyback PMD, brown or ruby Mercer's Micro Mayfly, Burk's HBI Nymph, Sparkle Dun, Paradun, Mercer's PMD Profile Spinner

Caddis (*Brachycentrus/Hydropsyche* spp.)
#12-16 brown Birds Nest, Copper John, Mercer's Z-Wing Caddis, Mercer's Glo-Bubble Caddis, Fox's Poopah, Morrish's Hotwire Caddis, Morrish's Super Pupa, Gordon's Prince Nymph, Mercer's Missing Link

March Brown (*Rhithrogena* spp.)
#12 brown Morrish's Dirty Bird, Birds Nest, Morrish's Anato-May, Haystack, Paradun

Sulphur (*Epeorus* spp.)
#10-12 yellow Mercer's Foam Parachute Sulphur, Neally's Brown Drake, Paradun, Haystack, Mercer's Poxyback Emerger

Trico (*Tricorythodes* spp.)
#20 black Mercer's Micro Mayfly, CDC Biot Spinner, Etha Wing Trico, Quigley's Hat Creek Spider

Little Yellow Stone (*Isoperla* spp.)
#14 yellow Morrish's Iron Sally, Quigley's Stacker Sally

Mahogany Dun (*Paraleptophlebia* spp.)
#12-14 rust Sparkle Dun, Mercer's Foam Parachute, Tilt Wing Dun, Paradun

Green Rockworm (*Rhyacophila* spp.)
#18 green Mercer's Z-Wing Caddis, Mercer's Glo-Bubble Caddis, Fox's Poopah, Morrish's Hotwire Caddis, Elk Hair Caddis, Cutter's E/C Caddis

October Caddis (*Dicosmoecus* spp.)
#8 Mercer's Tungsten October Pupa, orange Mercer's Psycho Prince, Morrish's October Pupa, Morrish's WMD, Stimulator, Madame X

Scuds (*Gammarus* spp.)
#16 olive/rust Hunchback Scud, Pregnant Scud, Sparkle Scud

the top spots for fish, and walk past the lesser water. In this way you will spend the most time fishing in the quality places.

Below the dead end on Hirschdale Road, the river enters a long canyon referred to as the Grand Canyon of the Truckee. The two primary ways to fish this water are to either hike up from the bottom or scramble down from I-80, which is not a great idea.

Trout expert Robert J. Behnke's explanation of how this part of the country evolved and brought forth special trout is provocative and striking to the imagination. The Truckee River flows between Lake Tahoe and Pyramid Lake, where the only native trout is the Lahontan cutthroat trout.

Lake Tahoe cutthroat trout were eliminated by 1940 due to a blockage of spawning tributaries and the introduction of nonnative lake trout, and the massive Pyramid Lake variation also went extinct that same year. Pyramid Lake produced the largest trout in the world as well as the official angling record for that species, which weighed 41 pounds. There are unauthenticated claims from Indian commercial fishermen of one Lahontan that weighed 62 pounds.

In ancient times parts of northern California, Nevada, and Oregon were covered in vast expanses of freshwater Great Basin lakes. Lake Lahontan was the second-largest of these, and is estimated to have been about the size of Lake Erie. Conditions in this huge body of water allowed the cutthroat trout to thrive at the top of the aquatic food chain and reach extraordinary sizes. Pyramid Lake is the sump (lowest elevation) of the ancient Lahontan basin. More and more water was being diverted from the Truckee, so spawning of Pyramid Lake cutthroat trout dwindled down to almost nothing.

According to Behnke, the last spawning run of these huge native fish occurred in 1938 in the Truckee River. There were spawning fish in the river when the last of the water was shut off. Witnesses counted 195 dying trout with an average length of 36 inches and average weight of 20 pounds each. In the 1800s the Lahontans in Pyramid Lake, Walker Lake, and Lake Tahoe would have had a total weight in the millions of pounds.

The Lahontan cutthroat trout in Pyramid Lake today are from non-Pyramid Lake parental sources, reared in a hatchery and stocked into the lake. While these trout provide a popular fishery for trout that are, by today's standards, big fish, they lack the hereditary basis to ever reach the proportions of the original, extinct strain.

There are efforts to reestablish self-sustaining populations of Lahontan cutthroat trout in the Truckee River basin, mainly in the headwaters of the Upper Truckee River. But if the historical profile of interaction between native species and introduced fish holds true in this case, the hardier nonnatives will likely prevail. Wild brown trout, now at the top of the Truckee River food chain, are especially difficult to extirpate, but they sure are fun to catch. ∎

Truckee Seasons

Though the Truckee is open all winter long, with sporadic exceptions, it begins to turn on in May when access to the river becomes easier and *Baetis* are hatching. During these times, especially when the fish haven't seen a lot of anglers, Truckee River fish will take tiny dry flies during the hatch, which often peaks just before dark. When the fish are feeding on the surface, a #18-

The Truckee holds plenty of fish larger than this one, but the abundance of these little guys only bodes well for the future of the fishery.

20 Quigley's Hat Creek Spider or Quigley Cripple will take fish. Nymphing in the afternoon can also be productive with Mercer's Glass Bead Micro Mayfly, Mercer's Poxyback Baetis, Mercer's Micro Mayfly, Morrish's Anato-May, Morrish's Hotwire May, or a Beadhead Pheasant Tail.

By June the river is usually in prime condition and hatches and feeding go with a vengeance. Be prepared to encounter Green Drakes, March Browns, PMDs, Golden Stones, Yellow Sallies, and various species of caddisflies. This can be a frustrating time for anglers and some people don't really know where to begin. At least Truckee fish on a feeding frenzy are not known to be that selective. Concentrate on fishing your nymphs or dry flies accurately and with a dead-drift, and you are likely to pick up fish, providing you are using a fly that might be taken as one of several of the naturals present.

The insects of June represent the major hatch period of the year, just before the river goes into torpor during the hot months of summer. Of course there are still bugs around, but the flush hatch activity of June will not be repeated until next year. But, the summer doldrums should not keep you from fishing, they just make the fishing less predictable. I've had great success at this time of the year fishing a #12 brown Birds Nest. I developed my own variation of this trusted pattern by adding a dubbing incorporating Australian opossum, teal wings and tail, and a tungsten bead. Veteran angler Andy Burk turned me on to Australian opossum years ago, and it's been a staple on my tying bench ever since. Other general nymph patterns worth fishing are Gold-Ribbed Hare's Ear, Pheasant Tail Nymphs, and Copper Johns. Scuds are also part of the mix, and the Hunchback Scud, Pregnant Scud, and Sparkle Scud may be good choices. Evening hatches can also be intense. Dry flies well worth fishing include Sparkle Duns, Paraduns, Mercer's Profile Spinner, and the Elk Hair Caddis.

The Truckee can be a great place to fish hoppers during late summer. Some days a well-fished hopper pattern will actually outfish nymphs under a strike indicator. There are, of course, a number of good hopper patterns out there, but I often find myself with a box of Sloan's Persuaders on hand, and they seem to do just as well as a hopper as they do imitating a Golden Stone, *Skwala*, or October Caddis.

The October Caddis hatch on the Truckee begins in September. The nymphs begin their migration toward boulders and stream banks during the afternoons, so nymphs such as Mercer's Poxyback Hare's Ear Nymph, Mercer's Tungsten October Caddis, Red Fox Squirrel Nymphs, and Mercer's Psycho Prince Nymph work well during the day. Dry flies for the evening spinner fall include Sloan's Persuaders, Morrish's October Caddis, Stimulators, or Madame Xs.

By October the warm temperatures of summer have passed and the days are beginning to get shorter again. The *Baetis* return for a second go, and they can provide some great midday dry-fly fishing. This is the last major hatch activity of the year before cold, snowy weather sets in again, but there are still a few good options, especially if you like big browns. Try spending a day on the Truckee fishing a sinking-tip line with Mercer's Rag Sculpin, Morrish's Sculpin, Woolly Buggers, and Haddon's Dead Drift Crayfish to catch some of the river's biggest fish.

The first time I fished the Truckee I escaped from an afternoon at Circus-Circus in Reno, dropping in to fish the Hirschdale area. In those days I expected browns, but had a banner day connected to wild rainbows instead. The day was especially sweet because there weren't any flashing lights or the protracted sounds of casino gambling anywhere to interrupt my serenity. I knew so much less about the river in those days and how to fish it. The good news is almost any reasonable angler can crack the river's code.

There is plenty of Truckee River to fish, and chances are you can find a place to have all to yourself. The fishing isn't easy, but then most things worth

Guide Jay Cockrum with a fine Truckee rainbow. Most of the fish are wild, but some stocked fish move down into the Glenshire area from the private club up above.

Big boulders often carve out deep holes providing the deeper habitat preferred by larger trout. Target these areas, making sure your nymphs are drifting deep enough.

cherishing seldom are. Parts of the river are within sight of historic railroad trestles and I-80, the entire river painting an artery on a landscape that has served Native Americans, pioneers, cowboys, gold miners, and devoted anglers. Perhaps we love some rivers for more than their great fishing. Maybe we love them because they're there.

Mercer's Tungsten October Pupa

Hook:	#8-10 Tiemco 2302
Bead:	Black tungsten
Thread:	Camel 8/0 Uni-Thread
Abdomen:	October Caddis Mercer's Buggy Nymph Dubbing
Rib:	Pearl Flashabou
Carapace:	Dyed brown marabou
Underwing:	Dyed brown clump of marabou
Overwing:	Shimazaki Aero Dry Wing
Antennae:	Pair of natural ring-necked-pheasant-tail fibers
Hackle:	Golden brown mottled hen back
Collar:	Same as abdomen
Head:	Dyed brown ostrich herl

Mercer's Glo-Bubble Caddis (Olive)

Hook: #12-18 Tiemco 3769
Bead: Copper
Thread: Olive 8/0 Uni-Thread
Body: Olive Midge Tubing and light olive
           Z-lon (kinky)
Legs: Golden brown mottled grouse
           or hen-back fibers
Wing Case: Brown Thin Skin
Thorax: Peacock herl

Mercer's Biot Epoxy Dark Stone

Hook: #6-12 Tiemco 2302
Bead: Gold
Thread: Camel 8/0 Uni-Thread
Antennae: Brown turkey biots
Tail: Same as antennae
Underbody: Round lead-substitute wire strips
           down both sides of hook shank
Abdomen: Brown turkey biots
Wing Case: Golden brown mottled turkey tail
           coated with 5-minute epoxy
Thorax: Dark Stone Mercer's Buggy
           Nymph Dubbing
Legs: Golden brown mottled hen-back
           feather
Head: Same as thorax

Mercer's Stubby Stone

Hook: #8-14 Tiemco 2499SP-BL
Bead: Black tungsten
Thread: Dark brown 8/0 Uni-Thread
Tail: Rusty brown turkey or goose biots
Rib: Black Ultra Wire
Carapace: Black Thin Skin with strip of pearl
           Flashabou down the center
Abdomen: Golden Stone Mercer's Buggy
           Nymph Dubbing
Thorax: Peacock herl
Wing Case: Black Thin Skin
Legs: Brown Mini Centipede Legs
Head: Peacock herl
Antennae: Same as legs

John Barr's Copper John

Hook:	#10-20 Tiemco 3769
Thread:	Black 8/0 Uni-Thread
Bead:	Gold
Tail:	Brown goose biots
Body:	Copper wire
Thorax:	Peacock herl
Wing Case:	Thin Skin and pearl Flashabou with a drop of 5-minute epoxy
Legs:	Hen back or Hungarian partridge

Haddon's Dead Drift Crayfish

Hook:	#8 Tiemco 5262
Thread:	Black 6/0 Danville
Eyes:	1/8-inch chrome bead chain
Weight:	.020 lead or lead-free wire
Mouth-parts:	Hot orange rabbit
Antennae:	Ring-necked-pheasant-tail fibers and orange Krystal Flash
Back:	Mottled-oak orange Thin Skin
Claws:	Gold variant rabbit strip
Rib:	Black Ultra Wire (small)
Body:	Olive Wapsi Sow Scud Dubbing
Hackle:	Natural brown saddle hackle

Cal Bird's Birds Nest (Brown)

Hook:	#8-16 Tiemco 3761
Thread:	Brown 8/0 Uni-Thread
Tail:	Wood-duck fibers
Rib:	Copper wire
Abdomen:	Brown Australian opossum
Legs:	Wood-duck fibers
Thorax:	Same as abdomen

Brad McFall lifts a brown for client Luc Paquet. Fall is not only a great time to fish Owens Valley streams, but brown trout get much more aggressive at this time of year.
BRAD MCFALL PHOTO

FLY FISHING
EASTERN SIERRA

Eastern Sierra Fly Shops and Guides

East Walker River

Brad McFall
P.O. Box 2515
Mammoth Lakes, CA 93546
(209) 484-1114
mammothflyfishing.com

Ken's Sporting Goods
P.O. Box 544
Bridgeport, CA 93517
(760) 932-7707
kenssport.com

Owens River Fly Shop
2212 North Sierra Highway
Bishop, CA 93514
(760) 872-3830
owensriverflyshop.com

Pat Jaeger
Eastern Sierra Guide Service
(760) 872-7770
jaeger-flyfishing.com

Reel Mammoth Adventures
(760) 924-0438
reelmammothadventures.com

The Trout Fly
2987 Main Street
Mammoth Lakes, CA 93546
(760) 934-2517
thetroutfly.com

Upper Owens River

Brad McFall
P.O. Box 2515
Mammoth Lakes, CA 93546
(209) 484-1114
mammothflyfishing.com

(continued)

The high-desert area around the towns of Mammoth Lakes and Bridgeport is big country and an austere landscape. That it only has an average precipitation of less than ten inches and is seemingly devoid of much life makes the three fertile streams, rich with bugs and fish, covered in this section of the book seem completely out of place. Because of the severity of the landscape, the things that are here, mainly mountains and blue sky, take on a more dominate role. Big-city dwellers prone to claustrophobia flock here for the sheer openness of the territory, and many experience a renewed feeling of being able to breathe again. The air is light as a dry martini with a hint of sage.

The Walker River above Bridgeport Reservoir holds some of the biggest brown trout I've ever seen, a fact that seems doubly outrageous considering its relatively small size. The nutrient base in Bridgeport Reservoir produces an incredibly rich cocktail supercharged with vegetable sediment that renders the water a funky brown color healthy beyond belief.

The Owens arrives on stage rather suddenly, bubbling out of the earth in a crystal spring. A meadow stream, it saunters down the valley like a curious shopper in his favorite store going this way and that. Valley grasses gather along its serpentine course, producing an almost endless bounty of ants, grasshoppers, and beetles, and the trout gorge on them.

183

Upper Owens River (continued)

Owens River Fly Shop
2212 North Sierra Highway
Bishop, CA 93514
(760) 872-3830
owensriverflyshop.com

Pat Jaeger
Eastern Sierra Guide Service
(760) 872-7770
jaeger-flyfishing.com

Sierra Drifters
(760) 935-4250
sierradrifters.com

The Trout Fly
2987 Main Street
Mammoth Lakes, CA 93546
(760) 934-2517
thetroutfly.com

You can usually find solitude on the upper Owens, as long as you don't mind hiking a bit.

Hot Creek carries the distinction of having the densest wild-trout population of any stream in California. It is extremely small, yet extremely rich. Were it not for all the aquatic vegetation, you might mistake it as an extension of the Hot Creek Hatchery just upstream. But this marvelous creek does not need any help to produce wild trout packed as densely as cordwood within its banks and preferring aquatic insects to food pellets.

While tucked away from California's major population centers, this area is mainly a refuge for southern Californians, and the town of Mammoth Lakes has evolved to serve that user group. There's hardly anything you might want while away from home that isn't available in Mammoth winter or summer, including several good fly shops. The only trick becomes avoiding the crowds that flock to the eastern Sierra on weekends and holidays.

If you cannot fish except prime weekends, don't bother with Hot Creek. It's likely to be the first place to fill up with anglers. There is usually open water on the upper Owens provided you don't mind hiking a bit, and the mountain scenery is dazzling. The least likely place to fill up is the East Walker, but it's an hour haul north if you're headquartering in Mammoth. It's worth checking out the Miracle Mile section first, since you have to drive past it on your way downstream. But there is plenty of good water as you head downstream toward the Nevada border. Look for turnouts along the road where no other cars are parked.

The Eastern Sierra is big country with plenty of big fish under a big Western sky. It's also the perfect venue for a big escape, one of the most important reasons we go fishing in the first place.

Hot Creek

Owens River Fly Shop
2212 North Sierra Highway
Bishop, CA 93514
(760) 872-3830
owensriverflyshop.com

Pat Jaeger
Eastern Sierra Guide Service
(760) 872-7770
jaeger-flyfishing.com

Reel Mammoth Adventures
(760) 924-0438
reelmammothadventures.com

The Trout Fly
2987 Main Street
Mammoth Lakes, CA 93546
(760) 934-2517
thetroutfly.com

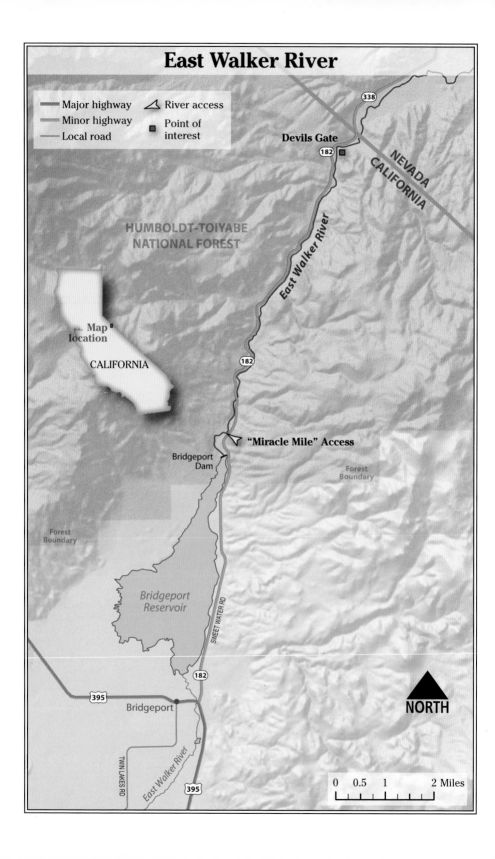

East Walker River

- Major highway
- Minor highway
- Local road
- River access
- Point of interest

Devils Gate

NEVADA
CALIFORNIA

338

182

East Walker River

HUMBOLDT-TOIYABE NATIONAL FOREST

Map location

CALIFORNIA

182

"Miracle Mile" Access

Bridgeport Dam

Forest Boundary

Forest Boundary

Bridgeport Reservoir

SWEET WATER RD

182

395 Bridgeport

TWIN LAKES RD

East Walker River

395

NORTH

0   0.5   1   2 Miles

CHAPTER 12

East Walker River

Every time I'm in the town of Bridgeport I get the wry sensation I may have seen too many spaghetti westerns as a youth. Walking out the door of Ken's Sporting Goods, if I weren't so excited about fishing the East Walker River, I might be tempted to give in to the fantasy: *At the end of the long, deserted street outside stands the lone figure of Clint Eastwood, waiting, a cheroot smoldering in his teeth and his poncho shifted to one side exposing the sweeping handle of his pistola.*

But if he's standing between me and fishing the East Walker, Clint might just have his hands full.

This quaint little Western town is nestled within view of the stunning mountains of the Eastern Sierra below Lake Tahoe and above Mammoth Lakes. It is the gateway to the East Walker River, and though it begins in the hills south of town, the real fishing begins below Bridgeport Reservoir. From the dam the river flows northeast about seven miles to the Nevada border and has earned a reputation for big wild fish—especially brown trout with the proportions of livestock. Considering what this amazing fishery has been through, it's a wonder there are any fish in it at all.

In 1988, shortly after I had fished the river for the first time and been captivated by it, a plume of sediment from Bridgeport Reservoir swept down the river completely destroying the fishery. Great efforts since then have brought the fishery back to its former glory, and it seems to be fishing better and better every year.

This is a year-round fishery protected by special angling regulations requiring barbless artificial lures or flies. Anglers may harvest one trout 18 inches or larger from the last Saturday of April through November 15. From mid-November until the last Saturday of April, anglers must release all trout. The water has a distinct brownish cast to it, and wading certain sections is reminiscent of northern California's Pit River. Bring a wading staff.

August can be very dry in the Owens Valley, and the sagebrush landscape takes on a grayish hue. Brannon Santos doesn't bother with waders during the summer since he will be dry within ten minutes of leaving the water.

Once you land a fish, do all you can to ensure the fish is ready to be turned loose. Not enough anglers devote enough time to this vitally important task. BRAD MCFALL PHOTO

Fishing Overview

Trout thrive not only on the diverse menu of aquatic insects, but also on several different varieties of baitfish that proliferate here. As a result anglers catch some very large wild rainbows and browns. The average trout probably goes a solid 15 to 16 inches. Biologists claim there are more browns than rainbows in the East Walker, but most days you will probably catch more rainbows. The most productive technique is usually indicator nymphing, but that doesn't mean dry flies or streamers are out of the question. In general it's a good idea to begin with nymphs, and let the river tell you if another technique is called for.

From Bridgeport take CA 22 north past the reservoir and park in any of the rough parking areas below the dam. Anglers refer to this stretch of river as the Miracle Mile, and it tends to get more fishing pressure than areas downstream. But when parts of rivers become popular, there's often a good reason for it. There are generally more trout in this well-oxygenated section, and lots of big fish. The water flows through gentle, rolling hills, and the fresh smell of sage is often in the air. Willows contain much of the river, and they contribute shady places for trout to hide and ambush terrestrials in late summer.

Almost a separate fishery in and of itself, the pool below the dam is referred to as Big Hole. This is typically a place where anglers are throwing big sculpin patterns and Woolly Buggers on sinking-tip lines hoping to connect with some of the river's more carnivorous trout. Intermittent reinforcement can be a powerful thing, and all it takes is one or two of these guys to hook into a monster trout to keep everyone coming back. JRs Baitfish, Conehead Kiwi Sculpin, Lawson's CH Woolhead Sculpin, and Morrish's Sculpin (#2-4) are great options. This routine is often more about fishing than catching, but the rewards, when they come, can be tremendous and well worth the effort. The best times are dawn and dark.

High-stick nymphing through a Miracle Mile run is a great strategy. Despite the often nearly opaque water, this upper section of the East Walker holds a tremendous number of wild rainbows and browns.

Below Big Hole the river twists and turns through the sage and willows in a pattern of riffles, runs, and occasional pools. The water up here is somewhat more difficult to read than other rivers because of the translucent quality of the flow. In late summer when the reservoir is in full algae bloom, translucent quickly becomes full-on opaque.

The other factor that affects water quality and often determines if fishing the river is a good idea at all is the river level. Releases from beneath the dam change frequently, and sometimes radically from month to month and year to year. Average flows stated here are based on the last seven or eight years, but at times can be radically different. Regardless of specific flows, the river is rarely unfishable. Go to Ken's Sporting Goods' website (kenssport.com) to click on a link that has daily flow information.

CA 22 crosses over the river, and from there the road is to the northwest side. The hills enclosing the river give way to more canyonlike surroundings, and the river cascades over many good pocketwater sections, which are also generally much less crowded then the water above. This section extends to the Nevada border and offers plenty of opportunities to get away from the crowds in a gorgeous, secluded desert landscape.

Short-line nymphing with two nymphs, caddis, or mayfly patterns is effective in this pocketwater. Using two to four medium size split-shot about 10 inches above the first fly, smack your nymphs down into the water driving them deep in the water column, then lift your rod removing all slack from your line and leader. Move the rod downstream as fast as you need to in order to keep slack out, and watch the end of your fly line for the slightest hesitation or twitch. This is fast, physical fishing that can bring outstanding results if you are fit and rugged. Don't fish too long in one place, but move fairly rapidly from spot to spot adding or removing split-shot as necessary to keep your nymphs on the fishes' noses.

Seasons

Beginning in February, the river often begins to show signs of coming to life. The potential for frigid conditions and nasty weather is still very real, but on some warmer days there may be tiny midges or *Skwala* stoneflies popping. This fishery is largely midge-driven during colder months, and anglers should never overlook the value of fishing #18-24 nymphs. Just about any reasonable midge pupa imitation is a good choice, and I keep a good selection of Beaded Zebra Midges, Brassies, Marlee Zebra Midges, and CB Frostbite Midges are in my box at all times. It's not uncommon for midges skating along the surface of the water to ball up into clusters gaining the attention of the fish. A good basic imitation like a #16 Griffith's Gnat is a great choice for these times. Good *Skwala* nymphs include #8-10 Mercer's Tungsten Skwala Nymph, Mercer's Stubby Stone, and Morrish's Cone Stone, and a #8-10 Sloan's Persuader is as good a dry fly as you're going to find should the occasion call for it.

Guide Brannon Santos with a small rainbow taken on a midge pupa imitation. A lot of anglers visit the water below the dam for the summer dry-fly fishing just before dark.

EAST WALKER RIVER HATCHES

	JAN	FEB	MAR	APR	MAY	JUN	JUL	AUG	SEP	OCT	NOV	DEC

Midges (Diptera)
#16-24 Zebra Midge, Brassie, Marlee Zebra Midge, CB Frostbite Midge, Quigley's Hat Creek Spider, Griffith's Gnat

Blue-Winged Olive
(*Baetis* spp.)
#18-24 Mercer's Poxyback Baetis, olive Mercer's Micro Mayfly, Morrish's Anato-May, Morrish's Hotwire May, Beadhead Pheasant Tail, WD-40, Quigley's Hat Creek Spider, Quigley Cripple, Quigley's Female Baetis Hackle Stacker

Skwala (*Skwala* spp.)
#8-10 Mercer's Tungsten Skwala Nymph, Mercer's Stubby Stone, Morrish's Cone Stone, Sloan's Persuader, Mercer's Flush Floater Foam Stone

Golden Stonefly
(*Calineuria* spp.)
#6-8 golden Morrish's Cone Stone, Mercer's Biot Epoxy Golden Stone, Superfloss Rubberlegs, Golden Stone, Idyl-Wired Stone, Mercer's Flush Floater Foam Stone, Stimulator, Madame X

Pale Morning Dun
(*Ephemerella* spp.)
#16-18 yellow Morrish's Anato-May, rust Morrish's Hotwire May, Mercer's GB Poxyback PMD, brown or ruby Mercer's Micro Mayfly, Burk's HBI Nymph, Sparkle Dun, Paradun, Mercer's PMD Profile Spinner

Sulphur (*Epeorus* spp.)
#10-12 yellow Mercer's Foam Parachute Sulphur, Neally's Brown Drake, Paradun, Haystack, Mercer's Poxyback Emerger

Green Rockworm
(*Rhyacophila* spp.)
#18 green Mercer's Z-Wing Caddis, Mercer's Glo-Bubble Caddis, Fox's Poopah, Morrish's Hotwire Caddis, Elk Hair Caddis, Cutter's E/C Caddis

Caddis
(*Brachycentrus/Hydropsyche* spp.)
#12-16 brown Birds Nest, Copper John, Mercer's Z-Wing Caddis, Mercer's Glo-Bubble Caddis, Fox's Poopah, Morrish's Hotwire Caddis, Morrish's Super Pupa, Gordon's Prince Nymph, Mercer's Missing Link

Little Yellow Stone
(*Isoperla* spp.)
#14 yellow Morrish's Iron Sally, Quigley's Stacker Sally

Grasshoppers
#6-8 Sloan's Persuader, Dave's Foam Hopper, Idylwilde Parachute Hopper, Neversink Hopper

As the weather continues to warm, flows will gradually increase from an average of about 50 cubic feet per second (cfs) in February to around 80 cfs in March. *Baetis* typically become active; and nymphing with #18-22 Mercer's Glass Bead Micro Mayfly, Mercer's Poxyback Baetis, Mercer's Micro Mayfly, Morrish's Anato-May, Morrish's Hotwire May, and Beaded Pheasant Tail Nymphs is effective.

It's much more common to take trout on nymphs than dry flies on the East Walker, but on some days you can tempt fish to the surface with #18-24 Quigley's Sparkle Stacker, Quigley's Hat Creek Spider, or a Quigley's Female Baetis Hackle Stacker. The water is never entirely clear on the East Walker, so you can get away with fishing 5X tippets with the tiniest of dry flies. Depend-

One deadly tactic on the East Walker is picking a small, likely looking spot and fishing it thoroughly. The brownish patina of the water allows careful anglers to get close to the fish. BRAD MCFALL PHOTO

ing on the water you're fishing, you may need to lengthen your leader by a few feet to get the drag-free drift you're looking for.

The fishing gets progressively better in April as more hatches come into play and flows continue their easy ascent into the 140 cfs range. The river is swelling and fish are less prone to pod up since they now have more habitat to work with. April usually signals the start of Golden Stones, Little Yellow Stones, *Brachycentrus* and *Hydropsyche* caddisflies, and Pale Morning Duns. Continue nymphing unless you notice actively rising fish, especially in the last hour of light when the sun is off the water. Rainbows generally spawn in late spring, so treat these fish with great care when releasing them so they may live to spawn again.

In May and June, the East Walker is in full bloom. In addition to most of the insects that were hatching in April, *Epeorus* mayflies and Green Rockworm caddis are added to the menu. The big Epeorus mayflies can inspire fish to start hitting on the surface, and if you're there at the right time, usually late morning, this hatch can be a hoot. Mercer's Foam Parachute Sulphur, Neally's Brown Drake, Paraduns, Haystacks, or Yellow Humpies (#10-12) are all good choices.

River levels enter the 240 cfs range in May, and then reach their annual zenith in June at around the 325 cfs range. Flows will gradually shrink from here on out, and there is more than ten times the water in the river in June as there is in November. June is the banner month for the river, with nymphs working well during the day and dry flies just before dark. Of course dry-fly fishing on the East Walker is never a sure thing, but if you're going to find rising fish, it's more likely to be on long June evenings.

Like a lot of desert trout streams, hatches stall a bit during the hottest months of the year. Not that you can't hit some great fishing on certain days, but the fish are clearly not as interested in feeding as they were in the spring. Due to the large proportion of browns in the river that feed at night, many anglers choose to fish at this time. The nighttime summer sky in this area is a sight to behold, with a million twinkling lights and frequent shooting stars. Evening is also an excellent time to encounter a rattlesnake or mountain lion in this neighborhood, so be careful.

Caddisflies seem to be more abundant during the summer season, so fishing caddis pupa imitations is a great idea. During the day, try fishing #12-16 Mercer's Glo-Bubble Caddis, Fox's Poopah, Mercer's Missing Link Caddis, or Morrish's Hotwire Caddis. While caddis is certainly king most summer days, the PMDs seem to own the night. My best success for the evening grab has been on #14-16 yellow Paraduns.

Not enough people fish terrestrials on the East Walker. During August and September there are plenty of hoppers, ants, and beetles around, and the

There aren't a lot of streams capable of sustaining good populations of wild browns of this caliber, but the East Walker is one. A lucky angler lifts this hook-jawed male before returning it to the water. BRAD MCFALL PHOTO

While better known for large wild browns, the East Walker holds some very nice rainbows as well. BRAD MCFALL PHOTO

fish know it. The river's high banks are just loaded with grass, brush, and trees hanging out over the water. On gusty summer afternoons quite a few of these land insects end up dog-paddling for the shore after an abrupt dunking. Trout will often murder these, especially hoppers, a moment or two after they hit the water. Delicacy is not needed. Just smack your fly down as close to the bank as possible, especially in areas of deeper water. The only difficult part of this fishing is in not breaking the fish off on the take. I go with 4X tippet and still break off some fish.

As early as September the browns in the river may welcome a juicy sculpin or Woolly Bugger twitched past their noses on a sinking-tip line and stout 1X tippet. Browns are always worthy fish, but when they get in that spawning mode, and for at least a month before, they develop an attitude. There are some truly impressive browns in this river. Back in the 1980s I clearly remember spotting a brown trout as wide as some of the fish I'd caught that day were long. I didn't have a sinking-tip line with me that day and only ended up putting the fish down with my sloppy casting. Fact is, the size of that fish freaked me out, and I'm certain my hands were shaking when I tied on the fly. I remember it slowly sounding, and sinking back down out of sight. Brown trout over 20 inches are not uncommon on the East Walker, and fish in the 27- to 30-inch range are caught each year. Even if I don't hook one of these, it's somehow good to know there are fish that size in the river, and my next cast could be the one.

Very often during November, December, and January, the dam is only releasing a trickle of water, which robs the stream of dissolved oxygen and causes the trout to pod up in the deepest places they can find. Fish hooked under these conditions must be treated very carefully, landed as quickly as possible, and not removed from the water for more than a few seconds at a time. Some understanding anglers just give the fish a little time off during these low-flow periods, and I'm not sure that's such a bad idea. Some years, snow and ice make winter fishing difficult or even impossible. But every angler understands that sometimes every passionate fly fisher just needs to fish. Most are willing to do so in the least intrusive manner possible, and catch-and-release with barbless hooks is no problem at all. Many of us fish this way all the time.

During the low water of winter, the fish can be very spooky. Give some thought to how you approach the stream, and be mindful of treading lightly. If there are any bushes or trees along the stream, try to use them for cover. Remember the fish are facing into the current; quietly sneak up from behind. There is little room for sloppy casting at times like this, and while few of us make perfect casts every time, pay particular attention to making smooth, liquid movements and avoiding being abrupt with anything except setting the hook.

Morrish's Sculpin (Brown)

Hook:	#2-4 Tiemco 3761
Eyes:	Dumbbell eyes painted white and black
Thread:	Black 6/0 Danville
Tail:	Pearl Flashabou Accent
Body:	Pearl Flashabou Accent
Underwing:	Pearl Flashabou Accent
Overwing:	Light brown rabbit zonker strip
Belly:	Dark brown rabbit zonker strip
Cheeks:	Brown dyed grizzly hen-cape feathers
Head:	Dark brown rabbit fur trimmed off hide and tied in dubbing loop

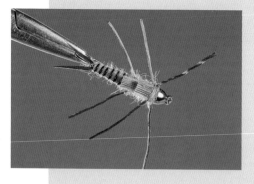

Morrish's Cone Stone (Golden)

Hook:	#4-8 Tiemco 5263
Cone:	Black nickel
Weight:	.020-.030 lead or lead-free wire
Thread:	Black 6/0 Danville
Tail:	Brown goose biot
Rib:	Black Ultra Wire
Abdomen/ Thorax:	Olive brown STS Trilobal dubbing and Tri/Hare-Tron Custom Golden Stone Blend
Legs:	Brown Lumaflex
Back:	White-tipped turkey tail coated with flexible lacquer
Wing Cases:	White-tipped turkey tail coated with flexible lacquer

John Engler's WD-40 (Ruby)

Hook:	#16-22 Tiemco 2487
Thread:	Red 8/0 Uni-Thread
Tail:	Partridge or other soft hackle fibers
Body:	Tying thread
Thorax:	Gray Super Fine or Ice Dub
Wing Case:	Same as tail
Note:	Black, gray, olive are other excellent colors

GB Brassie (Copper)

Hook:	#18 Tiemco 2487
Bead:	Gold
Thread:	Black 8/0 Uni-Thread
Body:	Copper wire
Thorax:	Peacock herl
Note:	Red and green are other good colors

Zebra Midge

Hook:	#16-20 Tiemco 2487
Bead:	Silver
Thread:	Black 6/0 Uni-Thread
Body:	Black tying thread
Rib:	Silver wire

CB Frostbite

Hook:	#10-18 Tiemco 2487
Bead:	Copper
Thread:	Red 8/0 Uni-Thread
Body:	Red Flashabou
Rib:	Silver wire
Thorax:	Peacock herl
Gills:	White poly yarn

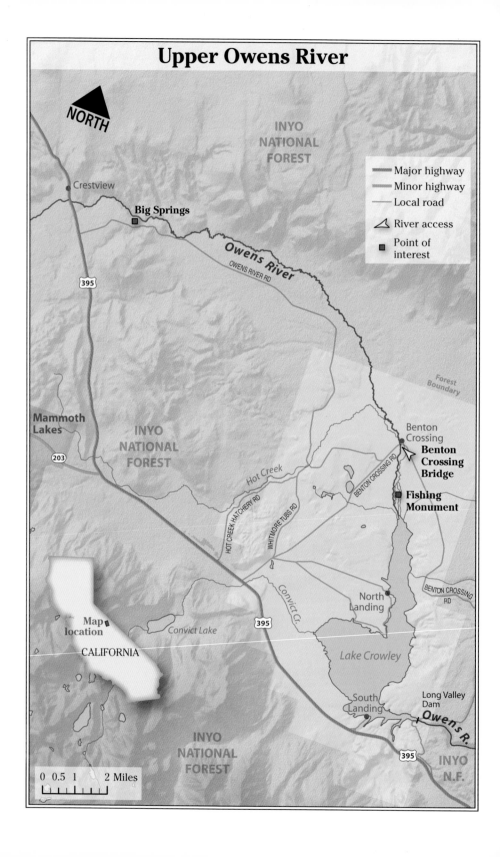

CHAPTER 13

Upper Owens River

The Owens bubbles out of the Earth and first glimpses daylight at a place aptly called Big Springs. From here it meanders through high desert meadows 15 miles before pausing in Lake Crowley before heading off again downstream to supply water to thirsty Los Angeles. Strangely, it is the connection to Lake Crowley coupled with the private ranches below Big Springs that allow this medium-size trout stream to contend for inclusion in the short list of California's best.

The Upper Owens has a lot going on for such a small, intimate trout stream. It has large wild rainbows and browns that run up from Lake Crowley much like steelhead. It has ample public access down low precisely balanced with private property above to protect wild fish. It has hatchery trout that provide great sport when the wild fish are in a glower mood. It has tremendous hatches and plenty of food for fish beneath a backdrop of the majestic Sierra Nevada on one side, and the White Mountains on the other. Yet it is some of these very attributes that conspire to make the fishing some of the toughest, and most rewarding, around.

This is flat, clear spring creek water. There is little by way of riparian habitat save the abundant grasses lining both banks. To put it simply, these trout can tell what color shoelaces you're wearing at forty paces, and there are no bushes to hide your approach. This little trout stream will test all of your skills and inspire you to learn the ones you haven't developed yet. On the other hand, these fish aren't impossible and wild fish average 12 inches, with many larger fish around. The Owens has tested positive for New Zealand mud snails so, despite the great fishing, hardly anyone wade fishes here anymore. The best strategy is to make longer casts standing well back from the stream.

High-stick nymphing is one of the best strategies for fishing the Owens, which is open year-round. JOHN SHERMAN PHOTO

How It Fishes

It helps to know there are lots of trout in this water, even if they are not cooperating on any given day. Biologists calculate at least 6,000 to 8,000 fish per mile, and some sections have more than that. Wherever you go on this river, you are in the right place for good fishing. Flat out, there are so many fish in this river it's almost funny to imagine getting skunked. On the other hand, the easy fish are hatchery-bred, and you can catch those in a lot of other places. The main event on the Owens is the healthy population of larger wild rainbows and browns, including some monster that has swum up from Crowley. The big rainbows are mainly there in the spring; the browns in the fall. The possibility of hooking a really large trout in skinny water maintains a devoted following on this river.

Open yearlong or not, it isn't always a good idea to fish the Upper Owens. Winters can bring subzero temperatures, lots of snow, and high winds. That's not to say you should stay home if you just have to fish, but proceed with

The upper Owens is a classic meadow stream sometimes offering tight meanders and great holding water beneath a backdrop of staggering mountain vistas.

In California many of the angling regulations are written so only Supreme Court Justices with a highly developed sense of ESP can interpret them. The regs can be a little intimidating on the Upper Owens. The public water between Lake Crowley and the private water above is divided about in half by the Benton Crossing Road Bridge.

The river above Benton Crossing Road Bridge is open to angling year-round and only barbless artificial lures or flies may be used. From the last Saturday in April through November 15, two fish may be harvested above the bridge, and none at all from November 16 until the last Saturday in April.

If you're fishing below Benton Crossing Road Bridge down to the Upper Owens River Fishing Monument, any method of take is acceptable and five fish may be harvested. This section is not open to fishing year-round like the water above, and it opens the Saturday preceding Memorial Day and closes September 30.

The last quarter mile above Crowley Lake, from the Upper Owens River Fishing Monument downstream, has a different season. From the last Saturday in April through July 31, five trout may be harvested. From August 1 through November 15 only barbless artificial lures or flies may be used, and two trout of 18 inches or over may be harvested. ■

Steer clear of trouble by fishing barbless hooks and releasing all you catch. Before releasing fish, spend time reviving them.

Greedy trout are apt to grab a well-drifted dry fly, but your approach to rising fish on the upper Owens needs to be low and quiet. Too much motion or vibration along the banks will put the fish down.

caution. Anglers have been known to access the river using snowmobiles. On the other hand, most of us have done crazier things. Snow is a probability through March depending on the year. In drier years there may be some great fishing to be had early in the year. But don't underestimate how cold it may get.

Tiny insects proliferate in the river. Midges are an important item on the trout's menu during all the cooler months. *Baetis* are also present during cool weather and are often active enough to get the trout feeding. #18-22 Zebra Midges, Mercer's Micro Mayfly, and Morrish's Anato-May are great choices for nymph fishing. If trout are rising, you may need to lengthen your leader to 12 feet and drop down to 6X, but tiny dry flies work well. Bob Quigley's patterns are a standby in my fly boxes because so few fly designers actually make flies sparse enough to look like the real thing. Quigley's Hat Creek Spider or his Quigley Cripple will pass for either midges or tiny mayflies. Any sparsely tied dry fly #18-22 will catch fish provided it is presented well.

The first big bug you're likely to see as soon as winter has passed is the Golden Stone. This isn't a really dense hatch on the Upper Owens, but there are enough of them around to grab the attention of the big wild fish and provide some exciting evening dry-fly action. Fish a #6-8 Madame X, Stimulator, or Sloan's Persuader.

By May, the hatches are in full bloom, but the river is swollen with snowmelt for at least six weeks. But that's no reason to stay home. Some of

One excellent place to find fish is the confluence of Hot Creek and the Owens. Your chances of finding rising fish here are good almost any time.

UPPER OWENS RIVER HATCHES

	JAN	FEB	MAR	APR	MAY	JUN	JUL	AUG	SEP	OCT	NOV	DEC

Midges (Diptera)
#16-24 Zebra Midge, Brassie, Marlee Zebra Midge, CB Frostbite Midge, Quigley's Hat Creek Spider, Griffith's Gnat

Blue-Winged Olive
(*Baetis* spp.)
#18-20 Mercer's Poxyback Baetis, olive Mercer's Micro Mayfly, Morrish's Anato-May, Morrish's Hotwire May, Beadhead Pheasant Tail, WD-40, Quigley's Hat Creek Spider, Quigley Cripple

Golden Stonefly
(*Calineuria* spp.)
#6-8 golden Morrish's Cone Stone, Mercer's Biot Epoxy Golden Stone, Superfloss Rubberlegs, Golden Stone, Idyl-Wired Stone, Mercer's Flush Floater Foam Stone, Stimulator, Madame X

Pale Morning Dun
(*Ephemerella* spp.)
#16-18 yellow Morrish's Anato-May, rust Morrish's Hotwire May, Mercer's GB Poxyback PMD, brown or ruby Mercer's Micro Mayfly, Burk's HBI Nymph, Sparkle Dun, Paradun, Mercer's PMD Profile Spinner

Sulphur (*Epeorus* spp.)
#10-12 yellow Mercer's Foam Parachute Sulphur, Neally's Brown Drake, Paradun, Haystack, Mercer's Poxyback Emerger

Green Rockworm
(*Rhyacophila* spp.)
#18 green Mercer's Z-Wing Caddis, Mercer's Glo-Bubble Caddis, Fox's Poopah, Morrish's Hotwire Caddis, Elk Hair Caddis, Cutter's E/C Caddis

Caddis
(*Brachycentrus/Hydropsyche* spp.)
#12-16 brown Birds Nest, Copper John, Mercer's Z-Wing Caddis, Mercer's Glo-Bubble Caddis, Fox's Poopah, Morrish's Hotwire Caddis, Morrish's Super Pupa, Gordon's Prince Nymph, Mercer's Missing Link

the largest Crowley trout are landed in the Owens in the spring and fall, usually on nymphs. *Baetis*, Golden Stones, Pale Morning Duns, and Sulphurs are all hatching and laying eggs, and the trout spend much of their time feeding. Of course, this phenomenon has not been lost on the considerable hosts of anglers in their last throws of cabin fever, so plan on having some company.

The effect crowds of people have on wild trout is worth mentioning. Few anglers would argue that trout tend to get more wary and selective as a reaction to heavy fishing pressure. But the truth is a trout wants to go on feeding unless someone gives it reasons not to. Tough fish require a heightened predatory instinct on the part of the angler. It's time to get back to basics. First, can the trout see you? If so, move. Find a place where you can make a good presentation without alarming your prey. Is your fly small enough? Are you using a light enough tippet? It's a good strategy to spot a specific fish or pod of fish and work to them.

If you spook a fish, you have a choice of either moving on to other fish, or waiting it out. They use to call this "hoarding the cast." The idea is not to whip the water into a foamy froth by repeated casting when the fish are clearly alarmed. It's better to wait for the fish to start feeding again before you make a very careful cast or two. Make them count. It's not even a bad idea to

In the fall, Owens brown trout begin to think about spawning and aggressively hit streamers. JOHN SHERMAN PHOTO

wait a bit between casts, just so the fish don't go into that state where they would even refuse a natural. With a little patience and skill, you can hook many wary trout.

When I go to the Owens I always look for rising fish first. Most evenings during the warmer months fish will rise for an hour or two before dark. The fish do rise at other times, but evening is almost a sure thing. During summer, caddis is king, and at least three different species hatch and lay their eggs at this time. Mating swarms are common in the air on summer evenings, making a perky Elk Hair Caddis or small Stimulator a great choice. If there are no fish rising, I generally fish two nymphs under a floating strike indicator. Most days your best chance of success will be fishing small mayfly nymphs or midge pupa imitations. Don't be afraid to fish tiny flies on this river. Even the big fish love them.

The hatchery fish in the system aren't such a terrible thing either. Perhaps it's because of the richness of the Owens River, but the extent to which they displace wild fish seems negligible. Truth is, it's not a bad thing to have some easier fish around once in a while. And who can resist the urge to hook one or two of these while on your way to and from areas with more wild fish? The hatchery fish are generally lower in the river, and they don't rise in the same way as wild fish do. They show no caution at all, much to the delight of every fish-eating bird in the vicinity.

In late summer grasshoppers are everywhere. Erratic wind gusts are common in this vast, open mountain landscape, so a lot of hoppers end up in the river and, of course, in the gullets of enthusiastic trout. Fishing hoppers in a meadow stream has a few differences from fishing standard dry flies during a hatch. First, when a hopper hits the water it's an accident; an unfortunate one for the hopper and a happy one for the trout. In other words, this isn't really a "hatch" as you might normally think of one. There will probably be no rising fish to signal time to tie on a dry fly. They do not land on the water gracefully like most aquatic insects. A hopper does not drift gracefully, dead-drift down the river; it kicks and struggles and sometimes produces its own wake trying to make it back to the stream bank. During hopper time, anglers can get away with breaking most of the so-called rules of successful dry-fly fishing.

Once stuck in the surface film a hopper is trapped and an easy target for fish. This is ambush fishing and a trout will often grab the bug as soon as it hits the water, before some other greedy trout gets it. A good approach involves looking for deeper water close to the bank, ideally with grass casting a protective shadow over the water. Your cast can land with a "plop," just like the naturals, and drifts should be short. Chances are the trout will grab your fly right away, or not at all. If trout are refusing your flies, try dropping down to a smaller size. Dave's Hopper, the Idylwilde Parachute Hopper, or Sloan's Persuader (#6) are great choices.

After the heat of summer, the browns enter the stream with spawning on the mind. They are hungry and cantankerous, but avoid targeting fish on redds or in the process of spawning. Nymphing with either caddis or mayfly imitations can be very effective. *Baetis* also return with the cooling weather, and some of the big fish in the stream at this time will take dry flies.

Eight- to 9-foot rods for 3- to 8-weight floating lines work well. There is little use for sinking or sink tip lines on a stream this small. Appropriate leaders for nymphing should run about 9 feet and taper to 5X or 6X. Fluorocarbon is not an absolute necessity, but it helps in this spring-creek water. Dry flies work well on tippets 5X to 7X, depending on conditions and how small a dry fly you are throwing.

Morrish's Hotwire Caddis (Chartreuse)

Hook:	#12-16 Tiemco 2457
Bead:	Black nickel
Weight:	.015 lead or lead-free wire
Thread:	Black 6/0 Danville
Abdomen:	Chartreuse Ultra Wire
Back:	Black Flashabou Accent
Wing Case:	Rust goose biots and pearl Flashabou Accent
Legs:	Brown Hungarian partridge fibers
Head:	Dark Stone (#15) Whitlock SLF

Morrish's Hotwire Caddis (Amber)

Hook: #12-16 Tiemco 2457
Bead: Black nickel
Weight: .015 lead or lead-free wire
Thread: Black 6/0 Danville
Abdomen: Copper Ultra Wire
Back: Black Flashabou Accent
Wing Case: Rust goose biots and pearl
           Flashabou Accent
Legs: Brown Hungarian partridge fibers
Head: Dark Stone (#15) Whitlock SLF

Morrish's Biotic Nymph (Olive)

Hook: #14-16 Tiemco 2457
Bead: Black nickel
Weight: .015 lead or lead-free wire
Thread: Black 6/0 Danville
Tail: Olive pheasant-tail fibers
Rib: Black Ultra Wire
Abdomen: BWO turkey biots
Thorax: Peacock herl
Wing Case: BWO turkey biots
Legs: Hungarian partridge fibers
Head: BWO turkey biots

Morrish's Super Pupa (Bright Green)

Hook: Tiemco 2457 (#8-12);
           Tiemco 2487 (#14-16)
Bead: Black nickel
Weight: .015-.025 lead or lead-free wire
Thread: Black 6/0 Danville
Rib: Copper wire
Abdomen: Caddis green Hare-Tron
Back: Green and black Flashabou Accent
Wing Case: Same as back
Legs: Brown Hungarian partridge fibers
Head: Black Hare's Ear Plus

Mercer's Psycho Prince (Orange)

Hook:	#12-18 Tiemco 3769
Bead:	Gold
Thread:	Camel 8/0 Uni-Thread
Tail:	Dark brown turkey biots
Rib:	Copper wire
Carapace:	Dark mottled golden brown turkey-tail slip
Abdomen:	Orange Ice Dub
Wing Tuft:	Electric banana Angel Hair
Wings:	Amber turkey biots
Collar:	Natural Arizona Synthetic Peacock Dubbing

Morrish's Dirty Bird (Rust)

Hook:	#6-16 Tiemco 3761
Bead:	Black nickel
Weight:	.020-.035 lead or lead-free wire
Thread:	Black 6/0 Danville
Tail:	Hungarian partridge shoulder feather fibers
Rib:	Copper wire
Abdomen:	Fox Squirrel Nymph (#2) Whitlock SLF
Hackle:	Hungarian partridge
Wing Case:	Pearl Accent Flash
Legs:	Pearl Accent Flash
Head:	Fox Squirrel Nymph (#2) Whitlock SLF

Morrish's Dirty Bird (Hare's Ear)

Hook:	#6-16 Tiemco 3761
Bead:	Black nickel
Weight:	.020-.035 lead or lead-free wire
Thread:	Black 6/0 Danville
Tail:	Hungarian partridge shoulder feather fibers
Rib:	Copper wire
Abdomen:	Dark Stone (#15) Whitlock SLF
Hackle:	Hungarian partridge
Wing Case:	Pearl Accent Flash
Legs:	Pearl Accent Flash
Head:	Dark Stone (#15) Whitlock SLF

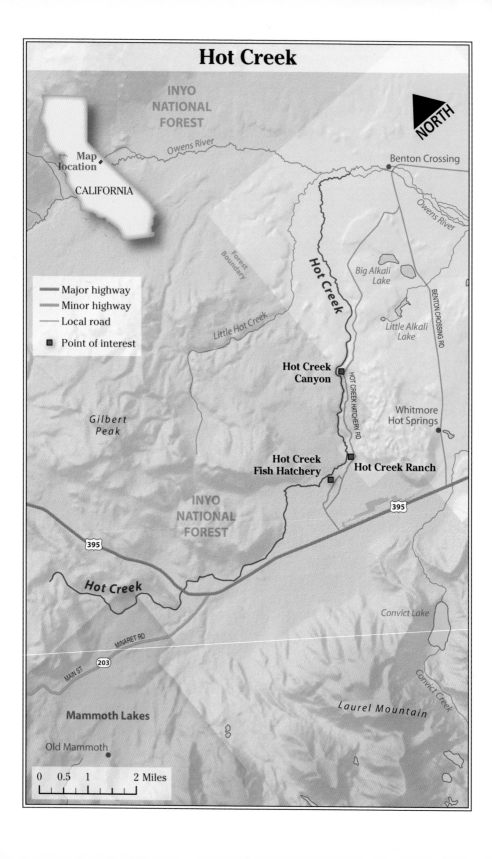

Hot Creek

INYO
NATIONAL
FOREST

NORTH

Owens River

Benton Crossing

Map
location
CALIFORNIA

Owens River

Forest Boundary

Hot Creek

Big Alkali
Lake

Little Alkali
Lake

BENTON CROSSING RD

Little Hot Creek

—— Major highway
—— Minor highway
—— Local road
■ Point of interest

Hot Creek
Canyon

HOT CREEK HATCHERY RD

Whitmore
Hot Springs

Gilbert
Peak

Hot Creek
Fish Hatchery

Hot Creek Ranch

395

INYO
NATIONAL
FOREST

395

Hot Creek

Convict Lake

MINARET RD

203

MAIN ST

Convict Creek

Mammoth Lakes

Laurel Mountain

Old Mammoth

0   0.5   1   2 Miles

CHAPTER 14

Hot Creek

Hot Creek seems better suited to an extraterrestrial landscape on one of the moons of Jupiter. Like other desert streams, it is surrounded by life that doesn't need much water. The strangely sterile landscape all around it stands in stark contrast to the tremendous richness of the river. Though it seems tiny compared with other wild-trout streams, Hot Creek contains huge numbers of wild rainbows and browns, many fish in the 16- to 18-inch range, as well as a few truly monstrous fish. There's about one mile of public water to fish. The obvious question is how could such a minuscule piece of water be counted among California's best? The answer has to do with math. Where else can you fish one mile of water, not counting the fish hatchery upstream, and potentially show your fly to 10,000 to 12,000 wild trout? Though there is only one mile of public water to fish, no other stream in California can rival that incredible density of fish per mile. In fact, the only trout stream in the United States that may surpass it is Utah's Green River.

Just think of it, 10,000 fish per mile. You would think at least a few would have to be nearsighted, unusually hungry, or just plain foolhardy. Selective, finicky trout or not, the numbers are on your side. With persistent effort, a reasonable fly, and just a little luck, chances are pretty good you're not going to get skunked at Hot Creek. Hot is also one of the few streams in California where fishing with a fly is the only option. Hooks must be barbless and all fish must be returned to the water unharmed. Few people wade Hot anymore because, like the Upper Owens, it has New Zealand mud snails. Great care must be taken not to transport this parasite to other waters. Fortunately Hot Creek is so small this is not a real disadvantage.

Finding Your Way

The Hot Creek anglers revere is really a transformed version of Mammoth Creek which flows eastward from the town of Mammoth Lakes above. Some of the water seeps through the porous ground beneath and is heated by hot

Hot's canyon section provides flat and broken water and plenty of aquatic vegetation. Every opening in the weeds is packed with trout.

lava magma from the Long Valley Caldera, the crater of a once-active ancient volcano, bubbling back into the river now known as Hot Creek. There is a short, public upper section to fish below Hot Creek Fish Hatchery, then the private Hot Creek Ranch property, and public water again below the ranch where the stream winds through Hot Creek Gorge before flowing into the Upper Owens River above Lake Crowley.

To get to the upper section, take CA 395 south from CA 203, the turnoff for Mammoth Lakes. Turn off CA 395 east on Hot Creek Hatchery Road. Just below Hot Creek Fish Hatchery park near the large bulletin board and fish either up- or downstream. This is a wide open meadow section, and with polarized glasses, you will be able to see many fish here. But if you can see the fish, they can certainly see you, so casting from your knees is a great idea. The water is a little less weedy in this section, and it doesn't normally receive the same fishing pressure as the river below the ranch.

To get to the river below Hot Creek Ranch, continue on Hot Creek Fish Hatchery Road past the sign for Hot Creek Ranch. Less than a mile farther

Upper Hot Creek is a classic meadow stream surrounded by natural beauty. In some ways it is just as satisfying to look at the mountains and big sky as it is the rich water.

The canyon section of Hot is not only known for great fishing, but Hollywood has filmed several old westerns here as well.

on you will notice several parking areas with signs stating the fishing regulations and warning you about the mud snails. Park in one of these and hike any of the many paths down to the stream. This section is often called the Hot Creek Gorge.

The gorge is the water most familiar to most anglers. At only about a hundred feet deep, the river continues to slowly chisel away at the rhyolithic lava flow forming the walls of the gorge, having escaped through a vent in the caldera about 300,000 years ago. Over time the creek has done its work to deepen and bleach the walls on either side, rendering them an almost pinkish hue. Above or below the scenery is stunning and almost enough to distract you from the fishing.

You know you've reached the downstream terminus of the good trout water when signs warn you of all the potential dangers of the actively volcanic area and misty steam rising off the water tells you something doesn't look quite right. Sober-sounding signs announce that 14 people have lost their lives or been seriously injured here since 1968. According to signs, a few of the hazards include scalding water, arsenic in the water, sudden temperature changes, sporadic high pollution, unpredictable eruptions, and unstable ground.

Happily, Hot Creek is mainly a dry-fly stream, primarily because the lush aquatic vegetation that is so important to bugs and fish is so lush that areas of open water are small. That isn't to say you can't fish nymphs at Hot Creek, but as the weather goes from cold to warm, the vegetation swells until sections of open water become smaller and smaller. By late summer, before the vegetation once again starts to recede, you have to fish fairly small areas between the weeds. Getting a proper drift in such confined spaces can be challenging. In fact, the smaller the area you're fishing, the more important casts are made with pinpoint accuracy so as to not get hung up in the weeds. This is fairly technical fishing, but there is also something almost addictive about it.

After challenging yourself against Hot Creek trout for hours at a time, it's common for your skill to take a nosedive at some point. Fewer and fewer casts will land on target and the percentage of time spent not fishing, showing your flies to fish in a lifelike manner, will skyrocket. This is a sure signal fatigue is setting in, and your brain simply refuses to give in to it. When that time arrives that you are no longer fishing Hot well, it's time to take a rest or head back in. Hot Creek trout will not suffer careless anglers for long, and your time is better spent doing something else. It's better to admit that everyone gets tired, and just call it a day.

Hot Creek's browns have a buttery gold cast to them and few spots. Guide Brannon Santos shows off a fish taken on a dry fly.

You have some options when there seem to be fish everywhere (there are), and you can't get a bite. Of course, if you insist on fishing Saturday mornings, plan on having a hard time. Realize how successful pummeling the water is in promoting the onset of lockjaw in wild trout. After 15 guys have flailed away on them already that morning, is it any wonder they aren't likely to cooperate? Saturday and Sunday mornings tend to get crowded on Hot, and there is so little water to fish anyway, I wouldn't even consider joining in on the madness.

When all else fails, there is the "try something really different" approach. I keep this as an absolute last resort and have only had to go this far a couple of time. After you've tried everything you can think of to match the hatch without success, try *not* to match the hatch. There are times, for reasons only understood by trout, when they will hit something really outlandish after passing up all the traditional fly patterns. Maybe they see something entirely different in the fly than we do. Perhaps the fish are just bored of the same old thing. Maybe it's better that some things should remain a mystery.

Another good option is to fish a small olive leech or #10 Woolly Bugger, especially if you want to try and attract larger fish. Sometimes the fish seem to want to chase something with some movement. I stay away from the beadhead versions I often fish elsewhere because of Hot's small size and incredible weed growth. Your fly should be light enough to keep from snagging on weeds with every cast.

When you spot a fish, stalk it carefully, carefully considering the best spot from which to cast, how visible you are to the fish, and what kind of a cast will result in the perfect drift. If you get lazy with your casts, dressing your fly often enough, or not fishing with a reasonable imitation of what's active in the stream at that time, your success will drop. Remember to keep a low profile as you stalk the fish. If you have to get close to the stream drop down to your knees to make the cast. These fish have seen it all, and there's no reason to make it easy for them to refuse your fly. ∎

Insect Bonanza

Hot, in addition to incredible fish numbers for its small size, has just about every aquatic insect imaginable in the West, but small insects are especially abundant. Trout feast on Hot's midges like popcorn, and #18-22 Beaded Zebra Midges, CB Frostbites, Chan's Chironomid Bombers, and Gold Bead Brassies are good choices when midges are active. When fish are rising try a Griffith's Gnat or Quigley's Hat Creek Spider #18-22 on a light tippet. A good coating of a powdered desiccant will also help your tiny dries float more naturally. *Baetis* also hatch with vigor on cooler days, especially when the weather is

Hot Creek below the hatchery is small water absolutely loaded with wild trout. Paths will take you up- or downstream, but before actually casting to rising fish, consider approaching the stream on your knees.

cloudy, and Mercer's Glass Bead Micro Mayfly, Mercer's Poxyback Baetis, Mercer's Micro Mayfly, Morrish's Anato-May, Morrish's Hotwire May, and a Beadhead Pheasant Tail will get results. During hatches try a small Quigley's Hat Creek Spider or Quigley Cripple.

The caddis get going early in the year on Hot, and several different varieties and sizes flutter around the stream as early as April. I've had my best success using smaller caddis dry flies when fish have repeatedly shunned #12-14 patterns imitating the naturals. Try a little #18 Elk Hair Caddis on a 6X

Some anglers take these shy, gentle gopher snakes for rattlesnakes. Mischievous anglers have been known to rattle their split-shot containers hoping to see their startled friends walk on water.

tippet if you can get away with it. If not drop down to 7X. A good bet for imitating the smaller caddis nymphs in the stream is a #18-20 Fox's Poopah. Scud patterns also begin turning trout in April.

By June things on Hot are really starting to pop. PMDs, Mahogany Duns, Tricos, and Green Rockworms add new layers to the aforementioned hatches. The abundance and complexities of numerous overlapping hatches has caused more than one angler to get caught up in fits of performance anxiety. But the best strategy is to relax and take a deep breath. While it's true these fish can become selective to one particular bug, or one particular stage of a hatch, they aren't all that way.

The summer Trico hatch lasts from mid-June through September. A morning hatch, it requires long, light tippets and perfect drifts with flies such as #20-22 Biot Spinners, Etha Wing Tricos, and Quigley's Hat Creek Spiders. When I tie my own Tricos, I make sure I have something more to look at than the almost invisible traditional Trico spinner patterns and tie in a sparse post of deer or elk hair in addition to the flat wings. I also sometimes fish a Haystack, which provides both the upright profile to watch on the water as well as the flush wings of a spinner.

Fishing pressure on Hot in July and August is generally light, yet the fishing can be great. With the absence of the weekend crowds, the fish are much less skittish and the experience is much more what you'd expect it to be. Fish are often rising in the open areas between lush blankets of vegetation.

The big fall hatches are the Mahogany Dun and the October Caddis, and they usually start sometime in September depending on the weather. Fall can bring with it warm, comfortable days and a noticeable reduction in fishing

HOT CREEK HATCHES

	JAN	FEB	MAR	APR	MAY	JUN	JUL	AUG	SEP	OCT	NOV	DEC

Midges (Diptera)

#18-20 Zebra Midge, CB Frostbite, Chan's Chironomid Bomber, GB Brassie, Griffith's Gnat, Quigley's Spider Midge

Blue-Winged Olive
(*Baetis* spp.)

#18-20 Mercer's Poxyback Baetis, olive Mercer's Micro Mayfly, Morrish's Anato-May, Morrish's Hotwire May, Beadhead Pheasant Tail, WD-40, Quigley's Hat Creek Spider, Quigley Cripple

Pale Morning Dun
(*Ephemerella* spp.)

#16-18 yellow Morrish's Anato-May, rust Morrish's Hotwire May, Mercer's GB Poxyback PMD, brown or ruby Mercer's Micro Mayfly, Burk's HBI Nymph, Sparkle Dun, Paradun, Mercer's PMD Profile Spinner

Caddis
(*Brachycentrus/Hydropsyche* spp.)

#12-16 olive or brown Birds Nest, Copper John, Mercer's Z-Wing Caddis, Mercer's Glo-Bubble Caddis, Fox's Poopah, Morrish's Hotwire Caddis, Morrish's Super Pupa, Gordon's Prince Nymph, Hot Creek Caddis, Mercer's Missing Link

Mahogany Dun
(*Paraleptophlebia* spp.)

#16 rust Morrish's Anato-May, Morrish's Hotwire May, Tilt Wing Dun, Mercer's Rusty Profile Spinner

Trico (*Tricorythodes* spp.)

#20 black Mercer's Glass Bead Micro Mayfly, CDC Biot Spinner, Etha Wing Trico, Quigley's Hat Creek Spider

Green Rockworm
(*Rhyacophila* spp.)

#18 green Mercer's Z-Wing Caddis, Mercer's Glo-Bubble Caddis, Fox's Poopah, Morrish's Hotwire Caddis, Elk Hair Caddis, Cutter's E/C Caddis, Hot Creek Caddis

Little Sister Sedge
(*Cheumatopsyche* spp.)

#18 brown Fox's Micro Poopah, Mercer's Glo-Bubble Caddis, Morrish's Super Pupa, Elk Hair Caddis, Cutter's E/C Caddis, Mercer's Missing Link, Hot Creek Caddis

Mahogany Dun
(*Paraleptophlebia* spp.)

#12-14 rust Sparkle Dun, Mercer's Foam Parachute, Tilt Wing Dun, Paradun

October Caddis
(*Dicosmoecus* spp.)

#8 Mercer's Tungsten October Pupa, Mercer's Psycho Prince, Orange, Morrish's October Pupa, Morrish's WMD, Stimulator, Madame X

Scuds (*Gammarus* spp.)

#16 Hunchback Scud, Pregnant Scud, Sparkle Scud

pressure. Mahogany Duns come off during the afternoons, and the October Caddis become active just before dark, just like on other streams.

Good nymphs to imitate the Mahogany Dun are #14-16 Morrish's Anato-May, Morrish's Hotwire May, or a brown Birds Nest. Good dry flies are #16 Mercer's Foam Profile Spinner, a Paradun, or Haystack. I only fish the evening October Caddis egg-laying session, so nymphs aren't necessary. Good October Caddis nymph pattern include #8 Morrish's October Caddis, Stimulator, Madame X, and Sloan's Persuader.

Down close to the water good observational skills really help. With polarized sunglasses you can often see trout feeding beneath the surface.

Path of Least Resistance

More than 20 years ago I was fishing the public water immediately downstream from the Hot Creek Ranch property. Despite numerous signs explaining that live bait wasn't allowed and fishing was catch-and-release, there was one defiant angler smoking a cigarette and fishing with a bobber and a gob of worms, a hefty stringer of trout flopping around on the end of his stringer.

I'm not sure how I sounded when I explained that bait fishing and killing fish weren't allowed here, but the response I got was not exactly what I expected.

"That so?" he replied with a penetrating stare and mocking grin on his face. "Well what the fxxx are you going to do about it?" I can't remember how I actually answered that question, but the reality was obviously "not a thing," and I stormed downstream in a torrent of anger. Feeling pretty upset about it, I spilled my guts to the first fisherman I ran into, an older gentleman with a knowing smile, who told me not to worry. He would take care of it.

He headed up around the corner and out of sight. Minutes later I saw the bait guy high-tailing it up the trail toward his truck, abandoning his stringer of dead trout.

"What did you say to that guy?" I almost shouted when the elderly man made his way back down. I was just about ready to believe the old gent was a seventh degree black belt or a ninja clad in waders.

"All I said was," the man replied, "Hey pal, there's a game warden heading up this way checking licenses."

I quickly saw the brilliance of his approach. Thanks to a man far wiser than I, I learned something that day. Since then I have used the same line several times with the same wonderful result.

New Zealand Mud Snails

Owens River and Hot Creek have New Zealand mud snails (NZMS). Contamination by these invaders from a foreign land is becoming more widespread throughout California and the West in general. As conscientious stewards of rivers that provide us with so much pleasure, anglers have a deep responsibility to do all we can to quell the spread of this scourge.

Mud snails eventually ruin a fishery by their propensity for multiplying in such numbers that they completely take over the environment. They are capable of consuming 80 percent of the available food in a river, leaving little for trout. Snails consumed by trout are capable of passing through the fish without hurting the snail or providing nourishment for the fish.

Gear like waders or boots provide rides for hitchhiking snails and can taint other waters. They are so small that they easily elude visual examination. Don't trust your eyes, just assume they are there and do something about it. Unfortunately, the little buggers are not easy to kill. The following is taken from Ralph and Lisa Cutter's California School of Flyfishing website:

Method 1. Freeze your gear solid. To be safe this may take 6 to 12 hours or more. It also requires sufficient freezer space and a very understanding spouse.

Method 2. Dry your gear completely. This option is only practical for anglers who don't fish an awful lot, since getting every bit of your gear entirely dry may take at least a month.

Method 3. Soak your gear in a 50/50 solution of water and Formula 409 degreaser/disinfectant. Note: Only the 409 degreaser/disinfectant product will work; not any other Formula 409 solution.

Method 4. Soak your gear in 3/4 teaspoon (3.8 grams) of 99 percent copper sulfate pentahydrate in one gallon of water. This is available online or from farm supply outlets. Soaking should completely wet your gear in a bucket or plastic bag for at least five minutes. When finished, rinse your gear outside with a hose, well away from lakes, ponds, or streams (copper sulfate is a highly toxic substance).

Method 5. Consider devoting one set of cheap waders and boots solely to those fisheries testing positive for the parasite.

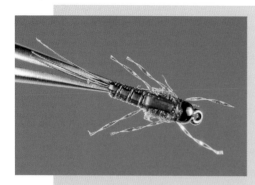

Morrish's Pickpocket (Golden Brown)

Hook: #12-18 Tiemco 3761
Bead: Black nickel
Weight: .015-.025 lead or lead-free wire
Thread: Black 6/0 Danville
Tail: Orange pheasant-tail fibers
Abdomen: Copper and copper brown
           Ultra Wire
Back: Amber goose biots
Thorax: Golden brown Ice Dub
Wing Case: Amber goose biots
Legs: Wine Krystal Flash

Morrish's Anato-May (Rust)

Hook: #8-16 Tiemco 3761
Bead: Black nickel
Weight: .020-.030 lead or lead-free wire
Thread: Black 6/0 Danville
Tail: Natural pheasant-tail fibers
Rib: Copper wire
Abdomen: Pale rusty brown Scintilla dubbing
Thorax: Pale rusty brown Scintilla dubbing
Back: Gold Krystal Flash
Wing Case: Gold Krystal Flash
Legs: Gold Krystal Flash
Head: Dark Stone (#15) Whitlock SLF

Morrish's Anato-May (Olive)

Hook: #8-16 Tiemco 3761
Bead: Black tungsten
Weight: .020-.030 lead or lead-free wire
Thread: Black 6/0 Danville
Tail: Natural pheasant-tail fibers
Rib: Copper wire
Abdomen: Olive Scintilla dubbing
Thorax: Olive Scintilla dubbing
Back: Root beer Krystal Flash
Wing Case: Root beer Krystal Flash
Legs: Root beer Krystal Flash
Head: Dark Stone (#15) Whitlock SLF

Mercer's Micro Mayfly (Electric Yellow)

Hook:	#14-20 Tiemco 3769
Bead:	Copper
Thread:	Yellow 8/0 Uni-Thread
Tail:	Dyed yellow ring-necked-pheasant-tail fibers
Rib:	Amber Ultra Wire (small)
Abdomen:	Electric banana Angel Hair
Wing Case:	Golden brown mottled turkey tail and a strip of pearl Flashabou coated with 5-minute epoxy
Thorax:	October Caddis Mercer's Buggy Nymph Dubbing
Legs:	Same as tail
Head:	Same as thorax

Mercer's Missing Link

Hook:	#13-19 Tiemco 102Y
Thread:	Camel 8/0 Uni-Thread
Abdomen:	Camel 8/0 Uni-Thread, ribbed with strand of pearl Flashabou, coated with Softex
Wings:	Dark dun Z-lon split with clump of peacock Ice Dub
Post:	Elk body hair
Hackle:	Dark dun dry-fly hackle

Mercer's Profile Spinner (PMD)

Hook:	#16-18 Tiemco 100
Thread:	Camel 8/0 Uni-Thread
Tail:	Blue dun spade feather fibers
Abdomen:	Rusty turkey biot
Post:	Orange and yellow macramé yarn
Wings:	Dun Z-lon (straight)
Thorax:	Rusty brown Super Fine
Hackle:	Blue dun dry-fly saddle hackle